THE BOOK
OF DREAMS

CONTENTS

Chapter 1

Chapter 2

Chapter 3

Chapter 4

Chapter 5

DREAM DICTIONARY

chapter one

DREAMING
THROUGH TIME

THE BOOK OF DREAMS

YOUR DREAMS AND WHAT THEY MEAN

Brian Innes

GRAMERCY BOOKS
NEW YORK

This 2007 edition is published by Gramercy Books, an imprint of Random House Value Publishing, a division of Random House, Inc., New York, by arrangement with Amber Books.

Gramercy is a registered trademark and the colophon is a trademark of Random House, Inc.

Random House
New York • Toronto • London • Sydney • Auckland
www.valuebooks.com

Printed and bound in Dubai

A catalog record for this title is available from the Library of Congress.

ISBN: 978-0-517-23057-2

10 9 8 7 6 5 4 3 2 1

*A*ll humans dream (and so, it seems, do many animals); yet the dream, as an experience, is something that remains difficult to explain, and still disturbs the most rational person.

In fact, within the terms of modern brain physiology, dreaming is harder to explain today than it was for the earliest humans. As the eminent anthropologist Sir Edward Tylor (1832–1917) wrote:

It seems as though thinking men, as yet at a low level of culture, were deeply impressed by two groups of biological problems. In the first place, what is it that makes the difference between a living body and a dead one; what causes waking, sleep, trance, disease and death? In the second place, what are those human shapes which appear in dreams and visions? Looking at these two groups of phenomena, the ancient savage philosophers probably made the obvious inference that every man has two things belonging to him, namely a life and a phantom.

From this beginning, Tylor suggested, developed the concept of the human soul, which moved and acted in the dream world, on the one hand; and, on the other, the idea of the gods, who watched – and in many ways controlled – humans' waking activities. This belief has persisted even into modern times: according to the Koran, for example, Allah takes the souls of sleepers every night, and returns them in the morning. What more natural, then, than to suppose that dreams were messages from the gods?

THE EARLIEST RECORDED DREAMS

The oldest written record to recount dreams is the *Epic of Gilgamesh*, written about 2000 BC on a series of clay tablets. Gilgamesh was a king who ruled Uruk in southern Mesopotamia around 2600 BC, and the story begins with his dream that he will befriend a man whom he will 'embrace as a wife'. In due course, a man named Enkidu comes to Uruk and, after a wrestling match with Gilgamesh, the two become firm friends, and set out to slay the forest demon Humbaba. On the way, Gilgamesh has another dream, that he is pinned to the ground by the weight of a god who falls on him, but Enkidu interprets this as indicating a successful outcome to their expedition. Eventually, however, Enkidu provokes the wrath of the gods, and dreams the foretelling of his own death.

Other records of dream messages emanating from the gods come from ancient Egypt. For instance, a pink granite tablet between the paws of the Sphinx at Giza describes the dream of the future Pharaoh Thotmes IV, who ruled in 1425–17 BC. One day, while still a prince, Thotmes rested during a hunting expedition in the shade of a huge statue of the sun god Re. As he slept, the god appeared to him in a dream, and told him he would inherit the kingdom of Egypt, and enjoy a long and successful reign – at the same time asking him to clear away the sand that had already half-buried the Sphinx. When Thotmes became pharaoh, he remembered the dream, and the tablet commemorates the fact that he fulfilled the god's request.

In Egypt it was generally the priests who practised the interpretation of dreams. The Chester-Beatty III papyrus, which dates from about 2000 BC, lists nearly 200 interpretations, such as:

If a man sees himself in a dream looking at a dead ox
– good, for it signifies the death of his enemies.
If a man sees himself in a dream looking at a snake
– good, it signifies abundance of provisions.
If a man sees in a dream his bed on fire
– bad, it signifies the rape of his wife.

The most famous account of dream interpretation in ancient Egypt is related in the book of Genesis in the Old Testament. It begins in the land of Canaan,

The sun god Re appeared in a dream to a young Egyptian prince, and told him he would one day rule Egypt. Re also instructed him to clear away the sand that half buried the Sphinx at Giza. The prince went on to become Pharaoh Thotmes IV, and the pink granite stone between the paws of the Sphinx commemorates his dream.

slavery in Egypt. For a time Joseph was an overseer in the house of Potiphar, the Pharaoh's captain of the guard, but then he was accused of trying to rape his master's

and concerns Joseph, the youngest and best-loved son of the patriarch Jacob. Joseph told his 11 older brothers how he dreamt 'we were binding sheaves in the field, and lo, my sheaf arose, and also stood upright; and behold, your sheaves stood round about, and made obeisance to my sheaf'. In a second dream, 'behold, the sun and the moon and the eleven stars made obeisance to me'.

Joseph's brothers were understandably furious at this suggestion that he was superior to them all, and they kidnapped him and sold him into

wife, and was thrown into prison. Two of his fellow prisoners were Pharaoh's butler and baker, and they asked Joseph if he could interpret dreams that they had had.

The butler had dreamt of a three-branched vine; he plucked the grapes, pressed them into Pharaoh's cup, and handed it to him. Joseph explained that the three branches signified three days, and that within that time, the butler would be freed from prison and be back in the royal household.

Hearing that the interpretation was good, the baker then told his dream: he had seen himself carrying three white baskets on his head; the top one was filled with cooked meats for Pharaoh, but the birds were eating them as he walked along. The baker was horrified to hear the interpretationt of his dream. Joseph said that, again, the baskets represented three days but that within that time Pharaoh would cut off the baker's head and hang him from a tree, and the birds would feed on his flesh.

Sure enough, three days later, on Pharaoh's birthday, what Joseph had predicted did indeed take place. Joseph himself, however, was left in prison for two more years. Then Pharaoh had a troubled dream, which none of his priests could interpret; the butler remembered Joseph and told Pharaoh about him. Joseph was brought from prison, and Pharaoh recounted his dream. He dreamt he stood on the bank of the Nile, and seven 'fatfleshed and well favoured' cows came out of the river and fed in a meadow. They were followed by seven more cows, 'poor and very ill favoured and leanfleshed, such as I never saw in all the land of

*'And Joseph said unto Pharaoh, "The dream of Pharaoh is one: God hath shewed Pharaoh
what he is about to do…"' (Genesis 41:25)*
Joseph Interpreting Pharaoh's Dream *by nineteenth-century French artist Gustave Doré.*

Egypt for badness'. And these cows ate the fat cows, but remained as skinny as ever. Later, Pharaoh said:

… seven ears [of corn] came up in one stalk, full and good: And behold, seven ears, withered, thin, and blasted by the east wind, sprung up after them: And the thin ears devoured the seven good ears …

Joseph explained that the dream was a warning that, although the region would enjoy seven years of good harvest, these would be followed by seven years of famine. Pharaoh believed him, and gave him the task of collecting and storing a fifth of all the corn that was harvested during the seven good years. Then, as the dream had predicted, came seven years of famine.

During this time, Jacob sent 10 of his sons to Egypt to buy corn, to help them survive the famine. By now, Joseph was governor over all the land, and his brothers went to him, and 'bowed down themselves before him with their faces to the earth'. And so Joseph's own dreams came true.

Another story from the Old Testament, the interpretation of King Nebuchadnezzar's dream by the prophet Daniel, includes a further complicating element: the king could not remember his dream when he woke, but Daniel – possibly in a dream of his own – was able to discover the details. He told Nebuchadnezzar that he had seen 'a great image' with a head of fine gold, breast and arms of silver, and belly and thighs of brass; its legs were made of iron, and its feet part iron and part clay. The figure was smashed to pieces by a stone, which grew into a mountain and filled the entire earth.

Daniel explained the symbolism of the dream. The golden head was Nebuchadnezzar himself, 'a king of kings', who ruled over a great kingdom. But after the King's death this kingdom would be succeeded by lesser kingdoms; and the last –

Nebuchadnezzar, King of Babylon, captured Jerusalem in 586BC and deported the Jews into exile. The prophet Daniel interpreted one of Nebuchadnezzar's dreams as a sign that his kingdom would eventually be followed by the kingdom of God.

strong like iron but brittle as clay – would collapse, and be followed by the Kingdom of God. 'Then the king Nebuchadnezzar fell upon his face, and worshipped Daniel.'

MESSAGES FROM THE GODS

One salient point emerges from all these accounts: most dreams were thought to foretell the future. For hundreds – indeed, thousands – of years, people believed that all dreams came from an outside source: they were images encountered by the sleeper's soul as it wandered in the night. They might be portents of great importance, visions of momentous happenings to come that were preordained by the gods; or, as in the Chester-Beatty III papyrus, predictions of relatively mundane events in the near future.

Sometimes messages would be brought by dream figures, often people that the dreamer had previously known, and who now appeared as phantoms. This is particularly true of dreams described in Greek and Roman literature. In Homer's *Iliad*, for example, as Achilles slept, the ghost of his dearest friend, Patroklos, 'appeared all in his likeness for stature, with the same lovely eyes and voice, and wearing such clothing as Patroklos had worn. The ghost came and stood by his head and spoke to him', and gave instructions for his funeral.

The gods could also send deceptive messages, as described in another passage in the *Iliad*. The Greek king, Agamemnon, had angered the supreme god Zeus, and Zeus gave his dream messenger the appearance of the aged Nestor, the King's most trusted adviser. On the god's orders, the dream figure told Agamemnon that the time had come to attack the city of Troy; he was favoured by the gods, and victory was absolutely certain. But when Agamemnon led his armies into battle, they were driven back time and again.

The temples of the gods were considered to be their visiting-places on earth and, throughout the Middle East, people would stay overnight there in the hope that dream messages would be received. This was known as 'incubation'. Sick people, in particular, travelled long distances to the temple of Asklepios, the god of medicine, at Epidaurus. After a rigorous diet (broad beans, especially, were believed to inhibit dreams) and a ritual washing, they made their offerings and prayed at the god's altar, and then slept – if they could, surrounded as they were by the non-venomous snakes that were the god's symbol.

If they were fortunate, the sleepers awoke to relate how they had been visited by Asklepios in their dreams, and given advice on how to treat their illness. Many 'miracle' cures were reported, and these reports have survived as inscriptions on the temple walls.

SCEPTICAL OPINIONS

The great Greek physician Hippocrates (460–377 BC) took a more modern view in his *Treatise on Dreams*. He wrote: 'Some dreams are divinely inspired, but others are the direct result of the physical body.' At the same time, he believed that dreams could predict coming disease. For instance:

If the heavenly bodies are seen dimly in a clear sky, and shine weakly and seem to be stopped from revolving by dryness, then it is a sign that there is a danger of incurring sickness …

A star moving upwards 'indicates fluxes in the head'; movement of the star towards the sea is a sign of disease of the bowels; and eastward movement indicates 'the growing of tumours in the flesh'. Hippocrates also noted other dream symbols: for instance, the colour black was a sign of physical sickness, while flying dreams indicated mental derangement.

Aristotle (384–22 BC) developed his opinions along much the same lines. He wrote three treatises – *On Sleep and Waking, On Dreams,* and *On Divination in Sleep* – which foreshadow much of modern psychological theory. Aristotle denied that dreams were divinely inspired, since, he said,

Fifth-century Greek dish depicting Achilles dressing the wounds of his gentle and amiable friend Patroklus. Achilles had refused to take part in battle in order to annoy Agamemnon, leader of the Greeks at the siege of Troy. Patroklus disguised himself in Achilles' armour and was slain by Hector, the noblest of the Trojan chieftains. Achilles was later to slay Hector, lash his body to a chariot and drag it three times around the walls of Troy in triumph.

Jean-Joseph Taillason's painting depicting Virgil reading The Aeneid *to the Roman Emperor Augustus and his sister Octavia. The Roman orator Cicero had foresight of Augustus's rise to power in a dream of a young man descending from the heavens on a golden chain. Unfortunately, Cicero made an enemy of Mark Antony, Augustus's ally following the assassination of Julius Caesar, and effectively signed his own death warrant.*

> *'Cicero is much to be pitied, who having excellently discoursed on the vanity of dreams, was yet undone by the flattery of his own'*

even the most unimportant and ignorant people – as well as animals – had them, and it was unlikely that the gods would choose them to transmit significant messages. He maintained that apparently prophetic dreams were due either to coincidence or to subsequent self-fulfilment. On the other hand, he accepted that dreams could give a clue to the dreamer's state of health, pointing out:

It is obvious that the beginnings of sickness and the other accidents that are produced in the body … are necessarily clearer in sleep than in the waking state.

However, Aristotle was well in advance of his time, and most people continued to believe that dreams came from the gods. Even the great Roman orator Cicero (106–43 BC), who poured scorn on prophetic dreams in his book *On Divination*, fell victim to the belief. He dreamt that a noble youth descended from the heavens on a golden chain, and stood at the door of a temple. Next day Cicero saw the young man from his dream at a ceremony in the Capitol, and recognised him as Julius Caesar's great-nephew, Octavian.

Convinced that his dream foretold a great future for Octavian, Cicero became one of his followers – and in due course, after the assassination of Julius, Octavian became the emperor Augustus. But Cicero had made an enemy of Mark Antony, and when Octavian and Antony became allies orders were issued for his execution. As the English essayist Sir Thomas Browne (1605–82) wrote, in *Of Dreams*: 'Cicero is much to be pitied, who having excellently discoursed on the vanity of dreams, was yet undone by the flattery of his own.'

THE FIRST DREAM DICTIONARY

The most complete work on the meaning of dream symbols that has survived from Roman times is the *Oneirocritica* (literally meaning 'the interpretation of dreams') by Artemidorus of Daldis, a second-century Greek. Little is known about him, except that he was a professional diviner, and travelled widely, collecting all the information that he could and recording more than 3000 dream events in what we now call a 'dream dictionary'.

Artemidorus defined five different types of dream: symbolic, prophetic, fantasies, nightmares, and daytime visions. He also distinguished between *insomnia* – dreams caused by physiological states or waking preoccupations – and *somnia* – those with a deeply symbolic reference to future events. In addition, he classified dream images into different categories, such as gods, animals, or parts of the body. At the same time, he made it clear that the individual images did not have a fixed symbolic meaning, but must be interpreted within the general context of the dream, and with specific reference to the dreamer.

Artemidorus was particularly concerned with prophetic dreams. He wrote, for example:

Seeing a tame, fawning lion that is approaching harmlessly is auspicious, and means benefits to a soldier from his king, to an athlete from his excellent physical condition, to a citizen from a magistrate, or to a slave from his master, for the animal resembles them in power and strength. But if the lion threatens, or is in any way angered, it arouses fear and portends sickness.

Some of Artemidorus's interpretations find an equivalent in modern psychological theory. Dreams of sowing, planting and tending crops, he said, represent a desire to marry and have children, and he identified the plough as a phallic symbol. Grain stores and ditches dug in the ground are symbols for women, wives or concubines. He also noted the possibility that dreams can go by opposites. Dreaming of the death of a brother portends the disappearance of an enemy, or that difficulties will be overcome. A dream of an earthquake is a sign that circumstances will improve, and a dream of illness promises a long life.

Most of the dream dictionaries published after Artemidorus drew extensively on his work, and when the *Oneirocritica* was published in English

Ancient Egyptian frieze showing a man ploughing in the fields. According to Artemidorus of Daldis, a second-century Greek, in his Oneirocritica, *a plough is a phallic symbol.*

translation in 1644, it went through some two dozen editions in less than a century.

However, most of the later dream dictionaries ignored Artemidorus's reservation that it was important to relate the dream to the individual, and set out to give specific meanings to dream symbols. For example, a French popular print of 1850 includes the following:

Picking grapes:	*Pleasure and happiness, wealth and good health.*
Gardening:	*Good health.*
Housework:	*Seeing someone spinning signifies prosperity.*
Usury:	*Profiting from money-lending foretells distress and loss.*
Selling fruit:	*Prosperity.*
Hunting:	*Accusation, or deception.*
Fire:	*Danger; putting out the fire, inheritance.*

Brigands:	*Death of a relative.*
Gentle breeze:	*Inconstancy.*
Music:	*Consolation in adversity.*
Blindness:	*Hard work to come.*

Many traditional dream dictionaries, readily available to the present day, follow the same lines of dream interpretation.

THE FOUNDATIONS OF RELIGION

Interestingly, dreams have played an important part in the foundation of several of the world's major religions. In his account of the life of Jesus Christ, Matthew tells us that when Joseph, who was engaged to be married to Mary, was troubled by her unexpected pregnancy, an angel appeared to him in a dream and told him of the child's

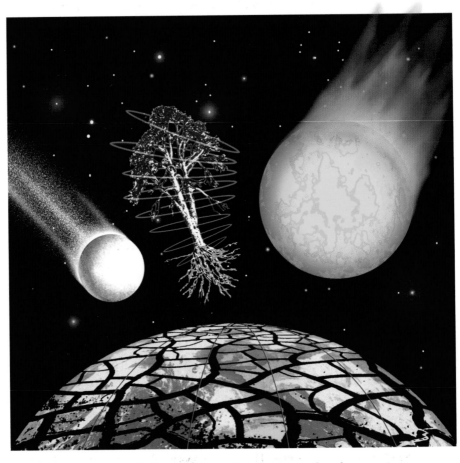

In the middle of the night Gopa had a series
of dreams. She saw the sun and moon,
haloed with their brightness,
fall out of the firmament

destiny. In another dream following the birth of Jesus, an angel came again to Joseph, warning him that King Herod was determined to kill the child, and that they should escape to safety in Egypt. Then, when Herod was dead,

an angel of the Lord appeared in a dream to Joseph in Egypt, saying, Arise, and take the young child and his mother, and go into the land of Israel: for they are dead which sought the young child's life.

The birth of Siddhartha Gautama, the Buddha, was similarly prefigured in a dream, but one that was highly symbolic. His mother, Maya, related her dream to her husband, king Cudhodana, and his soothsayers:

White as snow or silver, more brilliant than the moon or the sun, the best of elephants, with fine feet, well-balanced, with strong joints, with six tusks hard as adamant, the magnanimous, the very beautiful, has entered my womb.

The interpretation of the soothsayers was that Maya would bear a son to be a universal ruler, his sovereignty based on detachment and compassion, but that he would become a monk and give up all desire. Following this, the king had a confirmatory dream in which he saw the future Buddha 'leave the house in the peaceful night, escorted by a troop of gods, and then set forth, a wandering monk, clad in a red-coloured garment'.

Years later, when the Buddha announced his intention to fulfill his vocation as a monk, his wife Gopa had a fearful dream experience, as recorded in the Buddhist scriptures:

Gopa and the prince were both asleep, side by side, in their bed. In the middle of the night Gopa had a series of dreams. She saw the earth quaking, with its rocks and its peaks; she saw the trees that had been raised by the wind and uprooted fall back to the ground. She saw the sun and moon, haloed with their brightness, fall out of the firmament on to the earth. She saw herself cutting off her hair with her right hand, and felt her diadem fall to pieces. Then she saw herself, with both hands cut off, both feet cut off, and completely naked; she saw her pearls scattered, and the jewels of her girdle broken. She saw the four legs of her bed broken and lying on the floor; she saw the brilliant richly decorated shaft of the prince's parasol broken as well, his garments scattered, thrown down at random and carried away by the waters, all her husband's jewellery, including his diadem, pell-mell on the bed. She saw a meteor leave the town and the city plunged into darkness; then, in her dream, she saw the beauteous necklaces bedecked with pearls hang down and fall apart, the oceans raised, and Meru, the king of the mountains, shaken to its foundations.

These dreams reflected Gopa's distress that her husband was about to desert her but, when she awoke and told him, he gently reassured her, and explained each image as a favourable omen. According to the Buddha's philosophy, pain and anguish are experienced only on the plane of existence governed by desire and attachment. Gopa's horrific dream was a sign – as dreams can go by opposites – that she would be freed from grief and enter on to the plane of perfect bliss.

Dreams also played an important part in the development of Islam: the first part of the Koran was said to have been received from Allah by the prophet Mohammed in a dream, and the holy city, Mecca, was promised to the faithful in another. The prophet paid close attention to dreams, and every morning he would discuss and interpret his own, and those of his disciples. It was as a result of one of their dreams that the

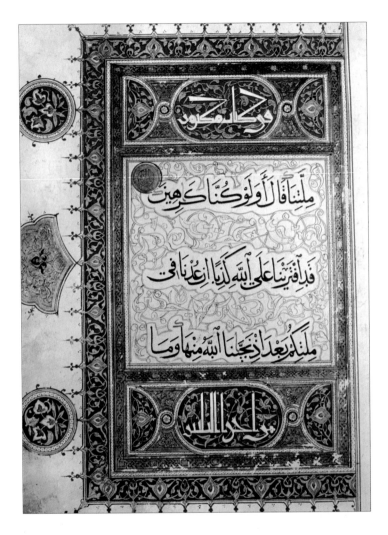

The first part of the Qur'an (Koran) was said to have been received from Allah during a dream.
This reading or Qur'an (Koran) became the legislative and doctrinal basis of the religion
of Islam. This is a fourteenth century frontispiece of the Qu'ran.

practice of the muezzin calling the faithful to prayer from the mosque was begun.

An early Islamic writing, *The Night Journey of Mohammed*, supposedly recounts – in no fewer than 114 chapters – one of Mohammed's dreams. In it, Mohammed was woken by the angel Gabriel and, riding Elborak, a silvery-grey mare, was taken on an awe-inspiring journey to the gates of Jerusalem, where he met Abraham, Moses and Jesus. After passing through 13 heavens, where he was welcomed by all the major prophets, Mohammed saw the Garden of Delights, and then the House of Adoration, where 70,000 angels paid daily homage to Allah. In a meeting with Allah himself, he was told to say his prayers 50 times a day but, with Moses's persuasion, he succeeded in bargaining this number down to five – a practice continued by the faithful of Islam to the present day. Then Mohammed remounted Elborak, returned to where he had been sleeping, and awoke.

The earliest Hindu writings had little to say about dreams, but later religious texts, known as the *Upanishads*, recognised their importance:

A man has two conditions: in this world and in the world beyond. But there is also a twilight juncture: the condition of sleep. In this twilight juncture one sees both of the other conditions, this world and the other world. When someone falls asleep, he takes the stuff of the entire world, and he himself takes it apart, and he himself builds it up, and by his own bright light he dreams. There are no chariots there, no harnessings, no roads; but he emits chariots, harnessings, roads. There are no joys or delights there; but he emits joys and delights. There are no ponds, lotus pools and flowing streams; but he emits ponds, lotus pools and flowing streams. For he is the Maker.

DREAMS IN OTHER CULTURES

For the Aborigines of Australia, there is no clear division between dreaming and waking, between past, present and future. The living world – including such phenomena as rain, wind and fire – exists because of the actions of pioneer heroes in the mythical past, the 'dreamtime'. But this past is also the present, and a living individual regards himself as emanating directly from one of the dreamtime heroes. In their initiation ceremonies, the Aborigines re-enact the doings of these heroes, and so become one with the past.

Dreams, therefore, are a way of entering the heroic past. By undergoing the experiences of the mythical heroes, Aborigines believe they will draw on the power of their ancestors, whose spirits are still present and will provide

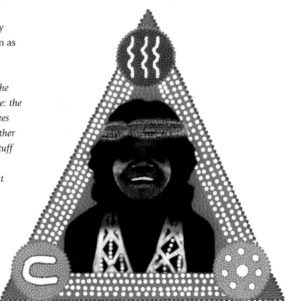

protection. At the same time, the Aborigines believe that life and death form part of a cycle that begins and ends in dreamtime. Past, present and future exist together: in the past, the dreamtime is made manifest in the heroes; in the present, in those who have been initiated; and, if the cycle is not broken, it continues in the future. Aborigines often fail to differentiate between dreaming and waking events; and many of their ceremonies have their origins in dreams experienced by inspired individuals.

The Australian Aborigines have developed as more than 500 separate tribal groups, each tracing its origin to a different heroic ancestor, and so it is difficult to generalise on their beliefs about specific dreams. However, most believe that the human spirit can leave the body during sleep,

and wander abroad, meeting up with other sleepers' spirits, or with the spirits of the dead. Many maintain that a sick person, or one in pain, can be relieved by the dream spirit of a dead friend. Some believe that dreams can warn them of approaching enemies, or inform the relatives of a dead man of his killer's identity.

Anthropologists have discovered some striking parallels between the dream symbols described by Artemidorus and those of other, entirely unconnected, peoples – evidence that supports the theories put forward by the psychologist Carl Jung.

For example, a 1926 report by A.G.O. Hodgson and H.J. Rose described the dream interpretations made by the elders of a tribe in Nyasaland (Malawi). According to Artemidorus, a dream of

fire in the sky was a warning of famine or war; and for the Africans a bush fire was a sign of coming warfare. Losing a tooth, said Artemidorus, was a sign that one would lose a member of one's household; for the Africans, it meant the loss of a wife or child. A dream of a flood, according to the *Oneirocritica*, signified a dispute, or the oppression of a bad-tempered superior; and it meant much the same in Nyasaland. And a dragon wound about the body, in Artemidorus's interpretation, symbolised bondage; while the Africans saw a snake around the leg as a symbol of slavery.

In North America, among native Americans, dreams are seen in a rather different light. Their significance can vary from tribe to tribe, but they are considered the most important of experiences, and can shape an individual's role within the tribe. Native Americans recognise that

the dream has a specific significance for the individual dreamer: whether it is favourable or unfavourable depends partly on its content, and partly on its effect upon the dreamer.

Among the Navaho of the southwestern USA, the implications of a bad dream can be avoided by praying on waking at sunrise. Many bad dreams are seen to have the opposite meaning as subsequent events develop – and the Navaho recognise that others have had similar dreams without serious consequences. However, particular kinds of dream, such as a dream of falling, are considered to be a sign of sickness, requiring interpretation and treatment. If a Navaho dreams that he or she is dead, it is a sign of having visited the spirits of the dead in the next world, and is not necessarily an unfavourable omen; but shaking hands with the dead is a sign that he or she will soon die.

The Mohave Indians take the connection between dreams and sickness even further: they believe that dreams can cause illness. Either the dreamer falls ill because of harmful events that have affected the soul during the dream; or the dream itself is so disturbing that it causes the dreamer to become ill in waking life. For instance, a Mohave woman suffered deep depression after a dream in which a dead relation had cooked a fish for her: it was only as she ate the fish that she realised that its head was that of her mother.

Rather like the Aborigines of Australia, the Mohave are said to interpret their culture in relation to their dreams, rather than interpreting their dreams in terms of their culture. They also believe that certain dreams can bestow power on the dreamer, as do the Yuma. The Yuma, another southwestern tribe, regard dreams as the basis of their religion and traditions, believing that they begin before birth, and are more real than waking experiences. The neighbouring Kamia people consider that dreams are best experienced by young persons, because the elderly can die during dreams.

In the northeast of the USA and Canada, theories of the significance of dreams are rather different. According to the accounts of seventeenth-century Jesuit missionaries among the Iroquois, for instance, a dream was generally regarded as a divine instruction that had to be obeyed in all its details. The Iroquois recognised that dreams reflected both the unconscious desires of the dreamer, and those of supernatural beings, and that frustration of these desires could result in mental or physical illness, death or disaster for the whole tribe, or even the end of the world.

Similar beliefs are found among the Ojibwa. For them, dreams are encounters with supernatural beings, frequently personified forms of natural phenomena such as the sun, wind or thunder. A satisfactory life depends not only on

> *the Mohave interpret their culture in relation to their dreams, rather than interpreting their dreams in terms of their culture*

good relations with other human beings, but also upon the assistance of these supernaturals.

THE SHAMANIC DREAM

Throughout northern America, and across the Bering Straits among the native Siberians, a particular form of dream was associated with the initiation of the shaman, or 'medicine man'. A nineteenth-century Russian anthropologist gave a detailed account of what was told him by a Siberian shaman. The man had been lying desperately ill with smallpox, and was so near death that he was unconscious for three days – in fact, he was about to be buried. In his feverish dreams, he saw himself descend to the underworld, and then was transported to an island, in the middle of which a young birch tree stretched up to heaven. He learnt this was the tree of the Lord of the Earth, and he received a branch with which to make himself the frame of a drum.

Later in the dream, the future shaman came to a mountain, inside which a naked man was working a bellows at a fire. The man caught him with a hook and cut off his head, setting it aside so that it could see what happened next. His body was hacked into pieces, and boiled in a cauldron

In his feverish dreams, he saw himself descend to the
underworld, and then was transported to an island, in the
middle of which a young birch tree stretched up to heaven

on the fire until it was reduced to bones. Then the skeleton was forged together again on an anvil, and covered once more with flesh. The shaman recovered consciousness to find himself in his tent, surrounded by his grieving relatives, cured of smallpox, and ready to begin his vocation.

Mircea Eliade, who was professor of the History of Religion at the University of Chicago, drew attention to the similarity between the later phases of this dream and the symbolism used by many sixteenth- and seventeenth-century alchemists in their description of the stages necessary to prepare the elixir of eternal life. It obviously comes from very deep within the human unconscious.

DREAMS THAT CHANGED HISTORY

Prophetic dreams have influenced political and military events at many times throughout history. Xerxes, the young Persian who invaded and conquered Greece in 480 BC, was advised by his senior minister, Artabanus, that the invasion was unwise. However, in a dream Xerxes saw a man, 'tall and noble of aspect', who told him to 'continue to tread the path that you chose yesterday'. The dream was repeated the next night, and Xerxes related it to Artabanus. He suggested that the minister should sit on his throne, and then sleep in his bed, in the hope that he might experience the dream himself. Artabanus agreed – although he pointed out that the apparition was unlikely to be deceived by the subterfuge.

However, as he slept, Artabanus had a similar dream, but this time the apparition reprimanded him for trying to change the course of destiny by dissuading Xerxes from his plan. The figure made as if to burn out the minister's eyes with a red-hot

Prophetic dreams have influenced political and military events at many times throughout history

iron, and Artabanus awoke with a fearful shout; he hurried to Xerxes, and admitted that his advice had been wrong. The invasion went ahead, the Greeks were defeated at Thermopylae, and the city of Athens was sacked.

The Persian occupation of Greece did not last long, however, and this, too, was prefigured in a dream. Xerxes dreamt that he was crowned with an olive tree, whose branches spread all over the earth. And then this crowning tree vanished. Soon after, the Persian fleet was defeated at sea, the Persian general was killed in a battle on land, and Xerxes fled with his remaining forces. And, as a fitting end to this story, he was later murdered – by Artabanus.

Alexander the Great, who conquered vast regions of Asia 150 years later, placed great value upon his dreams, and kept a personal soothsayer, Aristander, among his retinue. When his forces were attacking the city of Tyros, on the coast of Lebanon, in the summer of 332 BC, Alexander dreamt that a satyr (a woodland spirit) danced on his shield. He was worried about the significance of this dream, but Aristander explained that the Greek word *satyros* could be interpreted as meaning 'Tyros is yours'. Reassured, Alexander renewed his attack, and captured the city.

Julius Caesar was another military leader whose plans were confirmed in a dream. On the night before he crossed the river Rubicon, in his march to seize power in Rome, he dreamt that he slept with his mother. Caesar interpreted this powerful symbol of incest as a sign that he could dare to violate Rome, his mother-city, and he went forward to take the capital against little resistance. Sadly, he later paid no attention to the dream of his wife Calpurnia, that he should 'beware the Ides of March'; he was assassinated on that day – 15 March – in 44 BC.

An earlier attack on Rome was made by the Carthaginian general Hannibal. In 219 BC he had a dream that was later recorded by the Roman historian Valerius Maximus:

While he slept, Hannibal saw a young man, as beautiful as an angel, appear. He assured him that he had been sent from Heaven to urge Hannibal to invade Italy. Turning round, Hannibal saw an immense serpent, which violently and furiously overthrew and destroyed everything that got in its way. The sky behind this reptile was obscured by smoking clouds and pierced by lightning.

Sorely dismayed by this sight, Hannibal asked the handsome young man what it meant. 'You see' was his reply, 'the ruin of Italy and the disasters that await it. Go! The fates are about to be accomplished.'

'Is there any need' Valerius Maximus added, 'to recall the evils with which Hannibal ravaged Italy after he had this dream and obeyed its predictions?' Nevertheless, the dream prophecy was only partly fulfilled. Hannibal led an army of 40,000 men – and a troop of elephants – from southern Spain, across the Pyrenees and the Alps, and into Italy, but he was unable finally to crush the Roman forces. Recalled to Carthage, he was defeated there by the Romans, and fled into exile. When the Romans demanded his surrender, Hannibal committed

> *Caesar interpreted this powerful symbol of incest as a sign that he could dare to violate Rome*

suicide by poisoning himself.

In more modern times, most military leaders have hesitated to follow the dictates of their dreams, but it is said that even Napoleon paid attention to the ideas that came to him while he slept. On waking, he would try out his tactics, using model soldiers in a sandbox.

In the twentieth century, one particular dream had an outcome on the lives of probably more people than had been affected by all the dreams ever dreamt before. It occurred one November night in 1917, during World War I, at a place on the Somme front where the German and French trenches faced one another across a battle-scarred no-man's-land.

A group of German soldiers were asleep in their dugout when suddenly one of them, a 28-year-old corporal, woke from a horrifying nightmare. He had dreamt that he was buried alive beneath tons of earth and molten iron, with warm blood flowing across his chest. Still only half awake, he frantically struggled up, hurried out of the dugout, and climbed the parapet of the trench. As if he were still dreaming, he found himself stumbling out into no-man's-land.

The night was cold, and pitch dark, but he suddenly realised that he had placed himself in great danger as a possible target. He was about to

Hannibal saw a young man, as beautiful as an angel, appear. Turning round, he saw an immense serpent, which violently and furiously overthrew and destroyed everything that got in its way

turn back when there was a burst of rifle fire from the French lines, and he threw himself to the ground. As he did so, there was a huge explosion as a shell burst close by. When all was quiet again, the corporal turned and scrambled back towards the safety of the dugout. But it was no longer there: only a gaping crater in the earth showed where the shell had landed, and killed all his companions. The dream had saved his life, and saved him also for the future that lay before him. The corporal's name was Adolf Hitler

PROBLEMS TO BE SOLVED

Over the centuries, many creative people have discovered that problems they had been wrestling with in waking life were solved while they slept, and they awoke with everything suddenly made clear.

In the early seventeenth century, the French mathematician René Descartes had a succession of dreams whose outcome was to have a revolutionary effect upon scientific thought for hundreds of years. In 1619, the 23-year-old Descartes was spending the winter in Germany, and going through a period of emotional distress. He was troubled by difficulties with his sexuality and religious beliefs and, at the same time, he was struggling with a concept for a unified system of mathematics.

During the night of 10 November, Descartes experienced three dreams, which he later said 'could only have come from above'. The first two were filled with terrifying apparitions, violent winds, thunder, and flashing sparks. He interpreted these as representing the consequence of his failings and sins. The third was the most significant of all.

Descartes dreamt that he found and read a dictionary and also a volume of poetry. As a later biographer wrote: 'he not only decided while sleeping that it was a dream, but also interpreted

it before sleep left him.' To Descartes, the dictionary represented science, and the book of poetry represented philosophy. He believed that, while asleep, he had been visited by 'the spirit of Truth, which had wanted to open to him the treasures of all the sciences', and he realised that it was possible to apply mathematical methods to philosophical thought.

The young mathematician was so moved by his dreams that it was several days before he could begin to put his thoughts down on paper, but when he did so, he found that words flowed from his pen. For the rest of his life he devoted himself to developing his philosophy – which changed the course of Western thought. Yet, ironically, one of the conclusions Descartes eventually reached was that dreams are not a product of the rational mind, but represent mere fantasies and unfulfilled desires. As one later writer put it, his was 'the dream that would eventually put an end to dreaming'.

But other thinkers would not have agreed. An eighteenth-century philosopher, the Marquis de Condorcet, reported that he frequently left knotty problems incomplete, after he had been working many hours on them. He went to bed, and solved the problems in his dreams. And the nineteenth-century novelist Charlotte Brontë told her biographer that she often concentrated on a difficulty with her writing before she went to sleep, and woke up with the solution.

The American inventor Elias Howe had been struggling for years to develop a practical sewing machine. One night in 1844 he dreamt that he had been captured by a tribe of savages, whose leader roared: 'Elias Howe, I command you on pain of death to finish this machine at once.' Poor Howe found it impossible to obey, and the leader ordered that he should be put to death. But, as the savages advanced on him with their spears, he noticed that each spear had an eye-shaped hole

Descartes dreamt that he found and read a dictionary
and also a volume of poetry…To Descartes, the dictionary
represented science, and the book of poetry
represented philosophy

close to its tip. He awoke with excitement, sprang from his bed, and quickly went to work. And so the lockstitch sewing machine was born.

Other dreamers have had equally creative visions. In 1865 the German chemist Friedrich Kekulé was puzzling over the molecular structure of the compound benzene. He knew that it contained six atoms of carbon and six of hydrogen, but he could not work out how they were joined together. Then, as he later told a conference of fellow scientists:

I turned the chair to the fireplace, and sank into a half sleep. The atoms danced before my eyes … wriggling and turning like snakes. And see, what was that? One of the snakes seized its own tail, and the image whirled scornfully before my eyes. As though from a flash of lightning, I awoke. I occupied the rest of the night working out the consequences of the hypothesis.

The revolutionary solution was that the six carbon atoms were joined in a ring, or more exactly a hexagon, with one hydrogen atom attached at each corner. It was the beginning of a branch of chemistry that has brought us thousands of synthetic substances. And Kekulé concluded his account with words that would have scandalised Descartes – and no doubt scandalised many of those present: 'Let us learn to dream, gentlemen, and then we may perhaps discover the truth.'

Another chemist had an equally important influence upon modern understanding of atomic structure. He was Dmitri Mendeleev, a professor at the technological institute of St Petersburg. For years he had been searching for a logical way of tabulating the elements according to their atomic weights. One night in 1869, exhausted after wrestling with the problem, Mendeleev fell into an uneasy sleep. And he dreamt of 'a table where all the elements fell into place as required'. As soon as he woke, he wrote out the details of what

> *As soon as he woke, he wrote out the details of what is now known as the Periodic Table of elements*

is now known as the Periodic Table of elements – 'and only in one place did a correction later seem necessary'. Just as importantly, he was able, by considering the gaps in his tabulation, to predict the existence of three new elements; and within 15 years all three had been discovered.

Nearly 40 years later, the Danish physicist Niels Bohr, who was an important figure in the development of atomic energy, claimed it was a dream that gave him the idea for the hydrogen atom structure that is named after him. He also said that he had dreamt of the mushroom-shaped cloud that, years later, was produced by the explosion of the atomic bomb.

A problem of a very different kind faced H.V. Hilprecht, professor of Assyrian at the University of Pennsylvania. In 1893 archaeologists from the university excavated the Babylonian ruins of the Temple of Bel at Nippur, in what is now Iraq. They sent Professor Hilprecht detailed drawings of two fragments of agate, with inscriptions that they asked him to translate. After weeks of work he had to admit that he could not decipher the inscriptions, although he suggested that the fragments were from finger rings.

Then he had a dream in which 'a tall, thin priest, of the old pre-Christian Nippur, about forty years of age' appeared and took him into the treasure-house of the temple. It was a small room, with a low ceiling, and without windows. The priest explained that the fragments were not finger rings. King Kurigalzu, he said, had presented an inscribed agate cylinder to the temple; but later, when the priests were ordered to make a pair of earrings for the statue of the god Nimib, they cut the cylinder into three parts. Two were used to make the earrings. Said the priest: 'If you put the two together, you will have confirmation of my words. But the third ring you have not found … and you will never find it.'

When he awoke, Hilprecht told his wife of the dream, and when he re-examined the drawings, he found 'all the details of the dream precisely verified insofar as the means of identification were in my hands'. Later he visited the museum in Turkey where the two fragments were kept, but in separate cases. When he put them together, they fitted perfectly, and he was able to read the inscription.

DREAMS OF CREATIVITY

Charlotte Bronte was not the only writer to place great value upon dreaming. One of the most unusual pieces of poetry in the English language is *Kubla Khan*, by Samuel Taylor Coleridge, and, in a preface to an edition of his work, Coleridge described how the poem – incomplete as it was – came to be written. Kublai Khan was the grandson of the great twelfth-century

Mongol conqueror Jingis Khan, and emperor of China. The thirteenth-century Italian trader and explorer Marco Polo wrote a description of the wonders of the Khan's court, and Coleridge had been reading this before he fell asleep, after taking some opium 'for a slight indisposition'.

When he awoke, Coleridge had the text of a complete poem – some 300 lines long – in his head. He began to write it down, but then someone ('a person from Porlock') knocked at the door and, an hour later, when Coleridge was once more alone, he found he could remember no more.

There are many other examples. Geronimo Cardano, the sixteenth-century Italian

Spencer Tracy in one of many film adaptations of Robert Louis Stevenson's Dr Jekyll and Mr Hyde, *which came to the author in a dream.*

mathematician and philosopher, was living in poverty in Milan when he began to experience the same dream night after night. It was the idea for a book, a violent attack on the practices of the physicians of the city. He began to write the book, and continued to have the same dream as he wrote; in fact, it occurred more frequently when he rested from his labours – and it ceased entirely when the book was completed.

Robert Louis Stevenson, the Scottish author of *Treasure Island,* claimed that many of his shorter stories came complete to him in dreams, and in an essay he attributed his inspiration to the 'Little People' or 'Brownies': '[They] do half my work for me while I am fast asleep and, in all human likelihood, do the rest for me as well when I am awake and fondly suppose I do it for myself.'

Stevenson described how he came to complete one of his best-known stories, *The Strange Case of Dr Jekyll and Mr Hyde:*

I had long been trying … to find a body, a vehicle for that strong sense of man's double being which must at times come in upon and overwhelm the mind of every thinking creature … For two days I went about racking my brains for a plot of any sort; and on the second night I dreamed the scene at the window, and a scene afterwards split in two, in which Hyde, pursued for some crime, took the powder and underwent the change in the presence of his pursuers. All the rest was made awake, and consciously.

Musicians, also, have claimed to hear their compositions for the first time in their dreams, among them Mozart and Schumann. Richard Wagner wrote of such an experience in his autobiography:

I sank into a kind of somnambulistic state, in which I suddenly had the feeling of being immersed in rapidly flowing water. Its rushing soon resolved itself for me into the musical sound of the chord of E flat major, resounding into persistent broken chords; these in turn transformed themselves into melodic figurations of increasing motion, yet the E flat major triad never changed, and seemed by its continuance to impart infinite significance to the element in which I was sinking.

And what Wagner heard in this dream state became the leading motif of his immense operatic cycle, *The Ring of the Nibelung.*

The eighteenth-century Italian composer Giuseppe Tartini once dreamt that he found the Devil trapped in a bottle. The Devil swore to become his servant if Tartini would help him escape. When the Devil was free, Tartini handed him his violin:

What was my astonishment when I heard him play with consummate skill a sonata of such exquisite beauty that it surpasses the most audacious dreams of my imagination. I was delighted, transported, enchanted.

When he awoke, wrote Tartini:

I grasped my violin in order to play the music I had heard in my dream, but in vain. So I sat down to write what I had dreamed, and what I then composed is, without doubt, the best of my works. I called it 'The Devil's Trill Sonata'.

Nevertheless, it must be admitted that not all artists have been convinced of the creative power of dreams. At the height of his fame, the English novelist Charles Dickens was portrayed by a contemporary artist dozing in his study and surrounded by the vibrant characters of his stories. But Dickens denied the idea. 'It would be,' he said, 'like a man's dreaming of meeting himself, which is clearly an impossibility.'

chapter two

SLEEPING AND DREAMING

As much as a half of every modern home may be given up to rooms specifically devoted to sleeping (and the rituals normally associated with sleeping and waking, such as undressing and dressing, bathing, etc.), and, on average, the human race spends a third of its life asleep. Yet, despite many fascinating discoveries by scientists in recent years, the reason for sleep remains largely unknown.

It is not due just to the need for rest and recovery from exertion: many animals – and even humans – can sleep on their feet, and can wake in an instant to rapid movement if danger threatens. Nevertheless, some kind of sleep seems to be essential to all the more highly developed animals; it is said that if an animal is forcibly deprived of sleep for five days, it will die. Even lower forms of animal life seem to sleep at regular intervals, although it is difficult to tell whether this is similar to the sleep enjoyed by humans. If

sleep were not essential to the animal body, we could expect that it would long ago have been eliminated by natural selection because, even in the lightest sleep, animals are more vulnerable to attack by predators.

Among humans, the amount of sleep needed can vary greatly from person to person. Some people wake refreshed and ready for another day's work after a mere four or five hours; others feel deprived if they have slept for only nine or ten hours; and some are able to will themselves to sleep even longer. But, basically, an individual's sleep pattern remains the same. It has little relation to climate or place: whether in the long hours of the Arctic winter, or the 24-hour daylight of the Arctic summer, individuals seem to sleep for much the same length of time. The rhythm of 'normal' daily sleep tends to be dictated by the 24-hour cycle of the sun, and the need to rise at the same time every morning. On the other hand, people who have spent long

periods underground, isolated from events in daylight, generally sleep for nearly the same number of hours as usual, but find that their 'days' have become imperceptibly shortened, as they go to sleep a little earlier each day.

One thing is obvious: sleep is not a shutting down of the body's physical systems, nor of the brain's activity. All the metabolic processes continue, the heart continues to pump blood round the arterial system, the breathing is, on the whole, steady and regular. Although many of the muscles are relaxed, even immobile at times, there are between 20 and 40 periods, each of a

few seconds, during a night's sleep when they become active – the sleeper changes position, flings out an arm, clenches and unclenches the fingers, and maybe wakes briefly because of the movement.

Reactions to external stimuli, however, are considerably altered. In waking life, for example, coming into contact with something unpleasant – or, indeed, pleasant – provokes an immediate physical reaction. But it is not the same during sleep: the normal reaction may be suppressed, and the message to the brain converted in some way into a dream image that is related, but often only distantly.

Nearly all life on our planet is subject to a regular alternation of light and dark, warmth and relative coolness

The onset and duration of human sleep appear to be part of what is known as the 'circadian' rhythm – from the Latin *circa dies,* meaning approximately one day. Nearly all life on our planet is subject to a regular alternation of light and dark, warmth and relative coolness, and it is scarcely surprising that physiological processes should follow this pattern. In particular, the temperature of the body fluctuates throughout each day by something in excess of 1 °C (1.8 °F), reaching a maximum in mid-evening, and then falling rapidly until around 4 a.m., when it begins to rise again. There appears to be a direct connection between rising body temperature and alertness, and falling temperature is soon followed by sleepiness.

Another aspect of the circadian rhythm is the awareness of darkness and light. Until relatively recently – before clocks were common objects in the home, and when artificial lighting was still an expensive luxury – most people went to bed soon after sunset, and rose at dawn. It is the inbuilt biological 'clock' that causes the effects of 'jet lag', when we move rapidly from one time zone to another, and are forced to adapt to habits dictated by the local day-night cycle, while the body's own day-night cycle remains unchanged.

INVESTIGATING BRAIN ACTIVITY

Meanwhile, the brain remains active, even during the deepest sleep. Over the past 60 years, extensive studies have been made using electroencephalograph (EEG) apparatus. This records the variations in the electrical activity of the brain – literally, the 'brain waves' – during the waking and sleeping hours.

The early results of these studies led many scientists to believe that people fell quite quickly into a deep sleep, which gradually grew lighter as morning approached. Dreams, they suggested, were random events, generally very brief in length – even though they appeared to the dreamer to last much longer – which occurred shortly before waking.

However, an important discovery, which radically changed the theories of sleeping and dreaming, was made in 1951 by Eugene Aserinsky, a graduate physiology student at the University of Chicago. He was studying the sleep patterns of babies when he observed that the infants' eyes continued to move under their closed lids long after they had lapsed into sleep. The movements would cease for a while, and then begin again. Aserinsky wondered whether this cycle was an indication of lighter and deeper stages of sleep, and he went to his professor, Nathaniel Kleitman, with his observations.

Kleitman suggested that similar eye movements in adults could be compared with their EEG activity at the same time, and he and Aserinsky set up a 'sleep laboratory'. They began with observations of Aserinsky's 10-year-old son, and carried on for two years with a number of adult volunteers. They found that sleepers had periods of rapid eye movement (REM), which alternated with periods when the eyes were still, or moving only slowly. These periods occurred in cycles of approximately 90 minutes, some four or five times during a night's sleep.

Aserinsky and Kleitman also discovered that if they woke their sleepers during an REM period, they were able to recall dreams in extensive detail. Woken from non-REM sleep, however, the volunteers could usually not remember even a fragment of a dream. If they were able to recall anything, it was usually of an everyday nature, very different from the dramatic and often fantastic images of REM sleep.

Researchers from all over the world have now contributed to a detailed description of the sleeping condition. At the border between waking and sleeping, the individual enters what is known as the 'hypnagogic' state: the body's muscles relax, there is often the feeling of floating, the eyes roll slowly, and all kinds of unusual images seem to pass through the mind. At this point the EEG still shows the rapid, spiky 'alpha' waves of the wakeful brain but, as the individual drifts into the first stage of sleep, these give way to slower, more regular waves – known as 'theta' waves – which are characteristic of light sleep.

The first stage is very brief: it lasts from just a few seconds to 10 minutes at most. Gradually the theta waves die down, and become mixed in the

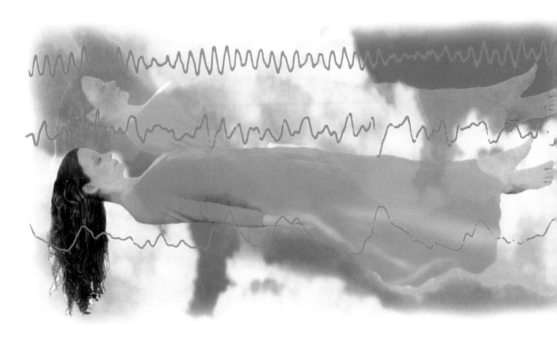

EEG trace with two other wave patterns: sharp, jumpy waves known as 'spindles', which indicate rapid brain activity, and 'K-complexes', which are waves that are large and steep. At this point – called stage two – the individual is certainly asleep; however, if he or she is woken, they may deny having slept at all, and assert that they have been 'thinking'.

Some 15 to 30 minutes after sleep has begun, large, slow 'delta' waves gradually replace the spindles and K-complexes. This phase has been divided into stages three and four. The sleeper is deeply asleep: if woken, he or she will feel disorientated and will have to struggle against the desire to return to sleep.

At the end of the first 90-minute cycle, the spindles and K-complexes of stage two briefly recur, and the brain then emerges from non-REM sleep into REM sleep. This phase is physiologically so different from both waking and non-REM stages of sleep that some researchers have called it a 'third state of existence'. The blood pressure and pulse rate increase, and the EEG trace is similar to that of a wakeful brain. At the same time, however, most of the body remains still; the eyes begin rapid movement, the facial muscles and the fingers and toes may twitch, but the principal muscles are temporarily paralysed.

This first major REM period can last from 10 to 15 minutes. The sleeper then comes close to wakefulness, before entering non-REM sleep once more. As sleep progresses, stages three and four become shorter, or may be omitted entirely, so that sleep alternates between non-

REM stage two and REM. The REM phases gradually become longer, and may last for as much as two-thirds of the 90-minute cycle; as a result, up to a half of a sleeper's dreaming time can occur during the last two hours of sleep, and may represent in all one-fifth of the total sleeping time. This means that the average person spends nearly five years of his or her life dreaming – and in that time it is estimated they will experience some 150,000 dreams.

Another of Professor Kleitman's former students, William Dement, carried out a series of experiments at Mount Sinai Hospital, New York, in 1959. For five successive nights he woke volunteer subjects each time they entered REM sleep. Each night they entered REM phases more often, until by the fifth night they were experiencing 20 REM phases a night. It was as if they had a biological need to return to REM, and experience a specific amount of dream time. Dement then gave them a 'night off', and found that they spent longer in REM sleep than normal – a true case of 'catching up on one's sleep'. However, other volunteers, who were woken during non-REM sleep, did not show any need for extra REM time.

Dement turned his attention to cats, which also show REM. He woke the cats at the onset of REM sleep over periods as long as 70 days, and the animals demonstrated marked changes in behaviour: some became merely restless, but others refused to wash themselves.

> *This phase is so different from both waking and non-REM stages of sleep that some researchers have called it a 'third state of existence'*

He described how insects were swarming over his
turntables, saw a rabbit on the windowsill, and complained
that cobwebs were clinging to his face

At the same time, Dement disproved the belief that dreams last only a few seconds. He showed that human dream time and real time were much the same: dreams took as long to be experienced as would the same events in waking life, sometimes lasting as long as 20 minutes. He also discovered that the rapid eye movement often related to actions in the dream. One subject was seen to move his eyes backwards and forwards horizontally many times: when he was woken, he said he had been watching a game of table tennis.

The year 1959 also provided Dement with a dramatic voluntary experiment in sleep deprivation. An American radio disc jockey named Peter Tripp announced that he would go without sleep for 200 hours, in return for listeners' pledges to a certain charity. His 'wakeathon' was supervised by a medical team of which Dement was a member.

For the first two or three days Tripp remained relatively coherent, but he then began to suffer hallucinations. He described how insects were swarming over his turntables, saw a rabbit on the windowsill, and complained that cobwebs were clinging to his face. At first he dismissed these events as products of his fatigued imagination, but after five days he became seriously disturbed, and began to view them as real.

Then he became paranoid: he accused the observing team of insulting him, and described one of them as wearing a suit of wriggling worms. He imagined that a cupboard burst into flames, insisted that the team had started the fire, and said that they had lied to him about the time he had already remained awake.

On the eighth day, the team decided to allow Tripp to continue, because his heart rate and blood pressure remained normal. However, as the 200 hours were reached, he accused one of

> *He imagined that a cupboard burst into flames, insisted that the team had started the fire, and said that they had lied to him*

the team of being an undertaker who had come to measure him for his coffin, and ran from the studio into the street, crying desperately for help.

Remarkably, Tripp rapidly recovered physical and mental health after only 13 hours of sleep, although he complained of a feeling of depression for several weeks following his 'wakeathon'. But it was clear that sleep, and the dreaming that accompanies it, serves an essential physical and physiological need.

THE SCIENCE OF DREAMING

All this research, which still continues, tells us a great deal about when dreams occur, and how long they last; it is also clear that dreaming is an essential part of sleeping, but what causes the dreams and why they seem to be necessary are still matters for debate.

One scientist, Ian Oswald at Manchester University (later professor of psychiatry at Edinburgh University), put forward a purely physiological explanation. He suggested that dreams are the result of the way in which the nervous system sets about repairing exhausted brain tissue. He showed that, during non-REM sleep, numerous growth hormones are released into the bloodstream, to restore bone and muscle cells after the labours of the day. As the REM phase begins, this flow ceases. Oswald proposed that a similar process then went on in the brain, and that dreams were no more than a by-product of this chemical activity.

Another, rather similar, explanation was suggested by J. Allan Hobson and Robert McCarley of Harvard Medical School. They began to make use of micro-electrodes in order to detect the activity of specific areas of the brain. Hobson wrote in 1988: 'Now, after thirty years of experience, we can begin to understand how brain activity may be organised.'

During REM sleep, the brain's cortex, the site of most higher brain functions – including movement and sight – is very active; but parts of the brainstem, the lowest part of the hindbrain where it meets the spinal column, are 'switched off'. This means, for instance, that although the motor cortex, which normally controls muscle movement, remains active, it cannot communicate signals to the muscles, and so the body is effectively paralysed during this phase. Because the brainstem is not operating fully, few incoming signals from the sensory system get through to the cortex. But the hindbrain and midbrain spontaneously generate signals that are indistinguishable from those that would normally come from the senses. These bursts of 'meaningless neural static' – rather like the 'jamming' of radio broadcasts – are received by the cortex, which interprets them as best it can. It identifies them as shapes, colours and other sensations, relates them to stored memories, and so makes up a story.

As their research continued, Hobson and his co-workers were able to distinguish 'REM-on' and 'REM-off' clusters of cells in the brainstem. The REM-on cells send messages to the higher areas of the brain by means of a chemical called acetylcholine. Hobson managed to set off 'artificial' dreams in volunteer subjects by injecting them with a chemical that mimicked acetylcholine, and was able to increase the amount of REM sleep by 300 per cent. He believed that he had, as he put it, 'found the dream nerve'.

Francis Crick – the Englishman who won a Nobel prize for his work on the structure of DNA – and Cambridge University mathematician Graeme Mitchison advanced another theory. As William Dement showed, and other researchers have confirmed, the sleeper who has his or her REM sleep interrupted needs to 'make up' what has been 'missed'. REM sleep obviously has a necessary function and, since many dreams are forgotten, the forgetting may be part of this function.

'We dream in order to forget.' In fact, he theorised that trying to remember a dream defeated its purpose

Crick and Mitchison pointed out that, during waking hours, the mind was bombarded with much information, both sensory and conceptual, that it had no need to retain. They suggested that during dreams the brain sorted through this information, storing what was necessary, and getting rid of the rest in a surge of activity that the sleeper perceived as a dream. As Crick put it: 'We

Ian Oswald suggested that mental activity during waking hours gradually reduces the brain's supply of essential chemicals

dream in order to forget.' In fact, he theorised that trying to remember a dream defeated its purpose. This theory, however, is at odds with the experience of many people: that memory information that seems to be lost for ever in waking life can be recovered in dreams. British psychologist Christopher Evans, who was also a computer expert, compared the working of the brain to a computer in his book *Landscapes of the Night* (1983). He described how his watch was stolen, but he was unable to give the police any details of its make. That night, however, he dreamt that he saw the watch in every detail, including the manufacturer's name. Evans pointed out that a computer processes, stores and retrieves information, just as the brain does. But the computer's operation becomes slower as more information is stored. Every so often, the computer operator must sort through its memory, 'tidying up' the information, transferring some to another store, and getting rid of what is no longer needed. In the same way, a dream sorts through accumulated information, as Crick and Mitchison proposed; it does not erase anything that might prove useful at a later date, however, but consigns it to a more distant storage area.

Some support for these theories – of both Crick and Mitchison, and Evans – comes from the observation that people who learn new skills during the day tend to experience more REM sleep at night. In this connection, it has been said that severely mentally disabled people have fewer dreams than normal people, suggesting that their limited ability to handle information reduces their need to dream. (However, since reporting one's dreams requires a considerable degree of conscious analysis, it may be that they merely find it impossible to describe what they have experienced.)

Dreaming also seems to be important as a regulator of the emotions. Those volunteers who were regularly deprived of REM sleep tended to become irritable and anxious, and found difficulty in concentrating. Ernest Hartmann, professor of psychiatry at Tufts University, Massachusetts, put forward a theory somewhat similar to that of Ian Oswald. He suggested that mental activity during waking hours gradually reduces the brain's supply of essential chemicals. REM sleep renews the supply, maintaining emotional stability and assisting the learning and memory processes.

On the other hand, it seems that too much REM sleep can have the opposite effect. Patients suffering from severe depression reach the REM phase more rapidly than healthy people, and remain in this phase longer. Experiments carried out at the Mental Health Institute in Atlanta, Georgia, revealed that many clinically depressed people showed a marked improvement when their REM sleep was regularly interrupted.

WHAT IS A DREAM?

At this point we can make only one valid generalisation: a dream is an event perceived by the brain during the REM phase of normal sleep. It may be a purely random response to chemical changes in the brain; or to confusing signals that have occasionally passed through the brainstem from the senses, or that have been generated in the hindbrain. It may be the means by which the brain sorts and classifies – and in certain cases rejects – information that has been received during waking hours. It may arise from a deep exploration of the memory. Or it may be due to a combination of all these factors.

Two centuries before physiologists began to experiment with the human brain, the French philosopher Denis Diderot (1713–84) advanced an inspired suggestion in his *Encyclopedia* that brilliantly foresaw what they were to discover:

We can only be said to be dreaming when we become conscious of these images, when these images imprint themselves on our memories, and we are able to say we have had such and such a dream, or at least that we have been dreaming. But, in the strictest sense, we are dreaming all the time; that is to say that as soon as sleep has taken possession of our mental operations, the mind is subject to an uninterrupted series of representations and perceptions; but sometimes they are so confused, or so dimly registered, that they do not leave the slightest trace, and this is in fact what we call 'deep sleep'; but we would be wrong to regard it as a total absence of any sort of perception, as complete mental inertia.

French writer Denis Diderot had his work burned by the authorities and suffered imprisonment in 1749. His 35-volume Encyclopedia, written 1751–56, was a major work of enlightenment.

Whatever the theory put forward to explain the occurrence of dreams, one indication seems to be common to all: dreams provide a mechanism for the necessary relief of emotion and stress during sleep – as Shakespeare's Macbeth puts it: 'sleep, that knits up the ravell'd sleeve of care'.

No matter what the dream's content, it represents an altered state of consciousness, very different from the waking condition. In many ways, a dream is similar to other altered states, such as those produced by deep hypnosis, meditation and trance, or various drugs. It is, however, a state experienced by nearly everyone, every night.

Allan Hobson noted the fine line between dreaming and insanity:

The five cardinal characteristics of dream mentation may also be seen in the hallucinations, disorientations, bizarre thoughts, delusions, and amnesias, of patients with mental illness. These mental symptoms collectively constitute delirium, dementia, and psychosis. Thus, were it not for the fact that we are asleep when they occur, we would be obliged to say that our dreams are formally psychotic and that we are all, during dreaming, formally delirious and demented … Dreaming could thus be the mental product of the same kind of psychological process that is deranged in mental illness … since all of the major signs of mental illness can be imitated by normal minds in the normal state of dreaming. The study of dreams is the study of a model of mental illness.

Two particularly dramatic types of dream have attracted the attention of psychiatrists: nightmares and night terrors. Nightmares generally occur during the latter part of sleep, when REM phases last longer, and dreaming becomes more vivid. They may last several minutes before the dreamer comes awake, short of breath and with heart pounding, after a terrifying experience. Psychiatrists believe that a nightmare is an intense dramatisation of the significance of problems or anxieties encountered recently in waking life: it draws on unconscious memories – particularly childhood fears of a world that seems incomprehensible and menacing – and builds them into a frightening and uncontrollable dream image.

Professor Ernest Hartmann wrote:'the common thread among those who have nightmares frequently is sensitivity.' In a series of experiments in Boston, he studied those who

Hell, *the right wing of Hieronymus Bosch's triptych,* Garden of Earthly Delights. *In the twentieth century, it is easy to see Bosch's work simply as a depiction of our worst nightmares and repressed fears. But in the Middle Ages, his paintings had a distinct moral purpose.*

> *Professor Ernest Hartmann wrote:'the common thread among those who have nightmares frequently is sensitivity'*

LUCID DREAMS

When subjects in dream experiments are woken during REM sleep, the dreams they report are generally mundane, lacking the bizarre nature of dreams that are described on normal waking after the last phase of sleep. This is probably because only the most unusual experiences are memorable: the more everyday the dream event, the less likely it is to be remembered in any detail.

What makes a dream memorable is its oddness. In waking life, we can be aware of being physically in a specific location, and at the same time aware of thoughts and mental images that are unrelated to it. This does not seem to occur in dreams. The psychophysiologist Allan Rechtshaffen drew attention to what he called 'the single-mindedness and isolation of dreams'. He wrote:

I cannot remember a dream report which took the form 'Well, I was dreaming of such and such, but as I was dreaming this I was imagining a different scene which was completely unrelated.' The imagery of the dream seems to overwhelm any independent consciousness: we are usually without any ability to exercise the imagination, and unaware that we are dreaming.

Now, however, psychologists are paying increasing attention to what is called 'lucid' dreaming. This is a relatively rare phenomenon, in which the dreamer is aware that he or she is dreaming. Often, they find that they are able – consciously, as it were – to influence the dream events and the people involved.

The first recorded reference to lucid dreams appears in Aristotle's treatise *On Dreams*, written in the fourth century BC. He wrote: 'Often, when one is asleep, there is something in consciousness which declares that what then presents itself is a

said they experienced nightmares at least once a week; many were creative workers in the arts, music or theatre. They often referred to themselves as 'different from other people'. Hartmann described them as 'very open and vulnerable … most had had stormy adolescences, sometimes followed by bouts with depression, alcohol, and suicide attempts.' He concluded that many had a deficient sense of personal identity, finding it difficult to separate reality from fantasy, and some were borderline psychotics.

Night terrors are quite different. They generally occur, not during the REM phase, but in the deep slumber of stages three and four. The sleeper wakes suddenly with a loud cry, sitting up terrified, but usually unable to remember what the cause was. The occurrence of night terror appears to be a hereditary trait, and researchers have suggested that there is some kind of genetic fault in the normal mechanism of waking. The usual progression from stages three and four to REM sleep does not take place, and the sleeper comes suddenly awake. Children, who spend longer in stages three and four than adults, often suffer from night terrors.

dream.' Over the centuries other writers, such as St Augustine and St Thomas Aquinas, made the same observation. And in the second edition of *The Interpretation of Dreams*, the pioneer Austrian psychologist Sigmund Freud wrote:

There are some people who are quite clearly aware during the night that they are asleep and dreaming, and who thus seem to possess the faculty of consciously directing their dreams. If, for instance, a dreamer of this kind is dissatisfied with the turn taken by a dream, he can break it off without waking up, and start again in another direction – just as a popular dramatist may, under pressure, give his play a happier ending.

The first examination of this type of dream was made by Hervey de Saint-Denis, a professor of Chinese at the Collège de France in Paris. In 1867 he published the results of 20 years' study and analysis of dreams in *Dreams and How to Control Them*. He stated that he had gained the ability to shape his dreams by careful recall of them, and by developing an awareness of being in the dream state and willing himself awake when he wished.

Nevertheless, at the beginning of the twentieth century most psychologists were highly sceptical about the possibility of lucid dreams. The Dutch researcher Frederik van Eeden, however, had himself experienced lucid dreams, and in fact coined the term in a paper he read before the British Society for Psychical Research (SPR) in 1913. One of his audience was Frederic Myers, a founder member of the SPR. He confirmed that he had had lucid dreams on three occasions, and suggested that they were a subject worth studying by psychical researchers.

Aristotle (right) with Plato. With Sigmund Freud, dream psychology had unmistakably arrived, but the the first reference to lucid dreaming is to be found in Aristotle's On Dreams.

In his paper, van Eeden described and analysed a total of 352 dreams. Of the lucid dream he said:

The re-integration of the psychic functions is so complete that the sleeper … reaches a state of perfect awareness, and is able to direct his attention, and to attempt different acts of free volition. Yet the sleep, as I am able confidently to state, is undisturbed, deep and refreshing.

He cited one particularly interesting example, recorded in his dream diary for 9 September 1904:

I dreamt that I stood at a table before a window. On the table were different objects. I was perfectly aware that I was dreaming, and I considered what sorts of experiments I could make. I began by trying to break glass, by beating it with a stone; I put a small table glass on two stones, and struck it with another stone. Yet it would not break. Then I took a fine claret glass from the table and struck it with my fist, with all my might, at the same time reflecting how dangerous it would be to do this in waking life; yet the glass remained whole. But lo! When I looked at it again after some time, it was broken …

I had a very curious impression of being in a fake world, cleverly imitated but with small failures. I took the broken glass and threw it out of the window, in order to observe whether I could hear the tinkling. I heard the noise all right, and I even saw two dogs run away from it quite naturally. I thought what a good imitation this comedy-world was. Then I saw a decanter with claret and tasted it, and noted with perfect clearness of mind: 'Well, we can also have voluntary impressions of taste in this dream-world; this has quite the taste of wine.'

Van Eeden said that 'the sensation of having a body – having eyes, hands, a mouth that speaks, and so on – is perfectly distinct; yet I know at the same time that the physical body is sleeping and has quite a different position'. There was a feeling of 'slipping from one body into another, and there is distinctly a double recollection of the two bodies'. He suggested that there was a connection with the 'astral body' that some psychics believe separates from the physical body during sleep or semi-trance states.

The difficulty in researching lucid dreams is that they occur to relatively few people, and even then only rarely. It was not until 1977 that any progress was made in this field. Stephen LaBerge, a young researcher in psychophysiology at the Sleep Laboratory of Stanford University, California, had experienced many lucid dreams as a child, and as an adult had them once a month or so. When he began his research, he developed a way of willing himself to have a lucid dream, and soon raised his total to more than 20 a month, with sometimes as many as four in a single night.

LaBerge then decided to devise a set of signals by which he could record, while he was sleeping, that he was experiencing a lucid dream. One was a double up-and-down movement of his eyes behind their closed lids. The other made use of the Morse code: he clenched his left fist for a dot, and his right for a dash.

The Dream by French painter, Pierre Puvis de Chavannes (1824–98). The interpretation is subjective, but it is tempting to see in this nineteenth-century painting a depiction of astral bodies – entities that separate from the physical body during sleep – paying a visit to a sleeping friend.

These methods made it possible to establish experimentally that lucid dreams occurred, and were not subsequently imagined by the sleeper. In order to make use of subjects other than himself, LaBerge devised a pair of plastic goggles, fitted with sensors that triggered a faint, pulsing red light as the sleeper entered an REM phase. This was just sufficient to make the dreamer aware that he or she was dreaming, without waking them. British research psychologist Keith Hearne developed a similar device, which he called his 'dream machine': a sensor attached to the sleeper's nostril detected the irregular breathing of the REM phase, and sent four mild electric shocks to the dreamer's wrist to indicate 'this is a dream'.

Towards the end of a lucid dream, the dreamer often dreams of waking up. As one experimental subject reported:

I dreamed that my wife and I awoke, got up and dressed. On pulling up the blind, we made the amazing discovery that the row of houses opposite had vanished, and in their place were bare fields. I said to my wife: 'This means I am dreaming, though everything seems so real and I feel perfectly awake.'

He was unable to persuade his wife that it was a dream, so he decided to convince her by jumping out of the window:

Ruthlessly ignoring her pleading and objection, I opened the window and climbed out on to the sill. I then

> ## 'Ruthlessly ignoring her pleading and objection, I opened the window and climbed out on to the sill. I then jumped'

jumped, and floated gently down into the street. When my feet touched the pavement I awoke … As a matter of fact, I was very nervous about jumping, for the atmosphere inside our bedroom seemed so absolutely real that it nearly made me accept the manifest absurdity of things outside.

SENSORY HALLUCINATIONS

Lucid dreamers, in particular, show a marked tendency to experience a form of synesthesia – the conversion of one kind of sensory signal into another: physical feelings into visual images or smells, sounds into colours – during the hypnagogic stage of entering sleep. In this stage, they may report hearing loud explosions or vague voices repeating their own names, seeing vividly coloured patterns, and experiencing the sensation of falling, while they may utter disjointed, meaningless phrases.

The Russian mystic Peter Ouspensky described a startling hallucination of this kind in 1912:

I am falling asleep. Golden dots, sparks and tiny stars appear and disappear before my eyes. These sparks and stars gradually merge into a golden net with diagonal meshes that moves slowly and regularly in rhythm with the beating of my heart, which I feel quite distinctly. The next moment the golden net is transformed into rows of brass helmets belonging to Roman soldiers marching along the street below … I smell the sea, feel the wind, the warm sun.

This flying gives me a wonderfully pleasant sensation, and I cannot help opening my eyes.

These hypnagogic images can seem so real that the sleeper awakes: the imagined smell of something burning, for instance, can send them to the kitchen to be sure that a pan has not been left on the stove. One woman repeatedly heard church bells and the sound of an organ as she fell asleep, and often got out of bed to open the windows, only to be met by complete silence outside.

Although hallucinations such as these can bring the sleeper awake with a sense of something wrong, most hypnagogic images are pleasant, or even mildly comic. One dreamer described 'a family of skulls driving along … I could tell it was a friendly family'.

However, it is difficult to wake someone from deep sleep, particularly in the REM phase. It has been found, for example, that a sound as loud as 80 decibels is necessary. Yet some relatively quiet sounds can register in the sleeper's mind. In experiments at Edinburgh University, a list of names, including those of boyfriends or girlfriends, was read to sleeping students. When the name of a friend was reached, the skin of the sleepers' palms registered a noticeable electric response.

The mind, however, can play some strange tricks. One student 'heard' the name of a former girlfriend, Jenny, a redhead. But he dreamt that he was trying to open a safe with a jemmy and that it was coloured 'a sort of red'. Another, when read the name Sheila, dreamt that he had left behind a book of poems by the German

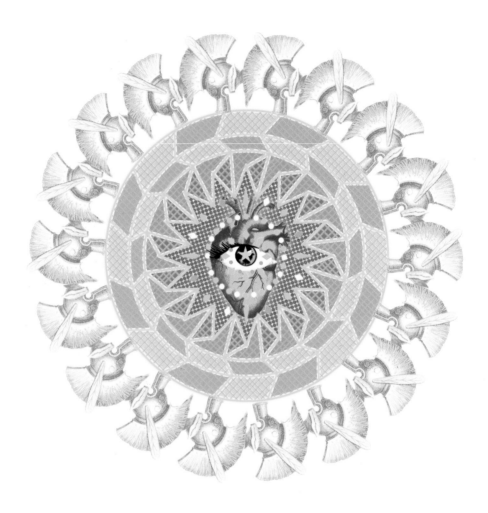

The next moment the golden net is transformed into rows of brass helmets belonging to Roman soldiers marching along the street below

writer Schiller. And a girl, hearing the name Robert, dreamt of a film in which a rabbit appeared.

Despite the theories of the physiologists that the sensory part of the brainstem is out of action during a major part of sleep, the mind seems capable of registering other sensory signals – although it may well change them into something different. Wetting the foot of a dreamer, for instance, may cause him or her to dream of wading in water; a gentle tap on the head may produce a dream of being attacked.

There is now plenty of experimental evidence that dreams are necessary for our health and wellbeing, but the reason for this is still in doubt. In waking life we try to present an ordered personality to those around us, but this often means suppressing many of our natural instincts – 'the real me'. Perhaps dreams are messages – warning, curative or even helpful – from this other self.

The problem is that these messages are in a code that we frequently cannot understand. As the Austrian philosopher Ludwig Wittgenstein (1889–1951) put it:

Austrian-born philosopher Ludwig Wittgenstein – who grappled in his early work with the nature and limitations of language and later concluded that language is essentially a toolkit – saw in the images of dreams a coded language in its own right.

There seems to be something in dream images that has a certain resemblance to the signs of a language, as a series of marks on paper or sand might have. There might be no mark that we recognised as a conventional sign in any alphabet we knew, and yet we might have a strong feeling that they must be a language of some sort, that they mean something.

So what do these bizarre images, very different from our waking experience, these ancient symbols, these puns and double meanings, have to tell us? It is important to know.

chapter three

SHADOWS
OF THE MIND

54

The first systematic psychological study of dreams was made by the nineteenth-century French physician Alfred Maury, who set out to show that dreams were caused by external sensations. His experimental approach, however, was largely limited to the preliminary, hypnagogic, stage of sleep. He had a colleague sit by his bedside who, as soon as Maury appeared to be asleep, produced external physical stimuli by shining a light at his closed eyes, ringing a bell, and so on.

Maury found the results confirmed his theory. A lighted match held under his nose resulted in a dream that he was sailing on a ship when its powder magazine exploded. The scent of eau de Cologne produced a dream of a bazaar in Cairo. And a drop of water on his forehead transported him to an Italian café, where he endeavoured to cool his sweaty body by drinking a glass of white wine. One of Maury's dreams has become particularly famous. He dreamt that he was involved in the events following the French Revolution, was condemned to death, and carried off to be beheaded by the guillotine. At the moment the guillotine blade fell he woke up – to find that the bedhead had fallen across his neck.

It was for such reasons that Maury argued that dreams were due only to external stimuli. The meaning of dreams, he wrote in *Sleep and Dreams* (1861), was of no more interest than the sound

> *The scent of eau de Cologne produced a dream of a bazaar in Cairo*

made 'by the ten fingers of a man who knows nothing of music, wandering over the keys of a piano'. Nevertheless, he made the intriguing suggestion that, as a sleeper sinks into slumber, he or she enters a state not unlike senility, regressing to a host of childhood memories. 'In dreaming,' he wrote, 'man reveals himself to himself in all his nakedness and native misery.' This was an idea that was to be expressed in a very different way by the psychoanalysts.

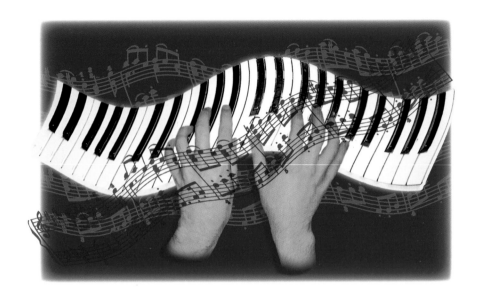

DREAMS AND THE UNCONSCIOUS

Psychoanalysis – the study and explanation of how our behaviour reflects, and is affected by, what takes place in the mind – was founded by Sigmund Freud (1856–1939). He was born in Moravia, which was then part of the Austro-Hungarian empire, and studied medicine in Vienna. He began specialising in neurology, but then learnt of the discovery by a senior colleague, Josef Breuer (1842–1925), that the disorder known as hysteria could be cured by making a patient

the disorder known as hysteria could be cured by making a patient recall unpleasant memories under hypnosis

recall unpleasant memories under hypnosis. As a result, Freud went to Paris in 1885 to train in hypnosis with the French neurologist Jean Martin Charcot (1825–93). On his return, he turned his attention to the study and treatment of pathological states of mind.

However, Freud found that hypnosis was inadequate for his purposes, and he developed the technique of 'free association'. The patient would be encouraged to lie down and relax – on the famous couch – and to ramble on, voicing his or her thoughts just as they came to mind. This usually brought to light a wealth of dream and childhood

The patient would be encouraged to lie down and relax – on the famous couch – and to ramble on, voicing his or her thoughts

recollections, the content of which convinced Freud of the awareness of sexuality in infancy. Freud's belief in this theory lost him Breuer's friendship, as well as many of his patients and the approval of the medical profession. Forced to work alone, he wrote *The Interpretation of Dreams*, the first edition of which appeared in 1900.

This book was a vast study of dream material, including Freud's own, from which he concluded that dreams are disguised representations of repressed desires that usually have a sexual origin. He became so obsessed with this idea that he saw all dream symbols as having a sexual significance. (He was not, however, the first to suggest this: the German Karl Albert Schermer had already made such a connection in 1861.)

Briefly, Freud's theory was that humans are basically selfish animals driven by what he called the 'id', comprising aggressive instincts and crude appetites for pleasure. In particular, he identified the 'Oedipus complex', named after the mythical

'A boy's best friend is his mother.' The chilling words of Norman Bates (Anthony Perkins) to Marion Crane (Janet Leigh) in Hitchcock's sly, dark classic, Psycho, *popular cinema's best-loved dalliance with the Oedipus complex.*

Greek king who (unwittingly) killed his father and married his mother. Freud postulated that every infant desired the exclusive possession of its parent of the opposite sex, even to the extent of wishing for the death of its same-sex parent. These impulses, at odds with the requirements of society, later became repressed by the 'ego' and the 'super-ego', which acted as 'censors'. But the primitive instincts were never fully conquered, and revealed themselves in psychotic behaviour and dreams.

A good example of Freud's thinking was his analysis of a dream experienced by Carl Gustav Jung. Jung (1875–1961) was a Swiss psychiatrist who met Freud in Vienna in 1907, and was for some years his enthusiastic collaborator. The two men were on a lecture tour in the USA in 1909 when Jung had his dream.

He found himself in an upper room of a grand old house, containing fine pieces of antique furniture and with valuable paintings on the walls. 'Not bad!' Jung thought to himself.

Although he had no recollection of having been in the house before, it nevertheless seemed familiar to him, and he believed it was his. Going downstairs, he entered an older-looking set of rooms, dark, with medieval furniture and red brick floors. Pulling open a heavy door, he found a stone staircase leading down to a vaulted chamber that looked as if it dated from Roman times.

The floor of the chamber was of stone slabs, and in the middle of one was an iron ring. Jung lifted the slab and descended another stone stairway into a low cave cut out of the rock. The floor was thick with dust, among which prehistoric fragments of bone and pottery lay scattered. Among them he discovered two human skulls. And then he awoke.

When Jung told Freud his dream, Freud immediately identified the house as a symbol of female sexuality. He was particularly interested in the skulls, which he said represented death. He pressed Jung to admit that he secretly wished for the death of two female relatives. The younger man did not wish to offend his revered colleague and eventually suggested that they were his wife and his sister-in-law – at which Freud, he noticed, was greatly relieved.

But Jung was sure that he had no hostile feelings towards the two women. He decided that Freud was unwise to relate everything to sex and the id, and this event was to lead to a parting of the ways between the two men. Jung himself developed a very different interpretation of his dream.

He decided that the house represented a model of his mind. The upper floor, with its luxurious furnishings, was his conscious self and its store of acquired experience. Below this lay levels of the unconscious, each darker and more alien than the one above. As he descended, he was passing back through human history, until he found an affinity with primitive ancestors and cultures. He later wrote: 'In the cave I discovered … the world of the primitive man within myself – a world that can scarcely be reached or illuminated by consciousness.'

Soon after this Jung had another dream. He came to a customs post in the mountains on the frontier between Switzerland and Austria, and saw an elderly, stooped official walk past him, with an expression that was 'peevish, rather melancholic and vexed'. A nearby person explained that the elderly man was not really there: he was the ghost of an official who had died years before – 'He is one of those who still couldn't die properly.'

Carl Jung, Sigmund Freud's one-time collaborator, who went on to found his own school of psychoanalysis, based on the Collective Unconscious with its archetypes of humanity's basic nature.

Jung realised that the disappointed customs official represented his own unconscious image of Freud himself. While recognising the value of Freud's work, he felt that it was already old-fashioned, and that he had to develop his own theories. Seeing Freud as a ghost did not express any death wish towards him (which would have been Freud's own analysis); indeed, the last sentence of the dream implied that the older man would be remembered for ever.

'A bulwark against what?' asked Jung. 'Against the black tide of mud' – and here Freud paused – 'of occultism'

Applying Freud's own principles of word association, Jung decided that the frontier represented not only the border between the conscious and the unconscious, but also the developing distinction between Freud's ideas (Austrian) and his own (Swiss). He also found the customs post significant, since it suggested the 'censorship' exercised by the ego and super-ego over the impulses of the id. What went on at customs – the opening of personal baggage and the search for illegal contraband – was rather like the process of psychoanalysis. The dream symbolically represented Jung's disillusionment with both Freud himself and his theories.

The final break between the two men came in 1910. During a conversation, Freud said: 'My dear Jung, promise me never to abandon the sexual theory. That is the most essential thing of all. You see, we must make a dogma of it, an unshakeable bulwark.'

'A bulwark against what?' asked Jung.

'Against the black tide of mud' – and here Freud paused – 'of occultism.'

Jung was disturbed by this conversation. He felt that Freud was demanding that he should blindly defend a theory, without full justification. And he knew to what Freud was referring. Jung had been raised in a family deeply concerned with psychical phenomena, and he himself had a lasting interest in such subjects as alchemy and spiritualism. By 'occultism' Freud meant not only this, but almost everything that religion and philosophy had to say about the workings of the mind that conflicted with his theories of repressed sexuality.

The disagreement between the two men became public knowledge at the Fourth International Psychoanalytic Congress in Munich in 1913. Both Freud and Jung stood for the presidency, and Jung won the election – in such a confrontation that the two never met again. But it was a bitter triumph: Jung sank into depression, and even contemplated suicide, keeping a gun by his bedside. He spent the next six years in an introspective investigation of the ideas and images that rose from his unconscious, recording them in a volume that he called the Red Book.

ANCIENT SYMBOLS

The most remarkable part of the Red Book was the series of detailed paintings in which Jung endeavoured to represent his dreams and the images that appeared to him during meditation. Some of these, he later decided, were forebodings

At the lowest level was the Collective Unconscious,
packed with images and motivations that were common
to people all over the world

> '*It is on the whole probable that we continually dream, but that consciousness makes such a noise that we do not hear it*'

Unconscious', a source of inner concepts that are common to all humankind.

At last Jung recovered from his long depression, and began to formulate his theories about the significance of dreams. He later wrote:

I do not know how dreams arise. I am altogether in doubt as to whether my way of handling dreams even deserves the name 'method' … But, on the other hand, I know that if we meditate on a dream sufficiently long and thoroughly – if we take it about with us and turn it over and over – something almost always comes of it. This something is not of a kind that means we can boast of its scientific nature or rationalise it, but it is a practical and important hint, which shows the patient in what direction the unconscious is leading him.

of the coming World War I; some have a resemblance to the visions of the English painter William Blake (1757–1827), while others seem to draw upon alchemical symbols, and world religions that included not only Christianity but also Buddhism and Hinduism. Jung concluded that these images did not arise from the events of his own life, but from what he came to call the 'Collective

A few years before his death, Jung claimed that he had carefully analysed about 2000 dreams a year. He recognised that dreams were a way for the mind to deal with previous experiences and current problems; they could spring from the unconscious mind in much the same way that solutions and decisions came from conscious deliberation. Indeed, he wrote: 'It is on the whole probable that we continually dream, but that consciousness makes such a noise that we do not hear it.'

In contrast with the complex sexual symbolism of Freudian theory, Jung came to believe that dreams were a fairly straightforward way for the unconscious to communicate – although they

could come from many levels. The uppermost level of the unconscious was the storehouse of individual memories and repressions – the level at which Freud worked. Below this came a level at which Jung thought more general impulses operated. At the lowest level was the Collective Unconscious, packed with images and motivations that came from the earliest experience of human beings, and that were common to people all over the world. As he put it:

If it were permissible to personify the unconscious, we might call it a collective human being, combining the characteristics of both sexes, transcending youth and age, birth and death, and, from having at his command a human experience of one or two million years, almost immortal …

Unfortunately – or let us say fortunately – this being dreams. At least it seems to us as if the Collective Unconscious, which appears to us in dreams, had no consciousness of its own contents … The Collective Unconscious, moreover, seems not to be a person, but something like an unceasing stream, or perhaps an ocean, of images and figures that drift into consciousness in our dreams, or in abnormal states of mind.

Jung proposed that these primal memories could be detected in myths and folklore, in children's fairytales, in Greek tragic dramas (as Freud had already suggested), in the symbols of magic and alchemy, and even in the modern rituals of church and state. They embodied all the elements of common human experience, such as birth, death, family life, and rites of passage from youth

primal memories could be detected in myths and folklore, in children's fairytales, in Greek tragic dramas, in the symbols of magic and alchemy

to adulthood, and they appeared in dreams as motifs that Jung called 'archetypes'. 'All consciousness separates,' he wrote, 'but in dreams we put on the likeness of that more universal, truer, more eternal man dwelling in the darkness of primordial night.'

Jung placed particular emphasis upon the figures that appeared in dreams, and that

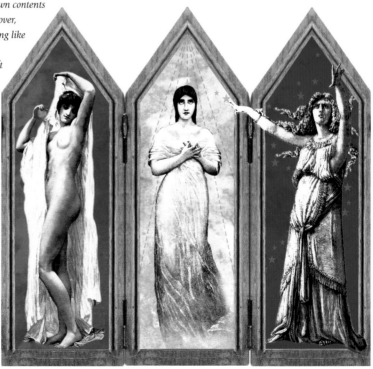

represented elements of the individual's personality. They could be the dreamer him- or herself, people the dreamer knew, or 'fictitious' characters or personifications. Other images were rarely as important. In the personality of a healthy individual, each archetype should occupy its own domain; any conflict that occurred where one domain met another should strengthen the character; and all should be integrated into a whole, the ultimate 'Self'.

The Self is the 'archetype of the future', representing the individual's potential development – a symbol, of the same sex as the dreamer, that beckons the way to achieving wholeness. This symbol can take many forms. In Hermann Melville's novel *Moby Dick*, for instance, Captain Ahab's pursuit of the white whale represents a search for the Self – a quest that, in this case however, ultimately proves destructive.

The male Self can be made up of a number of different forms, each of which may have positive or negative aspects. There is the Father, who represents authority and social conventions; the Eternal Youth, the seeker, wanderer and hunter; the Hero, and his counterpart the Villain; and the Trickster, and his counterpart the Black Magician. At a time when the dreamer is trapped in a seemingly desperate situation, the Wise Old Man – the Self of the future – will often appear.

The female Self can similarly embody a variety of forms. These are the Mother, the home-maker and protector; the Princess, the female equivalent of the Hero, whose negative aspect is the Seductress (frequently appearing in dreams dressed in classical costume); the Amazon or Huntress, representing the woman's intellectual qualities; and the Priestess, and her counterpart the Witch. The female equivalent of

The Self is the 'archetype of the future', representing the individual's potential development

the Wise Old Man is the Great Mother.

The Persona is the 'I' of the dream, the individual's self-image. In waking life, the need to express one's own personality, and at the same time to conform socially, leads to the repression of undesirable impulses that are regarded as 'not-I'. These rejected impulses are represented by the Shadow, a figure that the dreamer fails to recognise, or who stands behind his or her shoulder. 'Think of the person you most detest in the world' wrote Tom Chetwynd in *Dictionary for Dreamers* (1993), 'mix in the worst characteristics of anyone else you know, and you have a fair idea of your own Shadow.'

Two other Jungian archetypes of great importance are the Anima and Animus, which are each of the opposite sex to the dreamer. The Anima represents the feminine qualities in a man: the emotional and intuitive side of his personality. Developing an increased awareness of this feminine nature that is revealed in dreams will allow the individual to balance the male aggressiveness of his conscious state with sensitivity and adaptability.

The Animus represents the masculine qualities of a woman's personality. Recognition of the Animus in dreams will give a woman more discernment, increase her ability to think rationally, and develop her self-knowledge. Ignoring the appearance of the Animus will result in her becoming obstinate and opinionated.

Many of Jung's archetypes – with the possible exception of the Anima and Animus – regularly turn up in folkmyths and fairytales, and they can be seen to spring from the earliest experiences of all human beings – the Collective Unconscious. The Hero, and the Princess whom he must rescue, the Witch and the Trickster – these all appear in the tales handed down from generation to generation in every culture: Perseus and Andromeda; Cinderella and her Fairy Godmother; Red Riding Hood and the wolf; Brer Rabbit and Brer Fox.

It is instructive to compare the Freudian and Jungian analyses of a specific dream, as it was described by J.A. Hadfield in his book *Dreams and Nightmares* (1954):

I dreamt that I was staying in a country house, and after everyone had gone to bed I went downstairs to the sitting-room to get the coal that was left on the sitting-room fire, to take to my own bedroom. When I had taken the fire and reached the passage outside, I was met by a negro ... who threatened me. I tackled him and got him down, but then did not know what to do next. Then came a female form and said, 'Don't kill him, and don't hurt him, but send him to a reformatory'.

The Freudian, said Hadfield, would identify this as a dream about sexuality. The fire 'stolen' by the dreamer represents forbidden and repressed sexual desires. The black man and the female symbolise father and mother respectively, so that the successful attack on the man represents the Oedipus complex, the wish to be rid of the father and possess the mother. The suggestion of a 'reformatory' could be interpreted as a suggestion

> *These rejected impulses are represented by the Shadow, a figure that the dreamer fails to recognise*

that the father might be disposed of without the need for violence.

A Jungian interpretation would be very different. The theft of coals recalls the myth of Prometheus, who incurred the wrath of the gods by carrying off the fire of the sun and bringing it down to earth. He was sentenced to be chained to a rock for ever. The black figure is the Shadow, the dreamer's most primitive impulses; and the female is the Anima. The recommendation to put the black figure in a reformatory can be read as a suggestion that the conflicting tendencies in the dreamer's unconscious should be reconciled.

LATER DEVELOPMENTS

Psychoanalysts tend to be divided, in principle, into Freudians and Jungians, but both approaches to dream interpretation may be equally valid, and both schools of thought place great value on the analysis of dreams in therapy.

One psychotherapist who developed an even broader theory was Frederick Perls (1893–1970). Born in Berlin, he emigrated to South Africa shortly before the outbreak of World War II, and remained there in comparative obscurity for over 20 years. It was not until the mid-1960s, when he

For Jungians, the tale of Little Red Riding Hood is a classic example of a recurring
archetype. Freudians, on the other hand, have never been slow to draw
out its latent themes of burgeoning female sexuality and the predatory
nature of the male libido.

established a psychotherapeutic workshop at the Esalen Institute in Big Sur, California, that his theories began to be accepted.

Perls called his method Gestalt therapy. 'Gestalt' is a German word meaning a shape or pattern whose qualities are distinctly different from those of its components – a melody, for example, is something very different from the individual notes of which it is composed. Perls concentrated less upon the individual symbols in a dream than on how they contributed to the whole. 'I believe that in a dream we have a clear existential message of what's missing in our lives,' he said.

While most psychotherapists believed in quiet, one-to-one consultation, Perls developed a dramatic form of group therapy, in which the patient was encouraged to act out all the elements of his or her dream. For example, he recorded a workshop in which a participant named 'Carl' reported a recurring dream. Carl found himself lying in a desert, half-buried in the sand, under a blue-black sky from which the moon shone down. Beside him, a railway track stretched in a straight line across the desert. Then he heard a high whistle, and a high-speed train came rushing by. There seemed to be no end to it, and Carl, terrified, thought of death.

Perls told Carl to act out each of the symbols of his dream in turn in front of the group. As the desert, he immediately identified death. Then: 'I am a train, and I'm going somewhere, but it's nowhere … I have enormous direction … but there's no home, no resting place at the end.' And when he identified with the track: 'I'm lying on my back – and life is running over me.'

The desolation of Carl's dream was apparent, but Perls then set about a possible resolution of the problems that were obviously troubling him. He asked Carl to improvise a conversation between the track and the train. Gradually, Carl

Perls developed a dramatic form of group therapy, in which the patient was encouraged to act out all the elements of his or her dream

realised that the train was his mother, strong-willed and possessive. He began shouting that she should give up trying to control him, and leave him to live his own life. The meaning of the whole dream – its gestalt – was made clear. Perls recorded that, after further group work, Carl developed the will to insist on his independence from his mother.

Another psychologist, who developed his theories on the basis of Jungian therapy, was Montague Ullman, of the Albert Einstein College of Medicine in New York. Ullman proposed that dreaming first evolved a quarter of a million years ago, when humans slept in unprotected surroundings, as most animals still do. He pointed out that, as an animal sleeps, it must remain aware of sounds that warn of danger, and this awareness in the course of a dream will wake it. He compared this to the state of awareness of a soldier asleep on a battlefield.

In modern life, however, the most likely dangers are psychological – problems associated with social and emotional survival – rather than physical. Ullman suggested that the mind pondered these problems and – if successful – provided a possible resolution with the return of consciousness. He accepted the Jungian concept of archetypes, but believed that the store of myths

> *Ullman believed that our most vivid and memorable dreams are produced as the mind begins to revise these personal myths*

included everything that the dreamer had gained from waking experience, from patterns of behaviour imposed during infancy to stereotypes seen in films and on television. However, Ullman proposed that, as the individual matured, these personal myths did not become adapted to changing circumstances, and that dreams were a way of drawing attention to this. They were, he said, 'corrective lenses which, if we learn to use them properly, enable us to see ourselves and the world about us with less distortion and greater accuracy'.

Ullman believed that our most vivid and memorable dreams are produced as the mind begins to revise these personal myths. As an example he quoted the case of a young woman he named 'Maggie', who was shy and withdrawn, particularly in relations with men. Maggie suffered from a recurrent dream in which she was pursued by a huge shadowy monster; if she turned to face it, the monster would disappear. One night, however, she drew on her courage, and chased it. As she caught up with it, it changed into a beautiful horse, which she rode up into the sky – and found herself embraced by an attractive man.

Ullman interpreted this dream as a sign that Maggie had found a way of updating her personal myth – derived from her childhood and adolescence, rather than from the Collective Unconscious – that sex was something fearful and unpleasant. From that time on, he recorded, her relations with the opposite sex showed a marked improvement.

In recent years, the analysis of dreams has moved far from the psychologist's couch, and become once more the stuff of 'do-it-yourself' interpretation, as well as popular dream workshops. Of these, one of the best known is the Delaney and Flowers Center for the Study of Dreams, founded by psychologists Gayle Delaney and Loma Flowers in San Francisco. The process taught in this workshop is called 'dream incubation', and has a certain resemblance to the incubation practised by the ancient Greeks at the temple of Asklepios in Epidaurus, as well as the experience of many problem-solvers over the centuries. The individual is encouraged to keep a dream diary; on a chosen night, this is reviewed, and some notes are written about the events of the preceding day. Then the subject concentrates upon a specific matter with which he or she is concerned, examining every aspect of it, before falling asleep. In due course, they find they are able to control their dreams, experiencing lucid dreams in which they find the solution to their problem.

In the academic field, research into dreaming has increased greatly in recent years, and there

> *it changed into a beautiful horse, which she rode up into the sky – and found herself embraced by an attractive man*

are now sleep and dream laboratories in many parts of the world. Professional associations include the Canadian Sleep Society at Queen's University, Kingston, Ontario; the European Sleep Research Society, based in Finland; the Association for the Study of Dreams, in Vienna, Virginia; and the Sleep Research Society of Rochester, Minnesota.

EASTERN APPROACHES

In most Western theorising, the dream is regarded as symbolising aspects of reality – whether these are derived from everyday events or from some deep-down memory, repressed or unconscious. But many Eastern philosophers have suggested

'Am I Chuang-Tsu, who dreamt he was a butterfly, or a
butterfly dreaming he was Chuang-Tsu?'

that the opposite may be true: that the dream is the reality, and the waking life only its shadow. Chuang-Tsu, a Chinese philosopher of the fourth century BC, put the ambiguity very simply: 'Am I Chuang-Tsu, who dreamt he was a butterfly, or a butterfly dreaming he was Chuang-Tsu?'

Western philosophers – and certainly psychologists – have dismissed the possibility that dreams are the true reality

Another writer, Lie-Tsu, described an incident that exemplified the problem. In the province of Tcheng, a man out gathering wood discovered a stag, which he killed. He left the body there, covered with branches, and went home. The next day, when he went to recover the stag, he could not find it. After a long search, he decided that he must have dreamt the whole event.

The woodgatherer told other people how he had dreamt the incident. But another man went out into the forest and found the body of the stag, which he also left where it was. He said to his wife: 'Before me, a man who gathered fuel dreamt that he killed a stag, but forgot where he had left it. I found it. So was his dream real?' His wife suggested that maybe it was he who had dreamed the whole thing – to which he replied 'I have found a stag. What do I care whether it was the other man who dreamt it or I?'

But that night the woodgatherer had what was definitely a dream. He dreamt he saw both the place where he had left the body, and the man who had found it. In the morning he went to the man and claimed that the stag was really his. The two men took the matter before a local judge, who asked the woodgatherer: 'Did you in fact kill a stag, and afterwards did you not wrongly believe that you had seen it only in a dream? Or

did you in fact dream that you found the stag, and now you are wrong to claim that you killed it? Your wife maintains that you saw both man and stag in a dream … The fact is that there really is a stag before us. My decision is that the stag should be cut in two – and the prince of Tcheng must be consulted about the dispute.'

The prince of Tcheng was puzzled. He wondered whether the judge himself had dreamt that the stag should be cut in two. So he consulted his principal minister, who replied: 'Was it a dream? Was it not a dream? I cannot decide. To determine what is dream and what is reality would require the ability of someone like Chuang-Tsu. But he is no longer with us. Let the judge's orders be obeyed.'

The ambiguity continued to exercise eastern philosophy. In the fifteenth century, Lian-chi Ba-shi wrote: 'The old saying goes: living in this world is like having a great dream. And scripture says: when we come to look at the world, it is comparable to things in a dream.' And in his book *Hsiao-fu* (the House of Laughter), the seventeenth-century novelist Feng Meng-long related an amusing anecdote. 'A great drinker dreamt that he possessed some good wine … He was about to heat and drink it when he suddenly woke up. Remorsefully he told himself, I should have taken it cold!'

On the whole, Western philosophers – and certainly psychologists – have dismissed the possibility that dreams are the true reality. Nevertheless, in one of Plato's works, Socrates is described as asking his friend Theaetetus: 'What

71

proof could you give, if anyone should ask us now, at the present moment, whether we are asleep and our thoughts are a dream, or whether we are awake, and talking with each other in a waking condition?' And when Theaetetus cannot answer, Socrates points out: 'So, you see, it is even open to dispute whether we are awake or in a dream.'

SLEEP LEARNING

So far, we have discussed dream information that arises from images in the memory. However, it has been found that information can also go the other way: we can actually learn during sleep. The possibility was first put forward in a piece of science fiction in the magazine *Modern Electronics* in 1911, but not long afterwards it found a practical application at Pensacola naval academy in Florida, when cadets were successfully taught the Morse code through earphones while they slept.

During the 1930s, the technique was investigated principally in the Soviet Union, by Abram Moiseyevich Svyadoshch. He found that sleepers could memorise facts and figures, foreign words, and even whole speeches. His researches were not made public until 1953,

but soon after, as investigations into the phenomena of sleep began to gather momentum, they were taken up all over the world.

Sleep learning has been given the name 'hypnopedia'. Researchers have found that learning is most effective at the stage between wakefulness and sleep or during the light sleep of stage one, when an EEG records theta waves. Usually, an audio tape, with a lesson lasting some five or six minutes, is repeated several times, and the EEG then registers the recurrence of the alpha waves that are characteristic of the waking condition.

Hypnopedia cannot take the place of daytime learning. Sleepers can absorb simple facts, such as historical dates, mathematical formulae or foreign verbs, but appear incapable of more complex operations such as analysis and reasoning. However, even memorising facts immediately before sleep has been shown to be more efficient than attempting to memorise them some hours before. But what part dreams play in implanting these facts in the brain remains open to discussion.

Plato, who recorded in one of his works a dialogue between Socrates and his friend Theaetetus on the subject of sleep, which concluded with Socrates' assertion: 'So, you see, it is even open to dispute whether we are awake or in a dream.'

He found that sleepers could memorise facts and figures,
foreign words, and even whole speeches

chapter four

CAN DREAMS FORESHADOW THE FUTURE?

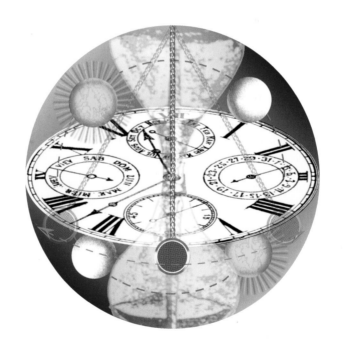

*I*n 1858, the famous American writer Mark Twain – author of (among others) *Tom Sawyer* and *Huckleberry Finn* – was still plain Sam Clemens, aged 23, and working as a pilot aboard the Mississippi paddleboat *Pennsylvania*. Sam's 20-year-old brother Henry was a clerk on the same boat. One night, while Sam was staying at his sister's house in St Louis, he had a vivid dream. He saw a metal coffin laid across two chairs, and in it was Henry's body. A wreath of white flowers lay on Henry's chest, with a single crimson bloom in the middle. Next morning, Sam mentioned the dream to his sister, and then forgot about it.

A few days later, Sam had a violent argument with the chief pilot of the *Pennsylvania*, as a result of which he was transferred to the sister boat *Lacey*, which was to follow the *Pennsylvania* up-river after a delay of two days. When the *Lacey* reached the town of Greenville, Sam learnt that the *Pennsylvania* had blown up just before arriving at Memphis, with the loss of 150 lives. Sam was somewhat relieved to be told that Henry was not among the dead, although he had been severely scalded by steam.

When the *Lacey* arrived in Memphis, Sam hurried to the hospital, where he found his brother unconscious and critically ill. He stayed at Henry's bedside day and night, scarcely sleeping, but his brother died on the sixth night. After a few hours of exhausted slumber, Sam went in search of Henry's body. He found it in a metal coffin, laid across two chairs. As he stood there, sadly regarding his brother's corpse, an elderly woman – unknown to Sam – came into the room and placed a wreath of white flowers in the coffin. And in the middle was a single crimson rose.

Mark Twain later wrote a description of his dream, and said that his sister had confirmed it. This is but one of many examples that seem to

American writer Mark Twain (1835–1910) had a vivid dream one night at the age of 23, which foretold his cousin Henry's death with extraordinary accuracy.

suggest that some particularly vivid dreams contain a vision of what is yet to happen.

The American President Abraham Lincoln often experienced dreams of this kind. During the Civil War (1861–65) between the Union and the rebel southern states, he had a recurrent dream of a damaged ship sailing away with a Union vessel in pursuit: in every case it prophesied a coming Union victory. However, one April night in 1865, when he was sleeping in the White House in Washington, Lincoln had a very different dream. He dreamt he was woken by bitter sobbing, rose from his bed, and went to see the cause. In the

One of America's most celebrated presidents, Abraham Lincoln, had a dream in which he witnessed people filing past his own coffin. He was assassinated a few days later.

East Room he found soldiers guarding a body that lay in state, while people filed past the coffin. Lincoln could not see the face of the dead person, and asked one of the soldiers who it was. 'It's the President,' said the man. 'He was killed by an assassin.' At which the mourners gave such a loud cry of grief that Lincoln came truly awake.

He told his wife Mary and several friends about his dream. A few days later, on 14 April, in Ford's Theatre, Washington, Lincoln was shot by actor John Wilkes Booth, and died the following day.

Another dream of an assassination, one that was to have even more tragic consequences, was

Archduke Franz Ferdinand of Austria with his wife. Their double assassination in Sarajevo sparked the First World War.

Princip fired six shots from his Browning automatic, killing Franz Ferdinand and his wife

At 3.15 a.m., the Bishop awoke from a terrible dream. He dreamt he had gone to his desk, on which lay a letter with a black border, sealed with black wax, with the coat of arms of the Archduke. Opening it, the Bishop recognised the handwriting of his former pupil. At the top of the letter appeared a small blue picture, and in this he saw the Archduke and his wife sitting in a car, together with a general and another officer. Suddenly, two young men sprang forward, firing pistols at the car. The letter read:

Dear Dr Lanyi, Your Excellency, I wish to inform you that my wife and I were the victims of a political assassination. We recommend ourselves to your prayers. Cordial greetings from your Archduke Franz, Sarajevo, 28 June.

experienced by Bishop Josef Lanyi, who had previously been tutor to Archduke Franz Ferdinand of Austria. On 28 June 1914, the Archduke was on a visit to Sarajevo, in Bosnia, while the Bishop was 500km (300 miles) away, at Grosswardein in Hungary.

Getting up at once from his bed, the Bishop wrote down the details of his dream. He was so troubled that he then said Mass for the couple. When the rest of the household awoke, he spoke of his experience to his servant, his mother and a guest.

At about 11 a.m., in Sarajevo, two Serbians, Gavrilo Princip and Tryfon Grabezh, attacked the Archduke's car. Princip fired six shots from his Browning automatic, killing Franz Ferdinand and his wife; the Bishop received the news in a telegram at 3.30 p.m. This assassination, tragic though it was, might have been dismissed as no more than a local incident – but its consequences were to result in the horrific carnage of World War I.

THREATENING DISASTER

One October morning in 1966, in the little Welsh village of Aberfan, 10-year-old Eryl Mai Jones made a rather curious remark to her mother Megan: 'I am not afraid to die.' When her mother said that she was too young to think of death, Eryl replied: 'But I shall be with my friends Peter and June.' Two weeks later, on the morning of 20 October, she told Megan of a dream: 'I went to school, and there was no school there. Something black had come down all over it.'

Next day, Eryl went off to Pantglas Junior School as usual. The building stood in the shadow of a gigantic mountain of wet coal-mining waste – and that day the mountain began to move. At 9.15 a.m., a black avalanche poured down through the classrooms and smashed its way through a row of houses across the street. A total of 144 people, 116 of them children, died. Eryl's body was eventually dug from the rubble, and buried with those of the other victims in a communal grave – between her friends Peter and June.

Among those who visited the scene of the disaster the following day was psychiatrist Dr J.C. Barker. He heard Megan Jones's distraught story, and wondered whether anyone else had had a premonition of the event. At his request, the London *Evening Standard* newspaper published an appeal asking for anybody who had experienced a forewarning to write in. In all, some 200 letters were received. Dr Barker himself received 76, and came to the conclusion that at

'I am not afraid to die...I shall be with my friends Peter and June'

least 60 were genuine. In 24 cases he was able to confirm that details had been related to others before the event.

One of the most vivid accounts came from Mrs Grace Engleton, of Sidcup, Kent – more than 500km (300 miles) from Aberfan. She wrote:

I have never been to Wales. Nor do I possess a television set. On the night of 14 October, I had a vivid, horrible dream of a terrible disaster in a coal-mining village. It was in a valley, with a big building filled with young children. Mountains of coal and water were rushing down the valley, burying the building. The screams of those children were so vivid that I screamed myself.

Mrs Engleton's neighbour confirmed that she had been told about the dream on 17 October, four days before the disaster. Other people reported dreams of screaming children, some saw falling mountains and black mud, and in three cases people named the village, or something close to it. Dr Barker was convinced by this overwhelming evidence that dreams could foreshadow coming events.

One of the most famous disasters was the sinking of the transatlantic liner *Titanic*, which struck an iceberg on the night of 14 April 1912, and went down with the loss of more than 1500 lives. In his autobiography *A Sort of Life,* the novelist Graham Greene wrote:

Dreams have always had an importance for me … On the April night of the Titanic disaster, when I was five and it was Easter holiday time in Littlehampton, I dreamt of a shipwreck. One image of the dream has remained with me for more than sixty years: a man in oilskins bent double beside a companion-way under the blow of a great wave.

Three weeks earlier, a London businessman, J. Connon Middleton, who had booked to sail on the *Titanic,* had had an even more specific dream: 'I saw her floating on the sea, keel upwards, and her passengers and crew swimming round her.' The dream recurred the following night but,

although he was upset by his dreams, Mr Middleton only cancelled his passage on receiving a cable from New York telling him to delay his departure for business reasons. It was then, a fortnight before the disaster, that he told his family and friends about his premonitory dream.

In May 1979, David Booth, an office manager in Cincinnati, Ohio, had the same dream for 10 nights in a row. It was so real that it did not seem like a dream: as he said, 'It was like I was standing there, watching the whole thing – like watching television.' He heard an airliner's engines failing, and then he saw a three-engined jet in American

No peacetime maritime disaster exercises such a hold over the human psyche as the sinking of the Titanic. *Many claimed to have dreamt of the disaster in advance, including the English author Graham Greene.*

Airlines colours swerve, roll over and crash into the ground. Each time he had the dream he woke up in horror, the explosion ringing in his ears. He said he could even feel the intense heat of the flames.

On 22 May, deeply troubled by his dreams, Booth telephoned both American Airlines and the Federal Aviation Administration (FAA) at Greater Cincinnati airport. He also told a psychiatrist acquaintance at Cincinnati University. But everyone pointed out that – whether or not they believed his dream predicted a coming disaster – there was nothing that could be done without further information, something that Booth was unable to provide.

A spokesman for the FAA, Jack Barker, described Booth's recurrent dream as 'uncanny' in its details

Three days later, on the clear, sunny afternoon of 25 May, an American Airlines DC-10 took off from O'Hare international airport, Chicago. Shortly after lift-off, the port engine and part of the wing broke away. At 100m (350ft) the plane turned over and plunged to the ground in a huge ball of flame. Everyone aboard – 258 passengers and 13 crew – as well as two ground crew, was killed instantly.

A spokesman for the FAA, Jack Barker, described Booth's recurrent dream as 'uncanny' in its details, all of which turned out to be correct. The FAA claimed that they had actually tried to match Booth's description with what they knew about forthcoming flights, but it was not until the disaster occurred that all the details fell into place.

Thirty or so years earlier, in 1947, a group of British doctors and psychiatrists had decided to keep a record of their dreams, which were reported in letters to the administrator of the group. They discovered that more than one member of the group was likely to have a dream that could subsequently be tied in with an event in the future.

One of Britain's first jet airliners, a BOAC Comet, exploded in the air off Elba, Italy, on 10 January 1954. As a result, all Comets were temporarily grounded for careful examination. Service was resumed on 23 March, and psychiatrist Dr Alice Buck, a member of the dream group, had planned to fly on this date. However, from the beginning of February, she began to receive letters describing dreams that suggested that another disaster was about to occur, and she decided not to take the Comet flight. By the beginning of April, the dream details included place, cause, number of passengers, and the amount of wreckage likely to be found. These were assembled in a document that was sent to the Ministry of Transport and Civil Aviation.

On 7 April 1954, a second Comet broke up, shortly after taking off from Rome airport. The death roll was 26. Officials at the Ministry confessed that they had not known what to do about the document: they had no idea of the date on which the disaster might occur and, in any case, they could hardly take the decision to ground the Comets once more on the basis of a series of dreams.

During the nights of 2 and 3 September 1954, Dr Buck dreamt of another air disaster. She recorded that the time of 3 a.m. seemed to be particularly significant. And on the night of 3 September another member of the group dreamt

Each time he had the dream he woke up in horror, the explosion ringing in his ears. He said he could even feel the intense heat of the flames

of travellers who were suddenly overwhelmed by water. Early in the morning of 4 September, a KLM Constellation crashed close to Shannon airport, in the west of Ireland. One newspaper report gave the following details:

Men and women died yesterday, trapped in darkness in the cabin of a crashed airliner, slowly filled with the muddy waters of the river Shannon. One man had clung for three hours to the tail of the almost submerged airliner, waiting for rescue.

The plane crashed at 3.40 a.m., but it was not until nearly two and a half hours later that the news was given to the airport, by a Second Officer from the flight, who swam to a mudflat, and then crawled painfully through 3km (2 miles) of mud and slime.

INDIVIDUAL DEATHS

A British housewife, Mrs Barbara Garwell, of Hull, Humberside, had a number of premonitory dreams during 1981. In the first, in March of that year, she described how she was travelling in a car with two men wearing the black uniforms of the Nazi SS. A large limousine approached from the other direction; it stopped, and from it stepped a man with a pock-marked face, whom Mrs Garwell tentatively identified as the English actor Trevor Howard. The two SS officers got out of their car, and one fired a number of shots at the actor, who fell. Three weeks later, on 30 March, US President Ronald Reagan had just emerged from his limousine in Washington when John Hinckley stepped forward and fired his pistol, seriously wounding the president.

On its own, this dream – taking into account the fact that it was only three months since former Beatle John Lennon had been murdered

The two SS officers got out of their car, and one fired a number of shots at the actor, who fell

in a similar manner in New York – was not particularly remarkable. There were, for instance, a number of differences from the attempt on Reagan's life: although he was a former movie actor, he bore no resemblance to Trevor Howard, and was not noticeably pock-marked; and only one man had been involved, rather than two as in Mrs Garwell's dream. On the other hand, it was later revealed that Hinckley had been a member of an American neo-Nazi movement in 1978, but had been expelled because his views were considered too extreme.

However, Mrs Garwell continued to dream. In September 1981, she had another vivid experience: she described how she saw 'a sort of stadium', in which sat a row of men 'with coffee-coloured skins', wearing dark suits. She identified the place as somewhere in the Middle East, because there was 'sand nearby'. As she watched, she saw two soldiers run forward and rake the row of seated men with bullets from automatic rifles.

Again three weeks later, on 6 October, President Anwar Sadat of Egypt, dressed in a dark blue uniform, was reviewing a military parade in Cairo. As an armoured personnel carrier passed the grandstand, four (not two) Egyptian soldiers jumped from it, one throwing grenades and the others spraying the seated dignitaries with automatic fire. Sadat was one of those killed.

In November, Mrs Garwell had a third disturbing dream. She saw a liner at sea, and two coffins sliding down 'a sort of rope gangway'. Two of her friends were shortly to take a cruise to South Africa aboard the Italian ship *Achille Lauro,* and she believed this could be the liner she had dreamt about. However, she decided not to alarm them – and, in any case, she did not feel that the coffins were theirs. Three weeks later – once more – on 2 December, fire broke out on the *Achille Lauro,* 160km (100 miles) off the Canary Islands. Mrs Garwell's friends were unhurt, but in the ensuing panic two other passengers died from heart attacks.

One man who was forewarned of his own death was the distinguished eighteenth-century

Did British housewife, Mrs Barbara Garwell, really have a dream during the summer of 1981 predicting the death of President Anwar Sadat of Egypt?

American merchant Robert Morris. One night he dreamt that he would be killed by a cannon fired from a ship at anchor that he was due to visit the next day. Because of his standing in the community, it was customary for a gun to be fired as a salute when he left a ship. Anxiously, he asked the captain of the vessel if the firing of the gun could be dispensed with, but the captain assured him that the salute would not be given until he was well out of range. In fact, said the captain, he would accompany Morris in the boat, and raise his hand as a signal to the gunner when they had nearly reached the shore. The boat set off, and Morris breathed a sigh of relief – but at that moment a fly landed on the captain's nose and, without thinking, he brushed it off. The gunner naturally took this for the signal, and fired. A fragment of the charge struck Morris in the arm; the wound became infected, and he died a few days later.

CHEATING DEATH

Try as he might, Robert Morris could not avoid the death that had been foreshadowed in his dream. But sometimes the dream comes more as a warning than a prediction, and the dreamer, or the subject of the dream, can take steps to avoid the outcome.

Nicholas Wotton was the English ambassador to France during the 1550s. Two nights running he dreamt that his nephew, Thomas Wotton, was about to take part in a project that, unless he could somehow be stopped, would result in his death and the ruin of his family. Wotton decided that the dream was a warning, and that he had to do something about it. Ingeniously, he wrote to the queen, Mary I, and requested her to send for his nephew, who should be interrogated, charged with some minor offence, and committed 'into a favourable prison'.

While Thomas lay in prison and protested that he was innocent of the charges against him, a plot against the queen was uncovered. Several of the conspirators, Thomas's close friends, were executed. And when Nicholas Wotton later spoke with his nephew, Thomas confessed that he had known of the conspiracy, and might well have been involved if his uncle 'had not so happily dreamed him into a prison'.

In more recent times, a very strange experience befell Sir

Victor Goddard, Marshall of the RAF, in 1946. He was attending a party held in his honour in Shanghai when he heard someone remark that he was dead. He turned round and found himself face to face with a British naval commander. The man turned red with embarrassment, and apologised profusely, before telling Goddard about a dream he had recently had. He had seen a transport plane forced down during a snowstorm,

and crashing on a rocky coast. Besides the RAF personnel it would be expected to carry, there were also three civilians, two men and a woman. They had escaped from the crash, but Goddard had not.

At first Goddard, who was due to fly to Tokyo shortly afterwards, was not unduly worried. But then the Consul General, his secretary (a woman), and a journalist (a man), asked if they could join him on the flight. Goddard agreed but, as the plane took off, he began to wonder whether he was about to die. Sure enough, the plane ran into a heavy snowstorm soon after, and the pilot announced that he would have to attempt a crash landing on a rocky Japanese island. However, everyone survived the landing – including Goddard.

In 1959, Edward Butler was a 25-year-old chemist, working for a New Jersey company on research into fuels for rocket engines. It was not until nearly 30 years later, on an American television show, that he related a remarkable recurrent dream.

In his dream, he was sitting in his lab in his shirtsleeves – a most unlikely condition, as laboratory workers normally wore fire-protective clothing. Suddenly, he heard a violent explosion: the neighbouring laboratory was in flames, and someone was screaming inside. He fought his way into the blaze and found another researcher, Rita Dudak, on fire from head to foot. She was alone – another unlikely detail, since she normally shared the laboratory with three others. Butler managed to grab Dudak's leg, and dragged her to a shower to put out the flames.

Over several months, the dream recurred at intervals. Then, one afternoon, Butler was sitting at his desk; he was doing paperwork and was therefore not wearing his fire-retardant clothing. Next door, Rita Dudak was working on an experiment when her apparatus suddenly exploded and engulfed her in flames. Two of her fellow workers were out of the laboratory, taking a coffee break, and the third ran away in terror, leaving her alone. The heat of the fire was so intense that Dudak's safety goggles were melted into her hair, and she was sure that she was going to die.

Butler rushed to the door, and struggled through the fire and smoke. When he found Dudak:

She was burning like a wick, she was completely in flames, her whole body … I guess I started acting like an automaton, because I was playing out the dream. I was able to grab her leg, drag her out of the flames, and pulled her into my laboratory … and put her into this deluge shower … It wasn't heroism. It was as though the dream had prepped me for this incident. I know that if I hadn't had the dream, I wouldn't have behaved as I did. People just don't walk into fires.

In her book *Hidden Channels of the Mind* (1961), the American parapsychologist Dr Louisa Rhine reported a case of a mother, who dreamt that she was camping with some friends beside a stream. Intending to wash some clothes, she carried her young son to the bank; then, realising that she had forgotten her soap, she left him there,

> *The heat of the fire was so intense that Dudak's safety goggles were melted into her hair*

throwing stones into the water. When she returned, she found the child lying face down in the water, drowned.

Later that summer, when the dream had faded from her conscious memory, she was in fact camping with some friends when she decided to do some washing, and took the young boy down to the water. Realising that she was without soap, she turned back towards her tent. At that moment the child began throwing stones – and her dream flashed back into her mind. Quickly she picked him up, and carried him away from the water.

SOLVING MYSTERIES

Dreams have also played a part in the discovery of dead bodies. One of the most famous of nineteenth-century crimes was the Red Barn murder, which took place near Bury St Edmunds in Suffolk, England. The barn stood on the property of William Corder, a young farmer, who met Maria Marten, the 25-year-old daughter of a local labourer, in 1826. They had an affair, and Corder promised to marry her. In May 1827 he told Maria's parents that he and Maria were to be married in Ipswich; she was to dress in men's clothing, so as not to be recognised, and cross the fields to the Red Barn, where he would have her own clothes waiting, and a gig to carry them to Ipswich. Maria took a fond farewell of her mother and father – and was never seen alive again.

Corder wrote to the Martens to tell them that he and Maria were well, and living on the Isle of Wight – in fact, he was married to another girl in London. For a year, nobody suspected anything, although Maria's mother was disappointed to hear nothing from her daughter. Then, in April 1828, she had a dream in which she saw Maria being murdered and buried in the earth floor of the Red Barn. The dream was so vivid that she convinced her husband to investigate, and very soon he discovered Maria's decaying body buried in a sack in the barn. Corder was arrested and found guilty of murder, eventually confessed to the crime in prison, and was hanged publicly in front of Bury St Edmunds gaol.

An intriguing case, which took place in the USA at the end of the century, was investigated by the psychologist William James, who obtained signed statements from all the people involved. In October 1898, a young woman named Bertha Huse disappeared from her home in Enfield, Vermont. When the alarm was raised, a squad of 150 men set about searching the woods, and the shore of nearby Muscova Lake. The only helpful information came from the blacksmith's wife, who said she had seen Bertha on Shaker Bridge, which crossed the northern end of the lake. On the following day, a diver was brought in to search the water below the bridge, but found nothing.

On the morning of the disappearance, Mrs Nellie Titus, who lived some 6km (4 miles) from the bridge, woke her husband in a distressed state, to tell him that a tragedy had occurred nearby. He dismissed her fears, but by evening everybody in the vicinity knew that Bertha Huse was missing.

After supper, Mrs Titus sat dozing in her chair by the fire. When her husband woke her, she exclaimed crossly: 'George, why didn't you let me be? I could have told you where the girl lays and

very soon he discovered Maria's decaying body buried in a sack in the barn

all about it.' But when they were in bed, George heard his wife mutter in her sleep: 'She's not down there, but over here on the left.' During the following night, Nellie Titus woke her husband and told him she knew where the girl's body was. She was so insistent that he agreed to take her to the bridge in the morning.

A local mill-owner, who had organised the search for Bertha, was so impressed that he fetched the diver back again. Mrs Titus led him on to the bridge and, pointing down, said: 'This looks like the place that I saw last night.' The diver protested that he had already searched thoroughly there, but Mrs Titus replied: 'No, you have been there and there, but not there. She is head-down in the mud, one foot sticking up, and a new rubber on it.'

Reluctantly, the diver went down again, and was visibly shaken when he surfaced: he had found Bertha's body, as described, in 5m (18ft) of water. 'I stopped short where I was,' he subsequently related. 'It is my business to recover bodies in the water, and I am not afraid of them, but in this instance I am afraid – of the woman on the bridge.'

DREAMS OF GOOD FORTUNE

Not all premonitory dreams are of tragedies; some, in fact, have very happy sequels. The English town of Swaffham in Norfolk still commemorates the pedlar John Chapman, who lived there in the fifteenth century. According to what is now only a well-worn legend, Chapman had a dream one night in which he was instructed to go to London and wait on London Bridge. It took him three days to walk to the city, and he waited a further three days on the bridge, but nothing happened. Those were the days when London Bridge was lined with shops, and eventually a curious shopkeeper came out to ask Chapman what his business was. Somewhat embarrassed, the pedlar told him of his dream – but did not mention his name, or where he came from. Said the shopkeeper:

I am very sorry for thee, my good friend. Now if I heeded dreams I might have proved myself as very a fool as thou hast; for it is not long since that I dreamt that at a place called Swaffham Market, in Norfolk, there dwells one John Chapman, a pedlar. He hath a tree in his back garden, so I dreamed, under which is buried a pot of money. Now, suppose I journeyed all the way thither, because of that dream, in order to dig for that money, what a fool I should be!

Chapman hurried home, and dug under the old pear tree in his garden. There he found a pot full of gold and silver coins, and on its grime-

> ## 'Now if I heeded dreams I might have proved myself as very a fool as thou hast'

encrusted lid the message: 'Under me doth lye/ Another much richer than I'. He dug further, and found a chest with an even greater treasure. He kept the money hidden, but when funds were needed to repair the town church he generously offered to pay for everything, including a new steeple. Whether or not the tale is true, it is a fact that one John Chapman, a local artisan of simple means, donated the money for the church's restoration. His story is told in the church's stained-glass windows, the figure of Chapman stands at the end of one of the pews, and a carved wooden signpost at the entrance to the town portrays 'Ye Pedlar of Swaffham who did by a dream find great treasure', together with his dog.

In *Hidden Channels of the Mind*, Dr Louisa Rhine reported a dream – if not quite so dramatic – of an amateur geologist. He dreamt that he found:

… a large, beautiful, agate-encrusted geode lying in shallow water quite near the shoreline of the W—- river … The exact location, shoreline, a long gravel bar, everything just as plain as though I were seeing it as it is, was clearly shown. When we arose on the following Sunday morning, I told my wife of my dream experience, and suggested we take our lunch and drive to the scene of my dream. We had only lived in this city approximately six months at the time, and I was unfamiliar with the particular location, but inquired along the way a couple of times, describing landmarks, etc., in detail; and, within a half-hour after we parked our car, we walked up to the big, beautiful geode lying exactly where I'd seen it in my dream. Later I was offered $300 cash for it, but did not care to sell.

But someone who had the most unexpected dreams of good fortune was John Godley, a young Irish undergraduate at Oxford University,

Chapman hurried home, and dug under the old pear tree in his garden. There he found a pot full of gold and silver coins

On 4 April, Godley was at home in Ireland and dreamt that he was looking at a list of winning racehorses

who was later to become Lord Kilbracken. On the night of 8 March 1946, he dreamt that he was looking at the following day's evening newspaper, which was open at a page giving the day's horse-racing results. When he woke, Godley could remember the names of only two of the winners: Bindal and Juladin.

Taking his breakfast at a café in the town, Godley met a friend and told him of his dream. Together they looked in the morning newspaper: sure enough, a horse named Bindal was running at one race meeting that afternoon, and Juladin at another. Godley became very excited, and told every acquaintance he met about his dream, and himself made arrangements to bet on both horses.

He waited impatiently for the arrival of the evening newspaper, and was delighted to discover that both horses had won their races. As a thoroughly amateur statistician, he calculated that the chances against both horses running on the same afternoon, and both winning, were greater than 1000 to one.

Naturally, the news spread through the undergraduate population – and no doubt reached some of the more sporting dons. Every morning in the days that followed before the end of term, Godley was asked if he had had any more dreams. He was happy to answer No,

because he realised that, if he dreamt again, all his acquaintances would bet heavily on the horse, or horses, he named – and, if they lost, they would never forgive him.

On 4 April, Godley was at home in Ireland for the Easter vacation, and dreamt that he was looking at a list of winning racehorses. When he woke, the only name he remembered was 'Tubermore'. His home was so far from Dublin that the daily newspapers always arrived one or two days late, so he telephoned the local postmistress. She told him that a horse named Tuberose was racing two days later in the English Grand National at Aintree. Godley, and members of his family, put money on the horse – and, listening to the radio commentary on 6 April, they were overjoyed to hear that Tuberose had won.

John Godley now decided that he would keep a record of his dreams. But he had to wait until 28 July, when he dreamt that he telephoned a bookmaker from a booth in an Oxford hotel and asked for the name of the winner of the last race of the day. He was told 'Monumentor' had won, at odds of five to four. Next morning, he even remembered how stuffy the phone booth had been but, looking in the newspapers, he could find only a horse named Mentores. Nevertheless, he decided to bet – and the horse won at odds of six to four.

A year passed before Godley had another similar dream. This time he was at a race meeting and saw a horse win easily. The jockey wore the colours of the horse's owner, the Gaekwar of Baroda, an Indian prince, and Godley recognised him. He was the famous Australian jockey, Edgar Britt. In the following race, everyone around Godley was shouting loudly for 'The Bogie', and the noise was so great that it woke him up.

Highly excited, Godley rose from his bed, quickly dressed, and hurried downstairs to

consult *The Times*. Sure enough, Britt was riding the Gaekwar of Baroda's horse, Baroda Squadron, that very afternoon, and the horse tipped to win the next race was – The Brogue. Godley bet heavily on both horses, and told several of his acquaintances. Then he wrote out an account of his dream predictions, and had it timed and witnessed by three friends. He took it to the nearest post office, where it was sealed in an envelope and time-stamped by the postmaster, and placed in the office safe. There would therefore be no doubt about the validity of his dream.

Both horses won, and Godley became instantly famous. The *Daily Mirror* published a two-page article about him, and shortly afterwards offered him a job as one of their horse-racing correspondents. People wrote to him from all over the world, and some even offered to share their winnings with him if he would give them exclusive advice.

Sadly, Godley's predictive dreams came to him only infrequently, and they were not always reliable. In October 1947 he dreamt of a horse named Claro; naturally he bet on it, but it lost. In January 1949, he dreamt once more that he was reading the racing results, and when he woke he remembered that one of the winners had been named Timocrat. Once again he bet, and this time he was successful.

As a racing correspondent, Godley naturally came to know more about racehorses, and to dream of them more often, but he came to the conclusion that his specific knowledge affected the content of his dreams, and few turned out to be startlingly predictive. His last success came in 1958, when he dreamt that a horse named 'What Man?' won the Grand National. One of the runners was Mr What; the horse won the race, and Godley won a large sum of money.

LONG-RANGE DREAMS

So far, the predictive dreams described have all occurred just a short time before the event they prefigured, often within only a few hours and never more than two or three weeks ahead. Very occasionally, however, years have passed between the dream and its outcome.

Anna Seward, the English poet, had a friend named Mr Cunningham. One morning in 1774, Cunningham told his companion, a Mr Newton, of two dramatic dreams he had experienced the previous night. In the first, he heard a horse approaching; as he watched, three men emerged from the bushes, stopped the rider, and searched his clothes and boots before taking him prisoner. At this point Cunningham awoke, but when he fell asleep again he dreamt that he was standing among a crowd before a gallows, on which the man he had seen arrested in the first dream was being hanged.

Later that morning, Miss Seward arrived on a visit, bringing with her a young British officer of Swiss-French descent named John André, who

but when he fell asleep again he dreamt that he was standing among a crowd before a gallows

was a newly commissioned captain, and about to join his regiment in Canada. Cunningham stared at André in amazement, and later explained to Newton that he was the very same man he had seen hanged in his dream.

In 1775 the American revolutionary War of Independence broke out. In 1780 Benedict Arnold, the American commander of the fort at West Point, began secret negotiations with the British to hand the fort over, and André was chosen by his commanding officer, Sir Henry Clinton, to handle the negotiations. On 21 September André met Arnold, and then set out to return to the British lines at New York, but he was intercepted by three men wearing British greatcoats. He showed them a pass from Arnold made out in the name of 'John Anderson', but told them his real name was engraved on the watch concealed in his boot. Unfortunately, the three were American militiamen; André was condemned as a spy, and was hanged at Tappantown.

SHARED DREAMS

Some researchers have suggested that premonitory dreams are in some unexplained way a form of telepathy. A degree of support is given to this theory by the most puzzling of

Some researchers have suggested that premonitory dreams are a form of telepathy

dream phenomena, in which two or more people have the same dream on the same night, or have dreams in which they encounter one another. One of the earliest accounts was written by St Augustine:

A certain gentleman named Prestantius had been entreating a philosopher to solve him a doubt, which he absolutely refused to do. The night following … he saw the philosopher standing full before him, who just explained his doubts to him, and went away the moment after he had done. When Prestantius met this philosopher the next day, he asked him why, since no entreaties could prevail with him the day before to answer his question, he came unasked, and at an unreasonable time of night, and opened every point to his satisfaction. 'Upon my word it was not me that came to you; but in a dream I thought my own self that I was doing you such a service.'

An interesting report appeared in the *Proceedings* of the British Society for Psychical Research (SPR) in 1887. A Mrs 'H' dreamt that she was walking in Richmond Park with her husband and a friend, Mr 'J', and saw a notice posted on a tree announcing that Lady 'R' was giving a party at her home in the country, to celebrate the Silver

Jubilee of Queen Victoria. Her husband remarked that he hoped they would not go, as it would be difficult to get back to London, but 'J' said; 'Oh, I will manage that for you.'

Mrs 'H' woke up, and found her husband also awake, eager to tell her of a dream he had just experienced:

I dreamt we were walking in Richmond Park, and I was told Lady 'R' was going to have a party. We were invited, and I was very troubled as to how we should get home, as the party was at 10, and the last train went at 11, when my friend 'J', who was walking with us, said 'Oh, I will manage that for you.'

A few years after this, an American woman, Dr Adele Gleason, dreamt that she was alone in the depths of a dark wood. Suddenly, she felt very afraid that a man she knew was about to arrive and shake the tree beside her, causing the leaves to fall in flames. When she awoke, she wrote a brief account of the dream, the time it had occurred, and the initials of the man, John R. Joslyn.

When Dr Gleason met Joslyn some days later, she told him: 'I had a strange dream on Tuesday night.' He said that he, too, had had a strange dream on that night, and had recorded it when he woke. 'Let me tell you mine first,' he said:

'he saw the philosopher standing full before him, who just explained his doubts to him, and went away'

St Augustine (354–430) taught in Rome, then Milan. His thinking was initially influenced by Scepticism, then Neoplatonism before he converted to Christianity in 387. His Confessions is a classic of literature and a spiritual biography as well as an original work of philosophy. His writings contain one of the earliest references to shared dreams.

I dreamed that I was walking at night in a remote spot, where I sometimes go shooting. Soon I saw in the bushes, about 12 yards from the road, one of my women friends apparently paralysed with fear at something that I did not see, rooted to the spot by the feeling of imminent danger. I came to her and shook the bush, upon which the leaves that fell from it burst into flames.

Many of these shared dreams occur when one of the dreamers is seriously ill, and are close to what the SPR named 'crisis apparitions'. Cromwell Varley and his wife were visiting the home of her sister, who was suffering from heart disease. On his first night in the house, Varley had a nightmare, in which he found himself completely paralysed. In the dream, his sister-in-law came into the room and said: 'If you do not move, you will die.' But, try as he might, he remained immobile, at which his

On his first night in the house, Varley had a nightmare, in which he found himself completely paralysed

sister-in-law exclaimed: 'I will frighten you, and then you will be able to move!'

After several vain attempts, she suddenly screamed 'Oh Cromwell, I am dying!', and Varley came immediately awake. His restless sleep had already awakened his wife, and he

Do not disturb. The gentle dreamer in this nineteenth-century engraving appears to be enjoying a multitude of dreams simultaneously. Or perhaps – as many people claim to have done – she is simply sharing her dream with a few of her friends.

told her of his nightmare. The time was 3.45 a.m.

Next morning, Varley's sister-in-law complained that she had passed a bad night. She said that she had dreamt of being in the Varleys' bedroom, and found Cromwell on the point of death. 'I only succeeded in rousing you by exclaiming "Oh Cromwell, I am dying!"' And when had this dream taken place? asked Varley. 'Between half-past three and four in the morning.'

Another account was vouched for by former American Congressman Robert Owen. It was related to him by Miss 'A.M.H.', who was one of his friends, and a prominent literary figure in mid-Victorian England. She dreamt that she travelled some distance to the town where her friend 'S' lived:

There, on his bed, I saw 'S' lying as if about to die. I took his hand and said 'No, you are not going to die. Be comforted, you will live.' Even as I spoke I seemed to hear an exquisite strain of music sounding through the room.

In the morning, Miss 'A.M.H.' told her mother of her dream. She also wrote to 'S' to inquire after his health, but did not mention the dream in her letter. Three years later, she and her mother met 'S' in London, and she described the dream. Her friend was astounded: he said that he had been very ill, shortly before her letter arrived, and had had a closely related dream. Feeling himself on the point of death, he had asked his brother, in his dream, for two last favours. 'Send for my friend A.M.H. I must see her before I depart. I would also hear my favourite sonata by Beethoven ere I die.'

And even as I spoke in my dream, I saw you enter. You walked up to the bed with a cheerful air, and, while the music I longed for filled the room, you spoke to me encouragingly, saying I would not die.

'Send for my friend A.M.H. I must see her before I depart. I would also hear my favourite sonata by Beethoven ere I die'

EXPERIMENTS WITH TIME

John William Dunne was an early aircraft designer, who built the first British military aeroplane in 1906 – but he was also fascinated by the many predictive dreams he experienced, and evolved a theory to explain them.

In 1902, Dunne was serving as a soldier with the British Army in South Africa, where the Boer population was fighting a losing battle for independence. One night, he dreamt that he was standing on the upper slopes of a mountain, which he recognised as an island volcano. Jets of vapour were spouting from the soil, and he exclaimed: 'It's the island! Good Lord, the whole thing is going to blow up!' He realised that the inhabitants were unaware of the situation, and that he had to try to save them.

In the next stage of his dream, Dunne found himself on a neighbouring island. He was trying to persuade the local officials, who were French, to send a fleet of boats; but they refused to believe him, as he went desperately from one to another. At the moment when he finally awoke, he was clinging to the heads of a team of horses. He was trying to stop 'Monsieur le Maire', who wanted to drive away to his dinner, and shouting;

'Listen! Four thousand people will be killed!'

Some time later, a bundle of newspapers arrived from England for the British forces, the *Daily Telegraph* among them. One headline read: 'Volcano disaster in Martinique. Town swept away. An avalanche of flame. Probable loss of over 40,000 lives.'

This was the terrible volcanic explosion of Mt Pelee, on the French island of Martinique in the Caribbean on 8 May 1902. As for the number of fatalities, Dunne said that his recollection was that the newspaper headline had given the figure as 4000; it was 15 years later when he discovered that it had been 40,000.

Two years after this dream, Dunne experienced another that was almost as dramatic. He was standing on 'a footway of some kind … beyond

In 1902, British aircraft designer, John William Dunne, had a dream that he came to believe predicted the volcanic disaster on Mt Pelee on the French island of Martinique in May of the same year.

which was a deep gulf filled with thick fog', through which he could see a wavering jet of water shooting from a fire hose. Suddenly,

the wooden plankway became crowded with people, dimly visible through the smoke. They were dropping in heaps; and all the air was filled with horrible, choking, gasping ejaculations … The evening editions brought the expected news. There had been a big fire in a factory somewhere near Paris. I think it was a rubber factory, though I cannot be sure … A large number of workgirls had been cut off by the flames, and had made their way out on to a balcony … the

he refused to accept any 'psychical' theory of anything like telepathy or clairvoyance

fire-engines had directed streams of water on to the balcony to keep that refuge from catching alight ... From the broken windows behind the balcony the smoke from the burning rubber or other material came rolling out in such dense volumes that, although the unfortunate girls were standing actually in the open air, every one of them was suffocated ...

More dreams followed. In the autumn of 1913 Dunne dreamt of a high railway embankment, which he was confident was just north of the Forth Bridge in Scotland:

I saw that a train going north had just fallen over the embankment. I saw several carriages lying towards the bottom of the slope, and I saw large blocks of stone rolling and sliding down. Realising that this was probably one of those odd dreams of mine, I tried to ascertain if I could 'get' the date of the real occurrence. All I could gather was that this was somewhere in the following spring. My own recollection is that I pitched finally upon the middle of April, but my sister thinks I mentioned March when I told her the dream next morning ... On April the 14th of that spring the 'Flying Scotsman', one of the most famous mail trains of the period, jumped the parapet near Burntisland Station, about fifteen miles north of the Forth Bridge, and fell on to the golf links twenty feet below.

Dunne recorded more than 20 dreams of this kind, as well as others of a more mundane nature. In 1916 he dreamt of an explosion in a London bomb factory. The actual explosion occurred at Silvertown, on the east side of London, in January 1917; in all, 73 workers were killed, and more than 1000 injured.

For years, Dunne puzzled over an explanation, persuading friends to keep similar records of their dreams. As an engineer, he refused to accept any 'psychical' theory of anything like telepathy or clairvoyance:

I was suffering, seemingly, from some extraordinary fault in my relation to reality, something so uniquely wrong that it compelled me to perceive, at rare intervals, large blocks of otherwise perfectly normal experience displaced from their proper positions in Time.

Dunne eventually developed a theory that he put forward in his book *An Experiment with Time* (1927), together with an account of some of his friends' dreams. Aware of Einstein's theory of relativity, which showed that time and the three dimensions of physical space are interdependent, he proposed that there was a further dimension of reality in which space and time were somehow combined. Dunne's explanation of his theory is complicated, but it can be exemplified in a relatively simple way. The individual is like someone aboard a train, travelling along a line that represents time. Other lines run parallel, each carrying a train that may be moving at a different speed. Looking out of the window, the individual may be able to see events taking place in the other trains, which are occurring in what, to him or her, is the future.

Interestingly, some present-day physicists, pondering the concept of time, have suggested the concurrent existence of an infinite number of parallel universes, each with its own different time-scale. We may suppose that, in the waking state, we are so preoccupied with current events that any perception of these other universes is obscured; but that, in dreams or trances, we somehow become occasionally aware of events in the future – or, indeed, in the distant past – that are occurring now in a parallel world.

ARE DREAMS TELEPATHIC?

When the Italian poet Dante Alighieri died in 1321, the last part of his epic poem *The Divine Comedy* was found to be incomplete. It seemed that the last 13 cantos of 'Paradise' were missing, and it was assumed that the poet had been overtaken by death before he could write them.

Dante's son Jacopo was himself a poet, though a modest one, and he was urged by friends to try to complete the work. According to Dante's fellow poet, Giovanni Boccaccio, who thought this 'a presumptuous folly', Jacopo had a dream one night, in which his father appeared 'clothed in the purest white, and his face resplendent with an extraordinary light'.

He took him, Jacopo, by the hand and led him into that chamber in which he, Dante, had been accustomed to sleep when he lived in this life; and, touching one of the walls, he said: 'What you have sought for so much is here'; and, at these words, both Dante and sleep fled from Jacopo at once.

Wildly excited, Jacopo dressed immediately and hurried through the night to rouse an old friend of his father, Pier Giardino. The two then went to Dante's former home, and sought out the room Jacopo had seen in his dream. Hanging on the wall was a small tapestry, and behind it:

… a little window in the wall, never before seen by any of them … In it they found several writings, all mouldy from the dampness of the walls, and had they remained there longer, in a little while they would have crumbled away. They found them to be the thirteen cantos that had been wanting to complete the Commedia.

This remarkable story was undoubtedly familiar to the Italian G.B. Ermacora, and encouraged him to investigate the possibility that dreams come to us by some form of telepathy. He carried out some interesting experiments at the end of the nineteenth century. He was acquainted with a

Italian poet Dante Alighieri (1265–1321). His Divine Comedy, *a journey through Hell and Purgatory, guided by Virgil, is considered to be amongst the highest cultural achievements of his age.*

Nineteenth-century French artist Gustave Doré's illustration of The Cross, one of the 13 'missing' cantos from 'Paradise', the concluding part of Dante's Divine Comedy. *After Dante's death, his son Jacopo discovered the cantos hidden behind a tapestry, after a visit from his father in a dream.*

medium named Maria Manzini, who had her four-year-old cousin Angelina staying with her. One morning, Angelina told Maria that she had dreamt of a little girl named Elvira. This astounded Maria: Elvira was the name given to her 'spirit control', and she was sure that she had never mentioned this to her cousin.

Angelina also said that Elvira had promised to appear in her dreams the following night, wearing a pink dress and carrying a doll. When Maria told Ermacora that this had indeed occurred, he decided to test the possibility that there was a telepathic communication between the two sleepers. On 59 separate occasions, he gave Maria a set of clues, of little direct meaning to her, but which she would consciously commit to memory. He reported numerous examples in which these clues had subsequently surfaced in the little girl's dreams.

There is, however, considerable doubt about the validity of Ermacora's experiments. He did not interview Angelina himself, and the alleged content of her dreams was relayed to him by Maria, who may well have been anxious to show that dream telepathy actually occurred – and not too meticulous about how she proved it.

Little further work in this direction took place until the late 1940s, when Wilfrid Daim, a young Viennese psychologist, decided to put such experiments on a scientific basis. He used waking 'senders' and sleeping 'receivers', sometimes taking part in the experiment himself; the dreamers were kept separate from the senders, and were sometimes miles apart.

The senders were given an image that neither they nor the receivers could know about before the test began, and were then asked to try to transmit it to the dreamers. As soon as the sleepers awoke, Daim recorded their experiences verbatim, before they were able to relate them to anyone else, or could be affected by other people's responses.

Elvira had promised to appear in her dreams the following night, wearing a pink dress and carrying a doll

A typical example was described in a paper Daim wrote for the *Parapsychological Bulletin* of Duke University, North Carolina. At 6.30 a.m. on 14 March 1948, sitting in a closed room, Daim selected an image from a set of sealed envelopes in front of him. Opening it, he found he was looking at a simple image of a red triangle on a black background. Concentrating his thoughts on this, he had, he wrote, 'a strange telepathic contact which is nearly impossible to describe. Then I energetically ordered the awakening of the receiver ...'

The receiver woke at 6.35 a.m. He reported that he had been experiencing a dream that involved music and soldiers, when:

... suddenly a three-cornered, glaring red fir tree pushes through the whole ... and remains unmoved for seconds amid all the former dream contents. It is not a fir tree out of nature, but such a one as one finds in children's primers; the trunk is black, colour distinct, while all the other dream contents are of a colourless grey.

It seems clear that Daim's concentration upon the image had successfully interrupted the receiver's dreams – but how it had done so remains open to interpretation.

THE DREAM
LABORATORY

Some 15 years later, Montague Ullman, an American psychologist who had developed theories of dreaming along Jungian lines, decided to investigate the phenomenon further. As director of the Community Mental Health Center at the Maimonides Medical Center in Brooklyn, New York, he was able to obtain funding for a programme of research in 1962. He enlisted the help of psychologist Stanley Krippner, and the project later became known as the 'dream laboratory'.

The structure of a typical experiment was as follows. A volunteer sleeper would arrive at the laboratory late in the evening, ready for sleep, and would be wired up to an EEG as they lay in bed. In a separate room, the experimenter sat watching the EEG read-out; and in a third room, soundproofed but connected by a buzzer to the experimenter, sat the sender.

When the EEG indicated that the sleeper was entering an REM phase of sleep (when dreams occur), the experimenter sounded the buzzer, and the sender opened one of a number of sealed envelopes that contained the 'target' image. The first series of experiments used simple geometric forms as targets. For example, on one occasion the target image comprised a set of three zigzag lines, which were 'sent' at 4.30 a.m. When the sleeper was awakened from an REM phase at 6.30 a.m., he reported;

Some people were standing around, and they had in their hands canes shaped like hockey sticks, used upside down, the curved part up. But they were shaped more like free form than plain hockey sticks.

After other successes such as these, Ullman and Krippner decided to use images with a strong emotional content – reproductions of paintings with archetypal elements and vivid colours, similar to the contents of many dreams. When the EEG indicated the end of an REM phase, the sleeper was woken by intercom, and told to describe his or her dream on a tape-recorder before returning to sleep. This procedure was repeated as many as five times in the course of a night. In the morning, the sleeper was asked to review the night's dreams, and add any related associations that came to mind. A transcript of the tape-recording, together with all the target reproductions – used and unused – was then sent to three independent scrutineers. They were asked to rank any correspondence between the targets and the dreams on a scale of 1 to 12.

Many of the results were inconclusive, but Ullman and Krippner concluded that they had a significant number of 'hits'. For instance, when one of the senders concentrated on George Bellows's painting *Dempsey and Firpo*, which represented the two prizefighters in a bout at Madison Square Garden, the subject reported 'something about Madison Square Garden and a boxing fight'. And when she targeted a painting of five women performing a ritual dance in a grove of trees, the dreamer remembered 'being with a group of people … participating in something … lots of mountains and trees … some sort of primitive aspect … I can almost see it as some sort of tribal ritual in a jungle.'

Ullman and Krippner found that one of their subjects, William Erwin, and one of the researchers, Sol Feldstein, were scoring a particularly high number of successes. In autumn 1964 they carried out a series of seven nightly experiments. The three scrutineers announced that five out of the seven had produced 'hits'. When, for instance, Feldstein targeted Degas's *School of the Dance*, Erwin dreamt that he was 'in a class … at different times, different people would get up for some sort of recitation or some sort of contribution … there was one little girl who was trying to dance with me'.

For the next phase of their experiments, the two psychologists chose a particularly dramatic demonstration in February 1971. They selected two psychic 'sensitives', Malcolm Bessent and Felicia Parise: Bessent was to sleep at the Maimonides Center under standard laboratory conditions, while Parise slept in her own apartment, but was woken every 90 minutes for a report on her dreams. Some 70km (45 miles)

> ## When the EEG indicated the end of an REM phase, the sleeper was woken by intercom

as the band played, a randomly selected art reproduction was projected on to the screen

away, the rock band The Grateful Dead were giving a series of six concerts before audiences of around 2000 fans. At 11.30 each night a message was flashed on to a screen above the stage:

You are about to participate in an ESP experiment. In a few seconds you will see a picture. Try using your ESP to 'send' this picture to Malcolm Bessent. He will try to dream about the picture. Try to 'send' it to him. Malcolm Bessent is now at the Maimonides dream laboratory in Brooklyn.

Then, as the band played, a randomly selected art reproduction was projected on to the screen to an audience (as Stanley Krippner later wrote) 'whose states of consciousness were dramatically altered … by the music, by the ingestion of psychedelic drugs before the concert started, and by contact with other members of the audience'. In fact, he had later to admit that 'this experiment does not prove that 2000 agents are better than a single agent'.

Nevertheless, Bessent scored very well on four nights out of six. For instance, when the picture on the screen was *The Seven Spinal Chakras* – a picture of a man sitting in the lotus position, with his seven chakras (energy centres) brightly coloured – Bessent dreamt of a man 'suspended

in mid-air or something … using natural energy', and he remembered 'the light from the sun … a spinal column'. On the other hand, Felicia Parise, who had not been mentioned in the message to the audience, scored no 'hits' that could not be attributed to chance.

After this success with Bessent, the psychologists decided to investigate whether he could dream future events. The experiment lasted 16 nights, each stage covering two nights. On the first night, Bessent would try to dream about a target picture that he would be 'sent' the following night; the next day, a member of the team – who had nothing to do with the first night's experiment – would select a picture to 'send' and Bessent would try to dream about that on the second night. The results were startling: he scored seven out of eight 'hits' in precognitive dreams, but none on any of the second nights.

Unfortunately, funding for the Maimonides study ceased in 1972, and the team dispersed to other projects. Other people tried to duplicate their results, with little or no success. David Foulkes, who led a research group at the University of Wyoming in Laramie, admitted that his team's extremely sceptical attitude could very well have had an adverse effect on their experiments, and inhibited their volunteer subjects. 'It proved hard to escape the role of protector of scientific purity, or guardian of the scientific morals. Were we sympathetic and encouraging observers, or scientific detectives out to prevent a crime being committed before our very eyes?'

So there is still no firm answer to the question whether dreams can foreshadow the future. There is a wealth of anecdote, from thousands of years of dreaming, to support the belief, but little in the way of scientific proof.

when the picture on the screen was
The Seven Spinal Chakras…*Bessent dreamt of a man*
suspended in mid-air

chapter five

GETTING TO GRIPS
WITH YOUR DREAMS

*F*or all those who are interested in the phenomenon of dreams and their interpretation, the news is good: every bedroom is a potential dream laboratory, and everybody can be a dream researcher. Our own dreams are as good a point to start as any other: they are available for analysis every time we awake, and – with care and practice – it is possible to learn to control and explore them while we sleep.

The study of dreams would not have advanced as far as it has, in fact, if the psychologists – led by Sigmund Freud – had not begun by analysing their own dreams. In 1895, Freud was still a struggling psychoanalyst with a small practice in Vienna. But, as he wrote to a friend, 'inside me there is a seething ferment, and I am only waiting for the next surge forward.' One afternoon, he was sitting on the terrace of the hotel Schloss Belle Vue, near Vienna, when he had his inspiration – and some time later he wrote to a friend:

Do you suppose that some day a marble tablet will be placed on the house, inscribed with these words? – At this house, on 24 July 1895, there was revealed to Dr Sigmund Freud – the Secret of Dreams.

Freud had been pondering a dream he had experienced the night before, and it is instructive to look at how he dissected it. Although different theories of dreaming have been developed since his pioneer work, Freud's analysis is an excellent example of how all the different elements of a dream must be examined. And in the Dream Dictionary (pp124–253) you will find a wealth of symbols that will help you in your own interpretations.

One of Freud's patients was a young widow named Irma, who suffered from a hysterical condition; her treatment had run into problems because she resisted Freud's psychoanalysis, and she had left Vienna for her country estate. One of her guests there had been a Dr Otto, a colleague of Freud, and on the day before the dream he had returned, reporting that Irma was 'better, but not quite well'. Freud had taken this as an aspersion on his professional abilities, and was very anxious about the case.

In his dream, Freud met Irma at a family party, and she told him she was suffering acute pain in her throat and abdomen. When he examined her, he found an unusual growth in her mouth and throat, and called another colleague, a highly respected physician, to take a look. They were joined by Dr Otto, and all agreed that Irma was suffering from a rare infection. The dream then revealed that the cause of the infection was an unsterilised needle that Otto had used in an injection for an earlier illness.

As Freud sat on the terrace of the Schloss Belle Vue, the significance of this dream suddenly became plain. First of all, it clearly symbolised his desire for revenge: against Otto for his implied criticism of Freud's treatment, and against Irma for her resistance to it. They were to blame, the dream implied, and not Freud himself. As he

Freud's analysis is an excellent example of how all the different elements of a dream must be examined

A typical example concerns an elderly woman who dreamed about May bugs in a box

wrote later: 'The dream represented a particular state of affairs as I should have wished it to be. Thus its content was the fulfilment of a wish, and its motive was a wish.'

Freud was able to explain some other elements of the dream as relating to incidents in his medical practice, but one or two resisted interpretation. However, he was particularly struck by the components of the injection given by Dr Otto: 'a preparation of propyl, propyls … propionic acid … and triethylamine (and I saw before me the formula for this printed in heavy type).' When Otto had visited Freud on the evening before the dream, he had brought with him a bottle of pineapple liqueur:

The liqueur gave off such a strong smell of fusel oil [amyl alcohol] that I refused to touch it … The smell of fusel oil evidently stirred up in my mind a recollection of the whole series – propyl, methyl, and so on … It is true that I carried out a substitution in the process. I dreamt of propyl after having smelt amyl. But substitutions of this kind are perhaps legitimate in organic chemistry.

Familiar as we are, nowadays, with the way in which everyday events can be carried over into dreams, these interpretations must seem obvious; but, at the time, such a careful analysis was

revolutionary. And it was when Freud began to consider the other component of the injection that he realised how it related to the theories for which he was to become famous. The formula for triethylamine appeared to his eyes in bold type:

What was it, then, to which my attention was to be directed in this way…? It was to a conversation with another friend [who] had mentioned among other things that he believed that one of the products of sexual metabolism was triethylamine … Irma's pain could be satisfactorily explained by her widowhood.

And we may note that the injection and the syringe used for it have an obvious phallic significance – although Freud himself did not record this at the time ('I have not reported everything that occurred to me,' he added in a teasing footnote.)

SEXUAL SYMBOLISM AND PUNS

As Freud developed his methods of dream analysis, he was able to find a sexual implication in almost all dream symbols. For instance, an adolescent girl dreaming of a snake, a church steeple, or anything that was long and pointed, revealed her fearful feelings about the male sex organ (and at the same time its fascination for her). Dreaming of a small and comfortable house nestling between two large mansions, said Freud, indicated a desire for sex. Climbing a ladder symbolised rising sexual excitement; and dreams of flying or playing the piano reflected the rhythm of intercourse.

A typical example concerns an elderly woman whose relationship with her husband had deteriorated, and who dreamed about May bugs in a box, which she tried to set free. Freud recorded

that the woman had been born in May, and married in May. She told him that, the night before her dream, a moth had drowned in her drinking glass; and she recalled that her daughter, when a child, had collected butterflies, sticking pins through them in order to mount them in a display.

Freud suggested that the dream was a sexual metaphor. He connected the May bugs with Spanish fly, reputedly a powerful aphrodisiac. Killing butterflies was cruel: did the woman equate sex with cruelty? And did the attempt to free the

May bugs represent a subconscious desire for freedom from her marriage?

Nevertheless, Freud occasionally allowed that some dream symbolism did not necessarily refer to sex. Dreaming of missing a train, he thought, was a good sign, because the train represents death. He was also struck by the way in which the mind seems to make puns on the words that describe some of the objects or events experienced in dreams.

For example, Freud was close to completing the treatment of a woman patient when she told him

she told him how she had dreamt of diving into a lake
'just where the pale moon is mirrored'

how she had dreamt of diving into a lake 'just where the pale moon is mirrored'. Ingeniously, he decided that this dream represented a play on the French word *lune* – which not only means 'moon', but is a slang term for the naked buttocks (and, indeed, this has crept into the English language in the expression 'mooning'). Since many young children supposed that babies were born from their mothers' buttocks, Freud proposed that the dream of diving into the moon could be interpreted as the representation of emerging into life – although this presupposed both a complicated pun and a symbolic action in reverse. He took it as a sign that his patient felt reborn, as a result of his treatment.

In another analysis, Freud interpreted a young woman's dream of violets as a sign that she was

fearful of being violated – both a sexual implication and a pun.

In recent years, many of Freud's more imaginative interpretations have come to seem almost laughable, particularly because of his obsession with sexuality, and his overwhelming desire to establish that his psychoanalytic treatments were effective. Nevertheless, many psychoanalysts continue to practice Freudian principles with success. And as you attempt the interpretation of your own dreams, you must ask yourself, honestly, whether the symbols could represent your own sexual impulses – or, of course, a play on words.

'BIG' AND 'LITTLE' DREAMS

The other principal approach to dream interpretation follows Jung's concept of the Collective Unconscious, and the ancient archetypes contained within it. He distinguished 'big' (significant) dreams, and 'little' (insignificant) dreams, and wrote:

We speak on the one hand of a personal and on the other of a collective unconscious, which lies at a deeper level and is further removed from consciousness than the personal unconscious. The 'big' or 'meaningful' dreams come from this deeper level … They employ numerous mythological motifs that characterise the life of the hero [or the heroine] … We meet dragons, helpful animals, and demons; also the Wise Old Man, the animal-man, the wishing tree, the hidden treasure, the well, the cave, the walled garden … all things which in no way touch the banalities of everyday. The reason for this is that they have to do with the realisation of a part of the personality which has not yet come into existence but is still in the process of becoming …

We all have our demons, and it seems there is a demon for everything. This sixteenth-century print depicts the Demon of the Plague. Carl Jung believed that demons dwelt in that place common to us all – the Collective Unconscious.

But why are [such dreams] not understandable? … The answer must be that the dream is a natural occurrence, and that nature shows no inclination to offer her fruits gratis or according to human expectations. It is often objected that the compensation must be ineffective unless the dream is understood. This is not so certain, however, for many things can be effective without being understood. But there is no doubt that we can enhance its effect considerably by understanding the dream, and this is often necessary because the voice of the unconscious goes so easily unheard.

the future, etc. If one believes that the unconscious always knows best, one can easily be betrayed into leaving the dreams to take the necessary decisions, and is then disappointed when the dreams become more and more trivial and meaningless. Experience has shown me that a slight knowledge of dream psychology is apt to lead to an overrating of the unconscious which impairs the power of conscious decision. The unconscious functions satisfactorily only when the conscious mind fulfils its tasks to the very limit. A dream may perhaps supply what is then lacking, or it may help us forward where our best efforts have failed.

> *The Wise Old Man may appear in your dream as one of your grandparents*

You may think that the interpretation of your dreams along such Jungian lines is a daunting prospect – but persevere. Very often the mind converts the archetypes into more identifiable symbols. The Wise Old Man may appear in your dream as one of your grandparents, or an acquaintance whom you respect for his or her thoughtful advice; the dragon may be represented by a dominating supervisor from your workplace; or the hidden treasure turn out to be a brilliant inspiration for a new way of life that you have been desperately seeking.

However, Jung sounded a warning note for all dream interpreters – although there are some who would disagree with certain of his reservations:

Many people who know something, but not enough, about dreams and their meaning … are liable to succumb to the prejudice that the dream actually has a moral purpose, that it warns, rebukes, comforts, foretells

SETTING ABOUT AN INTERPRETATION

In his *Dream Dictionary* (1990), Tony Crisp gives an excellent example of how a typical dream may be interpreted, and how, as Jung wrote, 'a dream may help us forward where out best efforts have failed'. The dreamer – named 'Ted' – reported how he found himself standing in the rain in the back garden of a house, which was one of a terraced row. Each garden was fenced, and ran down to a large drainage ditch, the water of which was backing up into the gardens, and rising up the dreamer's legs. It was quite hot. 'Ted' realised that this was because hot water was draining rapidly out of the baths and sinks in the row of houses. He felt that he had to get out of the gardens, not only because of the water, but also because of other people's reactions if they

> *Water symbolises the emotions, and there is a clear indication that the dreamer has been 'getting into hot water'*

saw him in their gardens. He managed to find his way into a farmyard, 'where I felt relaxed'.

Crisp then identifies the various symbolic aspects of the dream. The garden represents growth, in the sense of constructive changes taking place in the dreamer's life, and the row of houses represents other people. The rain is a sign of depressed feelings or difficulties, either the dreamer's or others'. Water symbolises the emotions, and there is a clear indication that the dreamer has been 'getting into hot water'. The fences represent social restrictions; and the escape to the farmyard symbolises the release of natural impulses.

When this had been explained to him, 'Ted' was able to understand the full meaning of his dream. He reported that he was 'going through a lot of changes at the moment... These are to do with allowing myself to have a warm but non-sexual relationship with women'. A few days before, he had attended a 'growth' group, in which he had previously made friends with a woman named Susan. In this particular session, the group work had involved some close physical contact, and 'Ted' and another man had worked with Susan. Shortly after, another woman in the group approached 'Ted', and emotionally accused him of having made love publicly to Susan.

For some days... I felt really blocked up emotionally – the blocked drainage ditch. I cut off any friendship toward Susan. When I realised that in the farmyard – the acceptance of natural feelings without neat little boundaries – I could feel at peace, I was able to allow my natural warmth again.

In its way, this is an outstanding example of a dream interpretation and its happy resolution. Notice, in particular, how the significance of each of the individual symbols becomes associated with the others: the rain causes the ditch to flood, but the 'hot water' of a social difficulty is attributed to the discharge from the row of houses; and the gardens of the houses are naturally separated by fences. As you begin to study the symbolism of your dreams, you must be constantly on the lookout for dependent connections of this kind.

One very important point to bear in mind is that the dream is yours, and reflects – except in those relatively rare cases of precognition – upon yourself. It most often will not be one of Jung's 'big' dreams, but you are the principal actor, and the dream is concerned with your physical, emotional and spiritual wellbeing. Other people in the dream, and even a house, a car, or an animal, are just as likely to represent certain aspects of yourself. Use the Dream Dictionary (pp124–253)

> *One very important point to bear in mind is that the dream is yours, and reflects upon yourself*

to identify the symbolism of your dream surroundings and actions, the objects you saw or made use of, the shapes and colours that seemed to play a significant part in your experiences.

KEEPING A DREAM DIARY

Some people maintain that they do not dream at all or, if they do, they can remember nothing of what took place. But this is certainly untrue – we all dream, every night, and in that time experience several dreams, in each of the 90-minute phases of REM sleep. Psychological experiments have suggested that those who cannot recall their dreams are deliberately refusing to recognise them, much as they try to avoid confronting problems in everyday life. To ignore one's dreams is to ignore an important part of one's psychological development.

The son of the American psychic Edgar Cayce once said that 'the most informative book you will ever read about dreams is the one you write yourself.' Keeping a diary of your dreams is an important way to understand them; and at the same time it builds up the link between the dreaming and waking self, strengthening the ability to recall dream events, and eventually helping to control their content. But be warned. One man decided to keep a record of his dreams while he was convalescing in hospital. In the end, he said, as he grew more practised, there were not enough hours in his waking life to write out everything that had happened while he was asleep – probably because he had little else to occupy his mind. Try to keep your records as succinct as you can, using abbreviations and other shorthand methods as much as possible.

The first essential in keeping a dream diary is 'a good night's sleep'. You will know how much sleep you usually need: try to go to bed at the same time, or allow yourself the same number of hours of sleep, every night. Regular habits are important. Some people complain of insomnia: in very many cases, investigation shows that, in fact, they have spent most of the time fast asleep, and exaggerate their awareness of wakefulness during the night. In any case, these wakeful periods are a good time to begin recording the dreams that preceded them.

There is a wealth of folklore about foods that provoke a restless night, but most of these are without foundation. However, try to take your last meal of the day some hours before going to bed and, if you eat anything late, make sure that it is easily digestible. Alcohol and other drugs can inhibit normal dreaming, and stimulants such as caffeine – which is found in both coffee and tea – may keep you awake.

Proper relaxation is essential. Your bed, presumably, is comfortable for your requirements – if not, change it! Make sure the room is at an acceptable temperature. Exterior sounds can be masked by the regular loud ticking of a clock, or the hum of an electric fan. If necessary, invest in an audio tape specially recorded to induce relaxation.

'the most informative book you will ever read about dreams is the one you write yourself'

*If writing seems to inhibit you, make a
drawing or two to represent what you 'saw'
in your dream*

Try to come awake slowly, keeping your eyes closed and remaining in the same position

When you awake, whether it is during the night or at your normal morning time, don't sit up immediately and begin writing what you can remember of your dreams. Try to come awake slowly, keeping your eyes closed and remaining in the same position, and recalling as many details as you can. Only then, when the dream experience has been transferred to your conscious, waking, mind, should you make the entry in your dream diary. Keep a note, also, of what happened on the previous day, and what you ate before going to bed. If writing seems to inhibit you, make a drawing or two to represent what you 'saw' in your dream.

As you become more experienced in keeping a diary of this kind, you may want to experiment. It is perhaps too extreme to suggest – as some writers have – that you should set an alarm to wake you at 90-minute intervals throughout the night. However, you may find that you get better results by setting the alarm for an hour earlier than your normal waking time. Make a record of your dreams, as detailed as possible, and add the time. Then relax – possibly reading a few pages of a book, or working on a crossword puzzle – and try to recover that extra hour of sleep. This may take practice. When you wake once more, you may be able to add extra details to your dream record.

Exterior sounds can be masked by the
regular loud ticking of a clock

INFLUENCING YOUR DREAMS

Some of the most interesting dreams are those known as 'lucid', in which the dreamer is aware that he or she is dreaming, and can carry out conscious experiments while continuing to dream. It may be some time before you experience this, but you can certainly learn to influence the content of your dreams.

Every night as you prepare for sleep, 'programme' your mind by telling yourself that you are going to recall all the details of your dreams: do this by imagining how you will wake in the morning and write everything down in your dream diary. Then decide what you are going to dream about: it may be a problem that is affecting you in waking life, an ambition that you have no conscious way of realising, or even a fantasy that it seems impossible to fulfil.

As you sleep, your unconscious mind will construct images that represent the concept you have given it. In due course, as you persist, you will find yourself apparently 'thinking' and rationalising within the dream. When you wake, do not try to relate your dream images immediately to what you decided to dream about; first of all, record them in your dream diary. Only then, when you read what you have written, will you discover how your unconscious mind has dealt with the concept. And, only then, may you recall that you have experienced a lucid dream.

The professional golfer Jack Nicklaus told a reporter in 1964 how a dream had helped him solve a long-standing deterioration in his play:

Last Wednesday night I had a dream, and it was about my golf swing. I was hitting them pretty good in the dream, and all at once I realised I wasn't holding

'programme' your mind by telling yourself that you are going to recall all the details of your dreams

the club the way I've actually been holding it lately. I've been having trouble collapsing my right arm [when] taking the club head away from the ball, but I was doing it perfectly in my sleep. So, when I came to the course yesterday morning, I tried it the way I did in my dream, and it worked. I shot a 68 yesterday, and a 65 today, and believe me it's a lot more fun this way. I feel kind of foolish admitting it, but it really happened in a dream. All I had to do was change my grip just a little.

British psychologist Keith Hearne had his first lucid dream some 18 months after starting research into the subject. His description is striking, and the outcome dramatic:

I was walking along the beach, which seemed to be Mediterranean perhaps. I looked down at the sand and saw some gold and silver coins. As I knelt down and started to dig them out, they expanded to become as big as plates. My immediate thought was 'This can't be real. This is a dream!' With that, I stood up and with total clarity looked around at the scenery. It was so astonishingly real. My vision was perfect – I could see individual grains of sand. Children were playing nearby and everything was so relaxed. I could feel the warmth of the sun on me, yet I knew that everything I saw, heard and felt was completely artificial.

After a short while, I decided to conduct an experiment, and so attempted to conjure up a dream companion whom I 'willed' to appear behind a stack of deck-chairs that was present. I walked over to the stack, looked down at the incredibly detailed sand, and as I raised my eyes I saw a young woman walking towards me. She was short, with black hair, markedly green eyes, and had a very pretty face. She approached directly, and said, 'Hello, my name's Jane'. We became quite close in the dream. Believe it or not, I actually met that same woman in waking life two weeks later, and we were together for two years. Her name was Jane, and she was identical to the dream woman.

Although Dr Hearne recognised this as a lucid dream, there is also a remarkable precognitive quality about it.

OVERCOMING DIFFICULTIES

As one dream expert has written, 'basically we have to learn to talk to our dreams; we have to get on good terms with them.' The same writer has suggested that, if dream recall is slow or difficult, you should try the Gestalt approach pioneered by Frederick Perls in California in the 1960s:

Put two chairs facing each other, and sit on one of them. Be yourself; look straight at the empty chair – in which your dream or an image from it is supposed to be sitting – and simply hold a question-and-answer session with it. You ask the question, then directly move to the other chair to let the dream answer. It's quite possible that you'll feel foolish to begin with, but you'll also find that the system really does work surprisingly well, given a chance.

Perhaps, despite your best efforts at interpretation, the meaning of a particular dream still eludes you. It may seem odd, but the best thing to do in such a situation is to 'ask' for another dream that will help you to understand. Your unconscious is working away all the time; if you send it your 'message' in those

moments when you are approaching sleep, it will frequently sort out a set of symbols that add to those in the first dream, and clarify its meaning.

Finally, do not hesitate to talk to your dreams, even argue with them. This is particularly valuable in nightmares and other frightening dreams. Be positive: don't think 'this threatening presence is going to do me harm', but concentrate deliberately on driving it away. And get out of the habit of saying to yourself: 'I had a dream last night'; this is a sure way to forget it. Tell yourself, instead: 'I remember one of the dreams I had. Then, turn to the Dream Dictionary that follows.

DREAM DICTIONARY

*A*s we have seen, the content of a dream is open to several interpretations. On the one hand, much of what is encountered while dreaming can be attributed to a sorting out and 'filing away' of recent experiences, or the mind putting forward solutions to problems that obsess the dreamer. However, the investigations of psychologists – particularly Freud and Jung – have revealed that there is a deeper symbolism that can be traced back to the earliest preoccupations of human beings. For the Freudians, many – if not all – dream symbols, however innocent they may seem at first, represent sexual elements. For the Jungians, most dream experiences are related to the ancient archetypes that seem to be shared by the whole human race. Finally, there is the unresolved question of whether some dreams are truly predictive.

Traditional 'dream dictionaries' tread a path between these different approaches. On the whole, they tend to be very specific, but usually what they promise is no more than increased wealth or poverty, good health or sickness, good news or bad news, success or failure in love and family relationships.

What follows is an attempt to cover all these different approaches to the interpretation of some of the thousands of different images – pleasant, troubling, puzzling, bizarre or downright terrifying – that are dreamt of every night, by people of all races throughout the entire world.

A word of warning. The interpretation of dreams is a difficult art: no symbol can be read on its own, and the circumstances surrounding it can seriously affect its meaning. In addition, dreams often go by opposites, and actually signify the reverse of what they may seem to. Lastly, there are the games that the mind plays, taking a word and making a pun on it. All these factors combine to make dreams a fascinating – if frequently frustrating – subject for study.

LOCATIONS

In dreams, events usually take place in quite clearly defined locations: we know at once whether we are in a building, the street, the countryside, or elsewhere. Very often the location is even more specific: a building for a particular purpose, a garden, a farm.
In general, the setting of the dream will reflect the mood of the dreamer, his or her emotional state, while a building of any kind generally represents the individual body and personality. Whatever the location, the weather conditions in which it is seen will affect the significance of the image. Is it bathed in warm sunlight? Hung over by threatening storm clouds? Or abandoned in the cold light of the moon?

Abbey The image of an abbey can take several different forms. It may be a great public place of worship, like Westminster Abbey in London; it may be a residential monastery ruled over by an abbot or abbess; or it may be a scene of romantic ruins. Traditionally, to dream of an abbey is not a good omen. If a priest bars the entrance, it is a sign that the dreamer's plans will be frustrated.

For a man to dream that he is an abbot is not a good sign: people are plotting his downfall. If he sees the priest at prayer, it is a warning that flattery and deceit will be likely to make him an unsuspecting victim of these plotters.
(See also: Altar; Church; Clergy)

Abyss The symbolism of the abyss springs from some of the most primitive, atavistic instincts. It yawns at our feet like a trap, and we teeter on the edge, fearful that we will lose our balance and plunge into its black, unfathomed depths. At one and the same time it is a threatening obstacle and a dangerous temptation. To dream of looking down into an abyss portends difficulties of many kinds: the possibility of loss of property, personal quarrels, everything that can make it almost impossible to face up to the problems of life. Falling in – a not uncommon dream – is a sign of desperation: how can one possibly hope to survive? But few dreamers reach the bottom of the pit, and fewer still find themselves trapped there, fighting vainly to get out. Somehow the fall is arrested, or a tiny passage of escape appears – hope survives. Even a dream of others falling into the abyss is a warning – to take care in all one's dealings.

Arch An arch can be an imposing part of an important building, or it may be standing alone as a memorial – often of military success. In either case, it symbolises distinction and honour.

Even the sight of an arch in a dream is often a good sign. Traditionally, if one passes through it, one can expect that people who have previously ignored one's abilities will come in search of favours and assistance. A broken or fallen arch, on the contrary, is a sign that one's hopes will not be fulfilled.

As with all other architectural symbols, the conditions in which the arch is seen play a part in the interpretation. For example, a memorial arch hung over with cloud, and through which lightning can be seen flickering in the distance, can denote the danger of a coming war.
(*See also: Bridge*)

Balcony Being on a balcony, with a view to the far horizon, or high above the crowd, perhaps making a powerful speech, would seem to be a symbol of superiority and domination. Freudians, however, think otherwise. For them, the balcony represents the mother's breast. The view from the balcony is romantic, and signifies a desire to escape from present-day troubles and return to the simple pleasures of babyhood.

Traditionally, dreaming of a balcony has similar meanings. Being on a balcony portends the loss of present position; and if the dreamer is there with a loved one it foretells that a long separation will follow.

Bank Half a century before Freud, Victorian euphemisms drew a parallel between money and semen. To dream of putting money into a bank, therefore – and more particularly into a safe-deposit box or vault – has an obvious sexual symbolism, for both men and women. In a more general sense, the bank premises can represent an emotional or spiritual store, rather than a financial one.

Dreaming of working in a bank – when that is

not the dreamer's occupation – is an indication that false promises are about to be made. On the same principle of dreams often going by opposites, dealing with a bank, or drawing money out, can portend financial losses.
(See also: Bankruptcy)

Bar Here, the mind may be playing word games. The bar is the dividing line between the customer and the proprietor, and the significance of the dream can depend upon which side of the bar the dreamer finds him or herself. Drinking alone at a bar can be a depressing situation, and can mean that an untrustworthy friend is not far away; drinking with others signifies the need to control one's appetites. A dream of serving behind the bar, on the other hand, while it is a symbol of having overcome initial obstacles, suggests that one may have to resort to questionable methods to advance further.

Bridge A bridge joins one piece of solid land to another; but it also crosses a cutting, a ravine or a river, or a dangerous place of some kind. In the first case, it symbolises a conscious transition from one stage of the dreamer's life to another. In the second, its significance depends partly upon what lies below it. If the dreamer crosses the bridge successfully from one side to the other, the problems will be overcome. But, if the bridge is broken, it signifies the frustration of plans for the future.
(See also: Arch; Rainbow)

Cabin In Shakespeare's play, Macbeth spoke of being 'cabined, cribbed, confined,

bound in to saucy doubts and fears'. The cabin can be a lone hut on the wild prairie, surrounded by threatening wolves, or an enclosed berth aboard a ship. It indicates that the dreamer, in waking life, is hiding away from emotional or business difficulties.

Castle A castle can represent unyielding and unapproachable authority, like the building that looms over Franz Kafka's novel of the same name. It can be the home of royalty, or of others who can bestow rewards and honour in recognition of achievement. Or it can be an impregnable fortress, but a place of safety if one finds oneself inside it. In this sense, it may represent woman, in her most forbidding aspect, but ultimately attainable.

Cathedral See Abbey; Church; Clergy

Cave Caves were the first homes of humankind, and they represent safety and protection from the outside world. In the same way, a cave is womb-like, and a dream of a cave may symbolise a desire

to escape from everyday responsibilities and return to the unquestioning comfort of existence before birth.

A cave can also represent the unconscious, the inner recesses of the mind. Descending into a cave may therefore symbolise the need to bring some hidden aspect of one's personality into the light. Dreams of killing a dragon or some other fierce animal that guards the entrance to the cave can represent a way of getting in touch with the Anima or Animus, who will help the individual to realise his or her true self.

Cellar Like the cave, a cellar can be a symbol of the unconscious mind. Going down into a cellar may be a search for repressed memories.
(See also: Cave)

Cemetery See Burial; Death

Chimney An obvious sexual symbol: the exterior is phallic, while the interior represents the female. A man who dreams of climbing inside a dark and frightening chimney is probably suffering from a fear of sex. In this connection, it is significant how one of the traditional dream dictionaries interprets a young woman's dream of descending a chimney: 'she will be guilty of some impropriety that will cause consternation among her associates'.
(See also: Fireplace)

Church Most churches are peaceful places in which to express one's religious beliefs. The dreamer may share in the peace, a sign that all is well and that prayers will be answered. He or she, however, may dream that they are disturbing this peace, a sign that they are struggling against the faith in which they were raised, or against other conventions that they have been taught to uphold.

If the church is seen in the distance, it signifies disappointment of plans that have been long cherished. And if the dreamer enters a gloomy church, this is an omen of a funeral to come soon.
(See also: Abbey)

Cinema During the 1930s, cinemas were built as 'picture palaces', fantastic edifices that reflected the desire of the moviegoer to be transported far from everyday cares. For many people, the cinema is still a symbol of the need to escape. The film being shown can be a secondary projection of other elements in the dream. It may be pleasant, dramatic or horrific. The dreamer may feel drawn into the action, possibly even a player in the story. All this is important in the dream's interpretation.
(See also: Acting; Platform; Theatre)

Circus The circus ring is a circle, and may have a related significance. On the other hand, the performers in the ring – acrobats, clowns, animals – may be the important element. There is also the implication that a circus is a superficial entertainment: did the dreamer feel that 'life is nothing but a circus'?
(See also: Acrobat; Animal Kingdom; Carnival; Circle; Clown)

City The significance of a city can vary considerably, depending upon the experience and beliefs of the dreamer. St Augustine wrote of the City of God; and the City of the Sun is the title of a sixteenth-century work describing a utopian state. A city, therefore, can represent the ultimate hoped-for destination, where the wanderer will be welcomed by the community. Or it can be a familiar place, where the dreamer feels at home. But it can also be a dirty, frightening maze of

streets and high buildings, where the dreamer is lost, and ignored by passers-by.
(See also: Maze)

Column This can be a simple phallic symbol. However, a column can also be raised to carry a statue of an honoured person; perhaps this symbolises someone whom the dreamer admires ('looks up to'). Other columns can support a roof or similar structure. The dreamer may be aware that his or her responsibilities are holding up a business or a family; and if the columns are crumbling and collapsing, this portends disaster.

Court A court is a place where judgments are made. The dreamer may be the judge himself, or appearing as an advocate, and in this case it may be that he or she is going to have to stand by an argument, or make a decision that will seriously affect someone else. But if the dreamer is in the dock – 'caught' – it is a sign that they feel guilty for something they have done, or perhaps misjudged.
(See also: Jury; Lawyer)

Ditch A ditch can be a boundary, marking the division between one piece of land and another, an obstacle that must be crossed, or part of a drainage system. Is the dreamer in the ditch? Has he or she been 'ditched' by a loved one? The land on either side of the ditch may represent two different aspects of the dreamer's life, and working in the ditch may symbolise a way of keeping them separate, or a way to drain boggy ground and allow both aspects to flourish.
(See also: Digging; Hedge)

Door The significance of this dream symbol is complex. It represents a way in: to new events or

prospects, to intellectual or spiritual understanding, or perhaps to the male or female body.

If the door is easily opened, or is already open, the omens are generally good – but what lies beyond the door? A closing door can portend frustration of one's plans; if it is the dreamer who closes the door – possibly forcing it shut against external pressure, even barring it – he or she is deliberately shutting off future developments. A locked door, since it is the dreamer who has produced the image, can equally represent reluctance and inhibition.
(See also: Entrance; Hallway)

Entrance In most cases, an entrance symbolises the female genitalia. What is happening at the entrance, whether it is wide and welcoming, closed – or even blocked by other people – can reveal the meaning behind this dream. On the other hand, emerging from a dark entrance into bright light may be connected with distant memories of the moment of birth.

(See also: Door; Hallway)

Exhibition What kind of an exhibition was it? An art show, or a similar event in a museum? A trade fair? Or a big national exhibition, packed with crowds? The objects being exhibited, or the purpose of the event, can also have significance.

Perhaps the dreamer feels they have 'made an exhibition' of themselves. Or they may have the need to put themselves on show, in order to attract the attention they feel they deserve. If the exhibition was very crowded and claustrophobic, it can be a sign that they feel unappreciated, and overwhelmed by the accomplishments of others.

Factory Working in a factory, even if it is not in the dreamer's experience, can represent the drudgery of everyday life. On the other hand, it may be a sign that the dreamer is an active person, working to a plan and capable of getting results; and, in this case, an accident in the factory suggests that the plan may not come to a successful conclusion.

(See also: Machinery; Workshop)

Fairground All sorts of activities take place on a fairground: rides, sideshows, tests of skill or strength, and sales of food and drink. Perhaps the dream is a reminder of the 'swings and roundabouts' of life, the roller coaster of emotions, or the 'tunnel of love'. Like other places crowded with symbols, the fairground can represent every facet of the dreamer's life.

(See also: Acrobat; Carnival; Clown)

Farm A dream image that is filled with different symbols: the domestic animals and birds, the concept of cultivation and nourishment, particularly in flourishing fields, and the idea of hard but rewarding labour. For many people, the dream of being a farmer may have surfaced from a childhood longing – before the realities of this demanding ambition were realised!

Because the dream symbols of the farm are so full of individual meanings, it is likely that one or two will appear more significant, and these must be interpreted within the overall context.

(See also: individual animals and crops; Digging; Ditch; Field; Hedge; Plough)

Fence A fence can be an obstacle, it can be built to enclose something, or it can keep something out. Which of these functions did it fulfill in the dream? If it was a fence against animals – whether they were inside or outside – it can represent the dreamer's struggle with primitive instincts. In other images, it is likely to indicate inhibition.

(See also: Hedge)

Fireplace From very early times, the fire has been the important centre of the home. Dreaming of an empty fireplace, or one in which the fire is dying, is therefore a sign of domestic troubles. And remember also the lines of the British writer Walter Savage Landor:

I warmed both hands before the fire of life;
It sinks; and I am ready to depart.

(See also: Chimney; Fire)

Fortress A fortress can be a place of safety and protection, or it can represent the dreamer's own body. If it is under attack, this may be a sign that illness is on the way. Dreaming of

storming a fortress can be a symbol of violent sexual desires.

(See also: Castle)

Garage The car is often identified with the dreamer's self, and so the kind of garage is significant. If it is the building where the car is housed, then it may well represent the individual's home. Other places can relate to the physical health of the dreamer: a garage where repairs are carried out has an obvious symbolism; we speak of 'recharging one's battery'; and even filling the fuel tank at a service station can symbolise nourishment and the recovery of strength.

Garden Gardens represent, above all, peace and pleasure, but they can also imply formality. As a dream symbol, they can present – like farms – a wide variety of elements: flowers and fruits,

lawns, paths, walls and gates, water in different forms, and the general image of growth. All these may have to be analysed separately.

The garden as a whole can be considered to represent the dreamer's self. If it was overgrown and choked with weeds, it signifies that the dreamer's thoughts, emotions or waking circumstances are in a similar untidy and confused state.

On the other hand, the garden may be the Garden of Eden, a lost Paradise. Perhaps the dreamer is hoping to find a place where man and woman can dwell together in loving harmony.

The presence of a gardener, perhaps an elderly man or woman wise in the ways of plants, is a symbol of a spiritual protector.

(See: individual flowers and fruits; Fence; Fountain and spring; Hedge; Lake and pond; Wall; Water)

Gate See Door

Grave See Burial

Hall Like other buildings, a hall can symbolise the human body. However, its purpose as a communal meeting place can represent social relationships, and if it is empty it can suggest that an important part of the dreamer's personality is not being properly expressed.

Hallway As the entrance to a building, the hallway is most likely to symbolise the vagina. However, it can also signify the approach to a new experience, further spiritual development, or a coming journey into unfamiliar territory.

(See also: Door; Entrance)

Hedge Like a fence, a hedge is a barrier; it may enclose something to be protected from outside influences, or it may prevent the dreamer from entering. However, it is not as solid as a fence, there may be openings or gateways through it, and it may be trimmed and cultivated to be an attractive part of a garden or park. The dreamer's feelings about the hedge, and the circumstances in which it was encountered (was the dreamer shut off from something pleasurable on the other side, for example?), can provide further clues to its significance.

(See also: Ditch; Farm; Fence; Garden)

Hospital As with all buildings, the hospital can represent the dreamer's own body. If he or she was there as a patient, the dream may give a clue to some developing ailment that has not yet become apparent; or perhaps it is a reflection of some injury – emotional or material – that has been inflicted upon the dreamer.

On the other hand, the dreamer may have been playing the role of a doctor or nurse. This can be a reference to some supportive function they are exercising in their waking life. Or it may be a memory of the semi-erotic games played in childhood.

(See also: Doctor; Nurse)

Hotel A place to stay when away from home, whether for rest and relaxation, or on a business trip. The dream may be a sign of a need to get away from familiar surroundings and

responsibilities for a time. If the dreamer was working in the hotel, it can represent the demands that are being made on them in waking life. On the other hand, if he or she was a pampered guest, this can symbolise the demands they are making on others.

House It is generally agreed that a house represents the dreamer's body and personality. Every aspect of the house can have significance. Was it being built, newly finished or redecorated, or in a dilapidated state? Was it the dreamer's home, a place of familiar comfort and refuge, or an ideal 'dream palace'? Or was it the house of someone else? Some houses seem threatening, even sinister, and what goes on inside is a dark mystery. And it should be remembered that the openings – the doors and windows – can each refer to parts of the human body.

The decorations and furniture are equally important. Were the rooms empty and echoing? Perhaps the dreamer was moving out, willingly or unwillingly, to begin a new phase in life.

What activities were taking place in the house? Was it crowded, possibly with people who were considering buying it? Was the dreamer kept at a serious meeting in an upstairs room, while a party was being held downstairs?

It is obvious that a dream concerning a house can have a wealth of meanings, and their significance will emerge only after very careful consideration.

(See also: Hallway; Room)

Island These scraps of solid land, entirely surrounded by water, have a great attraction for many people in waking life. The dreamer may be alone on the island, or with a few chosen companions, or welcomed by the friendly inhabitants. This can represent an ideal existence:

the land symbolises
security and personal confidence,
and the water is the unconscious.

But the island, particularly if it was a barren
place where the dreamer was stranded, can also
symbolise isolation. The dreamer is cut off from
emotional involvement and desperately awaiting
the arrival of a rescuer.

(See also: Ocean; Water)

Kitchen The kitchen can be considered the heart
of the home, and the source of nourishment –
which, in a dream, may be physical or spiritual.
Problems with the cooker can indicate the state of
the dreamer's health.

(See also: Food & Drink)

Laboratory
A place for
experiment, either in
the dreamer's waking life, or
with his or her inner beliefs or fears. The dream
can be a sign that the dreamer is too involved in
mundane matters, and it is time to open out a
little. The kind of experiment being performed
may provide other symbols that will help
interpretation.

Labyrinth See Maze

Library A library is a place where knowledge and
wisdom are stored. A dream set in a library
symbolises the dreamer's need to draw on these
resources, or search for a new meaning in life.
Sometimes, the dreamer is searching for a

particular book and cannot find it. Like many other searching dreams, this can be a sign that something is missing from the individual's spiritual development. The nature of the book can be an indication of what the dreamer lacks – sometimes, its title is a punning reference to the subject.

(See also: Book; Searching)

Lighthouse The lighthouse, symbol of a guiding principle that can bring the dreamer safely through the unknown waters and the storm of emotions, can represent the church to which he or she belonged in their youth. On the other hand, it may be a phallic form.

Maze A dream of being lost in a maze is likely to reflect some part of the dreamer's waking condition, in which they 'don't know which way to turn'. However, successfully finding the way out of the maze, or leading others out of it, is a sign that all will be well.

Mill The interpretation of this dream symbol will depend to a great extent on the conditions in which it was viewed. Was it a romantic windmill seen from a distance, a wished-for destination? Was it a watermill, with forceful streams of water gushing through – a rather obvious sexual symbol? Or was the dreamer inside the mill, surrounded by ominously rumbling machinery? The image of something being ground down can represent the gradual disintegration of obstinately held, but false, beliefs, and the emergence of true values.

(See also: Grinding; Machinery)

Mine A complex symbol. It combines the significance of the tunnel with the concept of exploration of the underworld, signifying the unconscious. Was the dreamer a worker in the mine, a lost intruder, or even someone trapped by a fall of rock?

(See also: Cave; Tunnel)

Monastery Since any building can represent the dreamer's self, dreaming of a monastery can symbolise either a desire to escape from the world into peace and contemplation, or a present condition of restriction and excessive discipline. Those in a monastery are exclusively male, so the dream – for either sex – will relate to the masculine side of the personality, and it may be a sign that the dreamer should show greater sensitivity. On the other hand, there may be a reference to the dreamer's sex life.

(See also: Monk; Nun)

Museum Museums around the world can be very different from one another, but they all have some characteristics in common. There will be a large number of exhibits, some of which are obviously important, while others have no apparent use or value. Somebody will have arranged all of the exhibits carefully, but in a few museums there seems to be no logic to the arrangement. And, even in the best-kept institutions, dust can gather in the corners.

The human memory is very like this, and the dream museum is likely to be filled with symbols of the dreamer's personality as it has developed over the years. Possibly one cobwebbed relic, discovered unexpectedly, will evoke feelings that have long been buried.

On the other hand, museums are also notoriously places where an acquaintance can be struck up with a stranger. Maybe the dream reflects the dreamer's desire to make new friends.

(See also: Exhibition)

Nunnery The female equivalent of a monastery, with similar implications.

(See also: Monastery; Monk; Nun)

Oasis The reality of an oasis is often very different from the way one is represented in illustrations or films. What the dreamer saw will therefore depend to a degree upon whether or not they have travelled to a real oasis. However, the symbolism remains very much the same: a place of rest and refreshment after the thirsty emptiness of the desert. If this was what the dreamer was seeking, it is a sign that he or she should take a break from everyday material concerns and turn their attention to their emotional and spiritual health.

Office A dream about the office in which one works is generally the result of a preoccupation with a specific problem in one's waking life. The office can also represent an important part of the dreamer's personality, and his or her professional reputation.

The significance of other offices will depend upon their nature. An unfamiliar office can suggest apprehension, or a feeling that the situation of other people is preferable to one's own. The office may be a specific one: that of a lawyer, a doctor, a tax inspector, and so on. In this case, the business of the office will provide further clues to the meaning of the dream.

Park See Garden

Parliament The interior of the individual's parliament building is likely to be fairly familiar from television and films. Dreaming that one was speaking there clearly indicates a need to draw attention to oneself, or to a matter that appears to be important – although, on later reflection, it may seem far too trivial to be discussed in parliament! The response of the parliamentary members may well go by opposites: an enthusiastic reception in the dream is likely to signify opposition in waking life.

(See also: Election)

Party Most parties in waking life dwindle down to a degree of disappointment and exhaustion; in dreams, they tend to end in disruption and chaos. This may very well symbolise conditions in the dreamer's waking life.

Path Whether it is straight or winding, smooth or rough, uphill or down, a path is laid out before us, and represents our destiny. It may provide an easy, pleasant stroll through a garden or park, each turn revealing something new, but with the end always in sight. Or it may require a struggle across rocks and through thorns until the goal is achieved. But one point must always be remembered: somebody – it may have been the dreamer, or someone else before them – made the path, and has been that way before.
(See also: Garden; Mountain)

Pit See Abyss

Platform The platform separates the speaker, or the committee, from the people below; it is also the place from which a plan or policy is declared, or prize results are announced. Was the dreamer one of those on the platform, looking down at the crowd? Did he or she make a rousing speech, to encouraging applause? Or did they feel exposed and likely to be held up to ridicule? They may even have discovered, on standing up to speak, that they were naked.
(See also: Acting; Nudity; Parliament)

Prison A prison symbolises constraint, guilt and punishment. The dreamer may feel 'shut in', with little or no opportunity for self-expression. Alternatively, he or she may understand that some actions or modes of behaviour have been unacceptable, or that certain anti-social feelings must be 'locked away'.

Quarry Quarries are often described as a 'scar' on the landscape. They are places where something has been taken away, leaving an unsightly gap. Perhaps the dreamer has recently ended a relationship, something that has left a scar on his or her personality.
(See also: Sand)

Race Was it a horse race, a motor race, a race on foot – or another of the many different kinds of race? In each case, the details of the race will provide specific symbols that will help to explain the dream's meaning. In general, if the dreamer was a spectator at the race, this may suggest that he or she is only a passive observer of the exciting things in life.

If the dreamer was one of those racing – rather than a spectator – the dream probably reflects waking preoccupations. Is the individual striving too hard, running risks, caught in the 'rat race'?
(See also: Betting)

Railway station A place of arrival and departure. Was the dreamer the traveller, about to leave on a journey or wearily returning from one? Or was he or she eagerly awaiting someone, or saying farewell to them? Missing – or just catching – a train can be a symbol of opportunities that could be lost.
(See also: Train)

Rehearsal Whatever the kind of rehearsal, the message of this dream is likely to be that the individual should be sure of his or her intentions before embarking on a new project. Was the dreamer capable of a competent performance, or did he or she stumble? Who was the director (perhaps even the dreamer)? And what was his or her reaction?
(See also: Acting; Audition; Dancing; Orchestra and band)

Restaurant A restaurant can be a pleasant rendezvous for a meal with a loved one or friends, or a daunting place where the dreamer feels at the mercy of the waiters. A dream set in a restaurant can therefore represent, depending upon the circumstances, the affirmation of social relationships, or a feeling of humiliation.

Also to be considered is the fact that a meal in a restaurant presents one with a wide choice of pleasure: for Freudians, its sexual connotations are obvious.

(See also: Food & Drink; Waiter)

Road A road can represent the course of the individual's life and his or her eventual destiny, or it can symbolise the more immediate future. If the road in the dream ran straight, then whatever is planned will come to a successful conclusion; if it was winding it signifies that the dreamer's plans are not sufficiently positive. In the same context, a choice of roads represents uncertainty, and a blocked road or a dead end signifies failure in that direction. The landscape through which the road ran is also of great significance.

(See also: Path)

Room A room can represent a specific area of the unconscious. Very often in dreams one room leads to another, and the objects in these rooms will have a particular significance. Freud maintained that, in men's dreams, a room was almost always a symbol for a woman. Alternatively, the room may be just a part of a house, which will prove to be the more important symbol.

(See also: Hallway; House)

Ruin A dream of a ruined building can represent a part of the dreamer's past, or the rejection of some previously held beliefs or way of life. Did

the dreamer view the ruin with nostalgia or relief?

School One of the prime experiences of school for every individual is the need to conform to conventions and restrictions wider than those encountered within the family, and the emotional impact is one that is never forgotten. Dreaming of being back in school may be a reworking of childhood memories, possibly getting the better of a sadistic bully; or it may represent a more recent humiliation. Whatever the events that take place, such a dream usually signifies the need to reconsider present conditions in waking life and to learn from past mistakes.

(See also: Professor; Schoolteacher; University)

Shop A place full of necessary or desirable objects, which are sold by the shopkeeper and bought by the customer. Which role did the dreamer play? Was he or she (like many an antique dealer) disposing of something they would rather have kept? Or did the articles they were buying represent something they desperately wanted?

(See also: Objects)

Skyscraper A symbol of ambition and achievement; and, because a building usually represents the dreamer, frequently a good omen. However, if the dreamer felt dwarfed by the height, it can signify that others are succeeding where the dreamer has failed, and possibly exerting a dominating influence. There is also the phallic symbolism to be considered.

(See also: Tower)

Spaceship According to Jung, spaceships have become the modern equivalent of angels in dreams. The alleged experiences of people who claim that they have been abducted aboard a spaceship by extra-terrestrial beings have all the characteristics of dreams, and probably are.

(See also: Angel)

Stable A place where horses – a powerful sexual symbol – are kept under control. Or has the dreamer 'shut the stable door after the horse has gone' – that is, left matters too late?

(See also: Ammonia; Horse)

Stairs A staircase is a place where one can walk up or down. In one respect, it can represent changes in the dreamer's social status or spiritual development. On the other hand, Freud maintained that walking up and down steps, ladders or staircases are representations of the sexual act.

(See also: Climbing; Descent; Ladder)

Swimming pool As with other water symbols, this is connected with Jung's archetypal Mother, and also with the unconscious – in fact, the swimming pool has been identified as representing the womb. The act of swimming, on the other hand, is said to symbolise sex.

(See also: Lake and pond; Water)

Tent There are many different kinds of tent – the lightweight model carried in a backpack, the broad, low tents of the Bedouin, a marquee for a party or a wedding reception, the huge tent of the circus – but they all have certain characteristics in common. In particular, a tent is the flimsiest possible division between the interior and the outside world, and is weaker and less secure than a house. If the tent was the dominant image in the dream, it probably signified that the dreamer was unsure about the strength of his or her personality, and felt likely to be at the mercy of outside infl-uences. On the other hand, the phallic significance of the tent pole should not be forgotten.

(See also: House; Pole)

Theatre Was the dreamer performing on the stage, or a member of the audience? What was the drama being played? Historically, the theatre was a place where the audience experienced the emotions of the characters at secondhand, and so became 'cleansed' of those emotions in themselves – a process the Greeks called catharsis.

Perhaps, in this way, the dreamer was playing out some inner emotion by projecting it into the action on the stage.

(See also: Acting; Cinema; Platform)

Tower A classic phallic symbol. Or perhaps the dreamer felt that he or she – or someone else – was a 'tower of strength' in some waking situation, and worthy of being looked up to. On the other hand, 'living in an ivory tower' describes a person who is out of touch with everyday reality. And, in fairy tales, princesses were often shut away in towers, from which they had to be rescued.

(See also: Prince and princess; Skyscraper)

Tunnel A common dream symbol for the vagina, and in this context the dream may be sexual (entering the tunnel), or a distant memory of the moment of birth. On the other hand, the dark tunnel can represent a time of anxiety in waking life. Was there a light at the end of it?

(See also: Cave; Mine)

University The circumstances of the dream will depend upon whether or not the dreamer has personal experience of university life. A university is a place of learning and research. Was the dreamer a student in search of knowledge, or a professor capable of imparting it? Remember also that those who have not been educated at university often speak of having attended 'the university of life'.

(See also: Professor; Schoolteacher)

Village Many people who live in towns have the wish to retire from the 'rat race' and settle down in a country village, and the dream may have reflected this desire. On the other hand, those who live in a country village know that it is likely to be a hotbed of jealousy and intrigue. The meaning of this dream can depend very much upon the dreamer's experience – or the lack of it – of village life.

Wall Like fences, walls can represent the individual's struggle with his or her more primitive instincts, and the social conventions that serve to inhibit them. They may also symbolise apparently insurmountable obstacles that prevent the dreamer realising his or her desires - the feeling that one is 'up against the wall'.

(See also: Fence; Hedge)

Window Was the dreamer looking out of the window, or looking in? In either case, there is an element of separation: from the common, everyday activities outside; or from the privileged, but isolated, status within. This is a dream that requires very careful consideration – especially if the dreamer felt the need to break the glass.

(See also: Glass)

Workshop The tradition of the honest, unselfconscious craftsman is long established. The dream probably reflects the knowledge and understanding that the dreamer has accumulated. Did he or she feel confident with the tools available, or daunted by the expertise that by implication was demanded?

(See also: Factory; Tool)

Zoo Above all, a zoo is a place where animals are confined and exhibited. Obviously, the individual significance of the captive animals seen in the dream is of considerable importance. But was the dreamer the keeper of the zoo, or did he or she identify with one of the animals? The keeper can be seen as someone who keeps animal instincts under careful control.

(See also: Animal Kingdom)

ENVIRONMENT & ELEMENTS

Nearly all dreams take place within some sort of natural environment – generally of a type that is familiar to the dreamer; but even one that is unfamiliar will contain aspects that enable the dreamer to identify it from his or her experience of reading, seeing films or paintings, or hearing the descriptions of others. The conditions in which the dream took place – by day or by night, in fine weather or foul, the time of day or the season of the year – will have a related symbolic significance.

Afternoon Traditionally, a calm, beautiful afternoon is a sign of good times approaching, and if the dreamer is a woman it denotes that she will form lasting and valuable friendships. A cloudy, rainy afternoon, on the other hand, portends disappointment. However, a foggy afternoon is a sign that one should continue to have faith in oneself, although it may mean changing one's plans for the future.

Autumn Most people regard autumn as a melancholy time, when the leaves fall from the trees, things are seen mistily, and the trials of winter are not far off. In this light, dreams of autumn are frequently due to an awareness of advancing age, and generally begin to appear in the middle years. There are consolations, however. Autumn is the time when fires are lit again, and the home seems ever more welcoming. For a young woman to dream of this season, for example, portends a happy marriage and a comfortable family life.

Beach See Shore

Cliff The dreamer may be at the foot of the cliff, possibly trying to climb it, or at the top, looking down from a terrifying height. If the cliff looms overhead threateningly, it can symbolise trouble in store for the dreamer. Trying to clamber up

the cliff represents a determination to overcome the obstacle, but the attempt may fail; perhaps it would be better to walk away to a safer place.
(See also: Abyss; Mountain)

Cloud A dream symbol that can take very many different forms. In everyday life, clouds foretell the weather to

come, and in dreams they can play a similar part. They may be a sign of calm in the near future, or threaten stormy days ahead. They can be a symbol of someone with their 'head in the clouds', or with a 'clouded brain': vague, impractical thoughts are drifting between the individual and the sun, which symbolises the active mind.

Clouds heavy with rain will bring refreshment, and can portend the nourishment of new ideas. But if the rain falls in a long torrential downpour, it can wash everything away.

(*See also: Rain; Sun*)

Cold The dream may involve merely a feeling of personal coldness, or it may take place in a landscape swept by freezing winds, deep in snow, or set into solid ice. In the first case, the simple explanation may be that the bedclothes are insufficient, or have fallen off. As for the second case, it could be an atavistic memory of the time when the first humans began to move northwards, as the last Ice Age retreated some 10,000 years ago.

As a symbol, coldness can have an equally simple meaning. It represents the dreamer's emotional personality and suggests that it has not been given the opportunity to develop fully.

(*See also: Ice*)

Comet and meteor These astronomical objects from outer space shine brightly in the sky for a short time, and then (in the case of a comet) shoot off, not to be seen again for many years or centuries, or (in the case of a meteor) burn up and vanish, sometimes falling to earth as tiny fragments. They can be a symbol of brilliant ideas that prove incapable of being seized, or they may reflect the dreamer's belief in extra-terrestrial beings.

In ancient times, a comet was regarded as a portent of violent events, while meteors were considered to bring gifts from the gods – which is how the concept 'wish upon a falling star' came about.

(*See also: Star*)

Darkness Throughout human history, the dark has been full of the terror of the unknown. The Spanish mystic St John of the Cross wrote of 'the dark night of the soul', and a dream of darkness can reflect apprehension, a pessimistic attitude to life, or a state of depression. However, there is always an element of hope, as in the phrase 'the darkest hour is just before dawn'.

(*See also: Black; Night*)

Dawn The sun rises, representing the hopeful development of the spirit, or a new project that is bound for success. Even a dark and stormy dawn can be an encouraging sign: eventually, the clouds will clear and bright day will follow.

Day It is believed that the time of day experienced in a dream reflects the dreamer's age; and the passage of a number of days signifies a period of that number of years.

A dream set in the morning will refer to the dreamer's youth; one set in the afternoon is connected with adulthood; and one set in the evening concerns old age.

(*See also: Afternoon; Dawn; Evening*)

Directions Many ancient peoples believed that gods or great spirits ruled the four cardinal points of the compass, and the direction in which dream events take place can still have a fundamental significance. The east, the direction of sunrise, is the source of birth and spiritual illumination; the south represents the full vigour of adult life; the west is the direction of death, because the sun 'dies' there every evening; while the north represents misfortune and evil.

By long-standing tradition, events on the left are regarded as bad – in Latin, sinister means 'left' – while the right is the side of good.

Earthquake A phrase from Ernest Hemingway's novel *For Whom the Bell Tolls* has become famous as a description of sexual climax: 'did thee feel the earth move?' In other respects, the sensation of the earth shaking, or opening up beneath the dreamer's feet, is a sign of a feeling of insecurity.
(See also: Volcano)

East The direction in which the sun rises, symbolising the dawn of new hopes or projects, or important spiritual development. A dream of the Orient may be a reflection of the dreamer's travel

experiences, or a result of their reading; if it concerned Chinese or Japanese philosophy it may also have a spiritual significance.
(See also: Directions)

Echo In ancient myth, Echo was a nymph who fell in love with the handsome youth Narcissus. When her love was not returned, she pined away until only her voice remained. Perhaps the dreamer is suffering from unrequited love.

In another sense, it is the dreamer's own voice that is being echoed, resounding in empty space. Do they feel that what they have to say is being ignored? Or are they surrounded by people who agree too easily, and do not contribute to the discussion of a problem?
(See also: Narcissus)

Electricity Despite its common availability in our homes, electricity is still a dangerous, and to some people a mysterious, force. In dreams, its significance can be closely related to how one regards it in waking life. Is the dreamer 'switched on', making use of the power? Or was there a sudden inexplicable failure? Does the dreamer feel that his or her 'batteries need recharging'? Did they get a shock?

Evening The end of the day can represent a number of different things. It can be a symbol of the last years of one's life; a period of rest and relaxation after labour; or a time of regret for matters that are unaccomplished.
(See also: Afternoon; Day; Night; Sun)

Fire A complex symbol, with a wide variety of meanings. Above all, it can represent passion and desire. It provides light, warmth and comfort, symbolising the home, but at the same time it is dangerous, and can destroy nearly everything. Fire can cause intense pain, yet it is also purifying – two aspects that are combined in the concept of the 'fires of Hell'.

Dreams of fighting a fire, therefore, can symbolise the calming of passion. Fire and water are opposites, and in this sense fire represents the conscious animal instincts, and water the cooling effect of the intellect and the unconscious. Other circumstances in the dream may give a clue to the inner conflicts involved.

(See also: Water)

Flood Because water represents the unconscious, a dream of struggling in a flood can symbolise being overwhelmed by repressed emotions, or by circumstances in one's waking life. In the sense of a bursting forth of liquid, a flood can also have sexual connotations.

(See also: Water)

Fog and mist An obvious symbol of being lost and confused, and of not seeing things clearly. Or it may be that the dreamer is deliberately obscuring something they would rather not recognise. As in so many other dreams of this type, the surrounding circumstances can help to explain its meaning.

(See also: Blindness; Cloud)

Fountain and spring The word 'fountain' can mean a flowing source of water, or a decorative jet and spray. In both cases, the water represents the emotions and the unconscious; the decorative fountain also combines the elements of air and light. Spring water refreshes the spirit, and the beauty of the fountain is like its expression, free but constantly controlled. In legend, drinking from the Fountain of Youth conferred eternal life, and this may be a symbol of spiritual fulfilment.

(See also: Lake and pond; River; Water)

Frost See Cold; Ice

Heat Much depends upon the dreamer's physical reaction to heat: was this the balmy warmth of summer, the oppressive, humid heat of the tropics, the welcome of a burning fire in autumn or winter, or the searing heat of a furnace? The dream may be merely an awareness of the temperature of the bed, or an expression of the strength of the dreamer's passions and emotions – even a sexual symbol.

Hill This dream symbol can represent a difficult task or obstacle in waking life – or, in Freudian terms, a woman's bosom – and whether it proves easy or difficult to climb can signify the dreamer's confidence in overcoming it. But the fairly common dream of climbing and climbing, never reaching the top, may be only a temporary setback, and (as dreams can go by opposites) a sign that success is on the way.

(See also: Climbing; Mountain)

Ice Ice is hard, cold and life-threatening, but it can also be a pleasant ingredient of a cooling drink, an ice cream, or a welcome relief when applied to a fevered brow or an injury.

A dream of icy surroundings can reflect the emotional state of the dreamer, even though they are unaware of their frozen feelings. They may be 'skating on thin ice', or possibly slip and fall – a sure indication of misfortune to come. If the dream is of an iceberg, it should be remembered that most of it is below the water's surface; perhaps the dreamer – or someone else – is hiding his or her emotional coldness beneath a superficial friendliness.

In its more pleasant aspects, ice is a difficult symbol to interpret. A tall drink, with ice cubes bobbing in it, can represent relaxation after a task well done; or it can symbolise someone whose

coolness – whether in love or business negotiations – the dreamer hopes to overcome. Ice cream, for some people, comes close to an addiction, and could represent a temptation that they know they should resist – or, with its childhood associations, it can symbolise a reward.

(See also: Cold; Crystal)

Lake and pond All water symbols have a close connection with the unconscious. Lakes are generally seen as placidly beautiful, stretching almost to the horizon, and can represent the dreamer's spiritual goal. But they can also appear dark and menacing, lying in a narrow cleft between hills – a sign that the unconscious is being neglected.

Ponds have a more domestic significance than lakes. They perhaps represent more accessible

spiritual stages, rather than the ultimate aspiration represented by the lake. And ponds reflect, not only the sky, but the objects or people on their banks.

(See also: Mirror; Water)

Light The symbol of emotional or spiritual insight – we say that we 'see the light' when the answer to a problem is suddenly revealed. A dream of being bathed in light has a very positive significance.

A dream of a narrow beam of bright light being shone on somebody or something is a sign that the dreamer should turn his or her attention that way; but if the beam is directed at the dreamer it is a warning that they should examine their own motives and shortcomings more closely.

(See also: Lamp)

Lightning A common symbol for sudden revelation. It may be a sign of spiritual inspiration and enlightenment; or it may represent a good idea that has just struck the dreamer – and, hopefully, it will be remembered on awakening!

But lightning is also destructive, striking trees and buildings and setting them on fire, and killing unwary people. Other circumstances in the dream will be an aid to its interpretation.

(See also: Fire; Thunder)

Meteor See Comet and meteor

Mist See Fog and mist

Moon A symbol of the feminine principle and the unconscious soul. The moon is the opposite of the sun, which represents active intelligence, but it also reflects the sun. The way in which its aspect changes can represent the rapid changes of mood to which most human beings are subject, or can symbolise death and resurrection. The phases of the moon – whether it was waxing, full, or waning – can have a specific significance.

In the Tarot pack, the card representing the moon is a symbol of uncertainty, warning us that we should not trust in appearances, even those things and people on which we most rely.

(See also: Night; Planet; Sun)

Morning See Dawn; Day

Mountain A daunting sight, as it looms above the dreamer. It symbolises obstacles that will require courage to overcome. Perhaps the dreamer is exaggerating the problem – 'making a mountain out of a molehill'. But climbing the mountain with confidence, and reaching the peak, represents the height of the individual's abilities and ultimate success.

(See also: Climbing; Hill)

Mud See Quicksand or quagmire

Night Was it a black night, in which the dreamer was lost and afraid, a night sparkling with stars, or one in which the moon shone calmly? Fundamentally, the night represents doubt, but other circumstances or events in the dream can lead to a more precise interpretation.

(See also: Darkness; Moon; Star)

Ocean The 'sea of emotion' that surges in the depths of the unconscious, as well as the all-enveloping influence of the archetypal Mother. Whether the water is stormy or calm; whether the dreamer is afloat in a boat, and possibly fishing; what fish or other animals are seen in the water – all these can affect the significance of this dream.
(See also: Boat; Dolphin; Fish; Fishing; Water; Whale)

Planet Astrology places great importance on the 'influence' of the planets, and each may have a particular significance in the context of the dream. The sun – the star at the centre of our planetary system – represents generosity, honour and vitality; and the moon (not strictly a planet, but a satellite of Earth) represents sensitivity, femininity and changeability. Mercury is the planet of quickness of intellect; Venus of grace, artistic ability and affection; and Mars of energy, courage and passion. Jupiter symbolises optimism, cheerfulness and nobility; Saturn, pessimism and self-restraint; Uranus, inspiration and individualism; Neptune, mystery and imagination; and Pluto the darker, unrevealed depths of the personality.

Quicksand or quagmire If the dreamer is caught in ground that seems to be sucking him or her down, 'that sinking feeling' may symbolise being faced with a situation in waking life that is beyond his or her control, or one in which emotions inhibit a rational response.

This may also be an image of repressed sexuality, particularly if the dreamer is dragging first one leg and then the other out of the clinging matter.

Rain Rain is a symbol of fertility and growth; it also cleans and refreshes. In dreams, if the shower is welcome, it can represent the washing away of old ideas, and the development of new ones. But heavy rain from an overcast sky signifies sadness and desolation.
(See also: Cloud)

Rainbow A universal symbol of hope and future promise. The clouds are clearing, and the sun is beginning to shine again.
(See also: Cloud; Sun)

River Rivers can represent the dreamer's life, with the twists and turns of fortune. If he or she was standing on the bank, it can be a sign that life is passing them by. On the other hand, the river may be an obstacle to reaching something desirable on the far bank, and in this context the association of water with the archetypal Mother may be significant.
(See also: Water)

Sand Was the sand on the seashore, in a sandpit, or a desert landscape? Seaside sand is most probably associated with images of the ocean. A sandpit can represent a desire to return to the simple pleasures of childhood, or it may be an industrial site, signifying that something has been taken out of the dreamer's life. A desert is a daunting symbol, and indicates a barrenness in the individual – but perhaps there was a distant figure approaching across the sand, signifying rescue?

If the sand was getting into machinery, or was an irritant in some way, it suggests that some person is creating problems in waking life.
(See also: Machinery; Ocean; Quarry; Shore)

Sea See Ocean

Shore The shore is the boundary between the land – the practical, 'down to earth' aspects of everyday existence – and the deep waters of the

unconscious. It can represent the place to which one returns after a voyage of self-examination, or from which one sets out on such a voyage.

(See also: Ocean; Sand; Water)

Sky Was it a clear blue sky, one speckled by cloud, or heavily overcast? Even a clear sky can have more than one interpretation: it may signify that 'the sky's the limit' in some project or, on the other hand, represent vague aspirations that the dreamer is unlikely to fulfil – 'pie in the sky'. Probably the most promising symbol is a sky in which beautiful clouds move majestically: this suggests that the dreamer's plans, despite minor difficulties, will come to completion.

(See also: Cloud; Night; Star)

Snow See Cold; Ice

Spring The season of expectation and the development of new ideas. Events set in a dreamtime spring are likely to be evocations of the dreamer's childhood.

(See also: Fountain and spring)

Storm Taking shelter in a storm is a sign that problems in the dreamer's waking life will soon be solved – perhaps they are only 'a storm in a teacup'. However, a violent storm may represent more serious difficulties.

(See also: Cloud; Lightning; Rain; Thunder; Wind)

Summer A symbol of the dreamer's early adulthood, a time when he or she is in 'the flower of youth'. Perhaps the feelings were of warmth, happiness and pleasure – or was the summer heat oppressive and uncomfortable? This dream can have something to say about past events, or present circumstances.

(See also: Heat; Sun)

Sun The sun is the ultimate source of energy for all life on our planet, and a symbol of consciousness and the active intelligence. The shining sun signifies good fortune, and the energy to embark upon new projects, especially if it is rising. The noon sun is a symbol of adulthood – and particularly masculinity – although its heat may signify a certain 'dryness' of personality. Sunset, on the other hand, represents the decline of physical and intellectual powers, and the approach of old age.

(See also: Dawn; Heat)

Thunder Perhaps the sound of 'Fate knocking at the door'. On the other hand, thunder was once supposed to represent the anger of the gods, and in a dream it may symbolise an inner, unexpressed rage.

(See also: Lightning; Storm)

Volcano A symbol of suppressed passions. A warning to the dreamer that he or she should express these feelings before a violent eruption occurs.

(See also: Earthquake)

Water In far-distant times, earliest life emerged from the waters to develop on dry land; and the child emerges from the waters of the womb. In this sense, water represents the unformed side of the individual's nature, from which new spiritual developments may grow. In the same way, it can also symbolise the

unconscious, the feminine side of the personality and the Jungian Mother.

(See also: Baptism; Flood; Fountain and spring; Lake and pond; Ocean; River; Swimming pool)

Wind A wind may be anything from a quiet breeze to a raging hurricane. In its gentlest form it symbolises the individual's spirit, the 'breath of life'. Stronger winds – 'the wind of change' – represent a transformation in the dreamer's life, or perhaps a turmoil of emotions connected with some waking situation.

Of course, a dream of wind may be no more than an awareness of indigestion!

(See also: Storm)

Winter A symbol of old age and declining powers. However, it can also represent a lack of spiritual strength, which may be only temporary: remember, 'if winter comes, can spring be far behind?'

(See also: Cold; Ice)

ONESELF, THE BODY & CLOTHING

In dreams, the body represents the individual, both physically and mentally. Children first discover themselves and the world around them through consciousness of their bodies, and the significance they attach to the various parts in infancy can recur as dream symbols in adult life. The upper part of the body represents the intellect, and the lower part the instincts. Any pointing or pointed part is held to symbolise the penis; while an opening – whether natural, like the mouth, or in an unnatural place on the dreamer's body – symbolises the anus or vagina.

On the other hand, a dream of sickness or pain in a specific part of the body may be due to the fact that the mind is aware of some developing disease, long before it is medically detectable.

Clothing covers the body, to protect it and keep it warm, and to conceal nakedness. But it is also an expression of one's degree of individuality. Those whose dress follows everyday convention reveal the need to conform, and 'get along' with others – or, perhaps, a lack of creative imagination. On the other hand, those who dress in a strikingly unconventional way may be (sometimes almost unconsciously) expressing their individuality, or deliberately forcing their intentions upon the attention of other people. Yet even the most conventionally dressed person reveals some particular element of their personality: in a club tie, personal jewellery, even a handbag or belt.

All these aspects of the body and its clothing can surface as dream symbols, and represent repressed or unconscious feelings.

Abdomen Traditionally, seeing one's own abdomen in a dream signifies great expectations. However, this does not mean the dreamer can relax and await good fortune; he or she should redouble their efforts to attain what is coming to them. Even a pain in the abdomen – dreamt, not physically felt – is a sign that affairs will be favourable. And a swollen abdomen signifies that, although there will be future troubles, they will be overcome, and the dreamer's efforts crowned with honours.

However, for a married person to dream of his or her spouse's abdomen is a sign of their unfaithfulness; and, for a lover, such a dream has similar significance.

(See also: Stomach)

Age To dream that one is old is generally held to be a sign of approaching illness, or at the very least of severe differences with relatives. To dream of other people who are old, however, can have several meanings. According to Jung's theory of archetypes, for a man the Old Man represents the Self,

and for a woman it represents the Animus. For a man, traditionally, a dream of a single elderly person can portend pleasure for himself; but for a woman it may be a sign that she is argumentative, opinionated and overly critical of others. To dream of a group of aged people, however, is said to be a portent of good health and fortune.

Ankle Every part of the human body has its own traditional significance. In astrology, the ankle is connected with the sign of Aquarius, which represents strong independence combined with an inquiring, analytical nature. Dreaming of an injury to the ankle, therefore, can be a sign that one's independence is likely to be affected in some way.
(See also: Accident; Foot)

Arm The arm is the symbol of human capability – we often speak of a person being someone's 'right arm'. In particular, husbands and wives in dreams are frequently seen as one another's arms. In Freudian psychology, the pointing arm is seen as a way of symbolising something that the dreamer finds embarrassing to acknowledge – the penis. To dream of an injured – even amputated – arm, therefore, is a signal of marital discord.
(See also: Finger)

Armour Rigid and constricting, any piece of armour, whether it is the historical breastplate and shirt of mail or a modern

'flak jacket' (it may even be no more than a tight shirt that cannot be removed), is a symbol of the danger of conforming too much to accepted views. There is no development of the individual personality: a truly individual person adopts convention solely for convenience, like a costume that can be worn or removed, and never identifies with it.
(See also: Uniform)

Back The back is the most vulnerable part of the human body. We cannot see directly behind us – we speak of someone 'stabbing us in the back' – and, even in a mirror, it is difficult to see one's own back clearly. So to dream of seeing one's back is usually not a good sign. It can signify that one has turned one's back on responsibility. On the other hand, it can mean that one is hoping for recognition of one's achievements – a 'pat on the back'. The sight of another person's back signifies

serious difficulties; if it is a young woman's, these will be problems in love.

Dreams of pains in the back are a sign of having taken on too much responsibility. If the back is bare, this can mean an awareness that others are not providing sufficient support or 'back up'.

(See also: Shoulder)

Baldness See Hair

Beard The beard is regarded as an outward sign of masculinity, and so it can represent Jung's archetypal Old Man. For a man to dream of losing his beard, or having it cut off, can represent the deep-seated Freudian fear of castration; and for a woman to dream of growing a beard is, in most cases, a sign of something undesired developing.

(See also: Hair)

Belly See Abdomen

Belt Throughout history, the belt has signified authority: in modern times, the highly decorative belt donned by a victorious boxer or wrestler still has this meaning. Putting on a belt, therefore, can signify a good future; if it is a new belt, it foretells recognition of one's abilities. But if the belt is too tight, it may mean that the dreamer is keeping something in that

would be better brought out into the open. On the other hand, the belt may be too loose, so that one's trousers or jeans are falling down: this is connected with a fear of loss of dignity and exposure.

(See also: Nudity)

Blindness As a dream symbol, blindness – or the sensation of being blindfolded – represents a lack of awareness, or a deliberate 'turning a blind eye' to a situation. It may also be a helpful warning that it is necessary to develop a sense of direction in one's waking life. Leading someone else who is blind is a sign of strange adventures to come.

In Freudian belief, on the other hand, a dream of blindness – like the loss of other powers – can be a symbol for the fundamental male fear of castration.

(See also: Black; Eye; Senses)

Blood Blood is the symbol of energy and vitality. To dream that one is bleeding, therefore, can represent the feeling that one has undertaken too much, and should take steps to conserve one's energy. For a man, this sense of being wounded can be yet another symbol of the fear of castration – whether the subconscious Freudian preoccupation, or a feeling that he is prevented from exercising his full powers in his waking life. For a woman, however, it may be no more than an awareness that menstruation is about to begin, or a symbol of the loss of virginity.

To see blood on one's hands is a very powerful dream symbol. It can be a sign of intense guilt – specific or general – or an omen of great misfortune. Conversely, to see others bleeding (and in particularly religious people this may be the sight of Christ's wounds) represents a cry for help.

Boot See Shoe and boot

Button Buttons fasten clothes, and the clothes may be too tight. We speak of someone being 'buttoned up', keeping their emotions too much under control. Perhaps the dreamer is losing buttons, a sign that they should 'loosen up'; or they may be completely unbuttoned, an embarrassment that indicates a little more formality is necessary in their lives. To dream of sewing on a button suggests that there is someone who needs help.
(See also: Armour; Nudity)

Cap Whether it is worn alone, or with other specific clothing, the cap is an item of uniform. It denotes an individual's position in society, and is a means whereby he or she can recognise others with the same function or standing. It may be a

symbol of a job accomplished, 'the cap put on it'.
(See also: Hat; Uniform)

Cloak Few people normally wear cloaks nowadays, except as part of ceremonial uniform. In a dream, a cloak is most likely to be a form of 'fancy dress', a stage costume, or an item of evening wear for a visit to the opera, or some other grand occasion. The dreamer wishes to disguise a part of his or her personality, or change it in some way.

Sometimes, however, the dreamer is caught up in an historical event, at a time when cloaks were everyday wear. Those who believe in reincarnation will identify this as an episode from one of the dreamer's previous lives.
(See also: Acting; Mask; Uniform)

Cosmetics A dream of using cosmetics can symbolise the desire to cover up faults, or it may be in preparation for a stage appearance. There can also be the concept of 'making up' – restoring good relations with someone with whom the dreamer has quarrelled.
(See also: Acting)

Deafness To dream of being deaf is a sign that one is trying to cut oneself off from the outside world. This can be deliberate, perhaps because of a desire for peace, or an unwillingness to be a part of some action; or it may be a warning that one's attitudes are too self-centred.
(See also: Ear; Senses)

Death To dream of dying, but without feeling any great distress, is a sign that some outworn part of the personality should be let go, and the spirit reborn. However, dreaming of someone else dying, particularly if it is someone dear to the dreamer, reveals a hostile, aggressive attitude

Brueghel's The Triumph of Death. *There is no mistaking the hellish terror intended here, but in dreams, as in the Tarot, death is often positive, signifying change or renewal.*

to that person, which has been repressed.

Disfigurement A complex dream symbol. Is the dreamer actually conscious of disfigurement, or is it something seen in a mirror? (A mirror image, after all, reverses reality.) If the scarring seems to be real, is it the result of an accident, or is it self-inflicted? The disfigurement may be new, in which case it is likely to represent a recent blow to the dreamer's personality. If it appears long established, the dreamer may have come to terms with it; while, if it is gradually healing, there is a hopeful outcome to the injury.

A dream of dismemberment, although much rarer, is of particular interest, because it reproduces the experiences of a shaman – a Siberian magician or North American 'medicine man' – in his initiatory trance. It has also been pointed out that the symbolism of this dream is very similar to that used by medieval alchemists in their description of the search for the elixir of eternal youth. It clearly goes very deep into the Jungian archetypes of the Collective Unconscious.

(See also: Eaten; Mirror)

Disguise See Acting; Cloak; Mask

Double Seeing oneself in a dream can be a disturbing occurrence; some people have even experienced it in waking life. The phenomenon has been attributed to 'astral projection', the separation of the soul from the body that is believed by some to occur during sleep or semi-trance states.

There are other explanations. Possibly the unconscious is commenting on the view the dreamer has of him- or herself. If the double appears altered in some way – in its physical appearance, dress or environment – this can be a suggestion that the dreamer should make similar changes in life.

praise. There is also the identification with money – 'filthy lucre'. In *The Meaning of Dreams* (1968), Raymond de Becker reminded his readers that excrement was one of the raw materials from which alchemists hoped to prepare gold.

(See also: Brown)

Eye There is an old and familiar saying that the eyes are 'the mirror of the soul'. To dream of something troubling one's eyes may be a sign of some deep spiritual problem. In a more general sense, the eye is a symbol of perception, knowledge, wisdom and enlightenment; for a man the Self and for a woman the Animus. Perhaps the dream was a suggestion to 'take a look at oneself'.

Was the dream of someone else's eyes? Were they kindly, fierce, crossed, blinded? The colour of the eyes may also be significant. A pair of red eyes staring out of the dark is a typical nightmarish image. To interpret it one should try to identify what it seemed the eyes belonged to.

(See also: Blindness; Senses)

Dress For a man to dream of wearing a woman's dress is not necessarily a sign of repressed transvestitism; it can signify an awareness that he should be more open and caring – expressing the female side of his personality – in his waking relationships.

Ear Perhaps because of its shape, the ear is often associated in the subconscious with women and sex. But it can also have a more direct meaning: in many cultures, magic words whispered into the ear are believed to bring about instant spiritual enlightenment. Or perhaps the dreamer is being warned that he or she should pay more attention to the advice of others.

(See also: Deafness; Senses)

Excrement The meaning of this dream can depend very largely upon the dreamer's experience as an infant. In adult life they will almost certainly regard it as something dirty, but in early childhood it may have been a matter of relief, success, even

Face King Duncan may have complained, in Shakespeare's Macbeth, that 'there's no art to find the mind's construction in the face', but in fact the human face can convey emotion more readily than any other part of the body. The face in the dream may be the dreamer's own, or that of someone else. If it was the dreamer's face – presumably in a mirror – its appearance can relate to problems that must be 'faced' in waking life. Another person's face can represent a relationship, and its expression symbolise the dreamer's attitude to the relationship.

(See also: Cosmetics; Eye; Lips; Mask; Mirror; Mouth; Nose; Teeth)

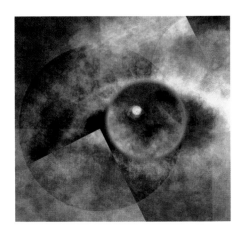

Finger In Freudian psychology, the finger is a phallic symbol. However, the use of the fingers in so many gestures can suggest other meanings: pointing the way forward, indicating a selected object or person, 'fingering' the guilty; the finger, which often wears a ring, can even refer to marriage. *(See also: Hand; Ring)*

Foot Without feet, we would find it difficult to stand upright and move about. For the Chinese, and practitioners of the alternative therapy known as reflexology, specific zones of the feet correspond to other parts of the body. Dreams of one's own feet, therefore, can be important. Pain in, or injury to, a foot may be a sign of sickness in another part of the body. Feet can also symbolise self-reliance – 'on one's own feet' – or doubts about one's 'standing'. We speak of 'putting the best foot forward', meaning undertaking something to the best of our ability.

Dreaming of having one's feet cared for, perhaps by a chiropodist, can have a specific significance for Christians, and symbolises a need for compassion. *(See also: Ankle; Heel; Leg; Shoe and boot)*

Fat A dream of becoming fat can have several different meanings. It may simply reflect a waking preoccupation of the dreamer or, in the case of a woman, it can also be due to either a desire for, or a fear of, pregnancy. Alternatively, it can represent the dreamer's awareness that they have over-indulged – and not necessarily in food or drink.

However, fatness is also connected with wealth and success – we speak of 'fat cats'. On the other hand, common parlance refers to something that is extremely unlikely as 'a fat chance', and to a fool as a 'fathead'.

There is also another, purely physical, explanation. Certain unusual chemical processes in the brain can produce the sensation during sleep that parts of the body have swollen, often to an enormous size.

Glove Like shoes, gloves can be strong sexual symbols, and their condition will often have a specific significance for the dreamer. Gloves may also be worn for comfort, or to prevent 'dirtying one's hands' – perhaps the dreamer has an unpleasant task to perform. Other connotations include wearing gloves to perform a

clandestine act, and having a fight with someone –
when the gloves may be on or off.

(See also: Hand)

Hair Hair has always been a symbol of sexual
potency. In the Bible story of the strong man
Samson, he lost all his strength when Delilah cut
seven locks from his head. Baldness is regarded as a
sure sign of the loss of virility – even though
modern research has shown that (at least in middle
life) it is often due to an excess of male hormones.
This significance is not restricted to men: many nuns
have their heads shaved as a symbol of their
renunciation of sex.

So a dream of losing one's hair – or of going to
the barber or hairdresser – can be a sign of preoccupation with failing sexual performance. Some
psychologists have equated the young boy's dislike
of having his hair cut with a fear of castration.

Conversely, a good head of hair is a sign of vitality
and seductiveness. A dream of having one's hair
properly cared for can be a symbol of self-confidence.

(See also: Beard; Nun)

Hand The hand is second only to the face as a
means of communicating concepts and emotions. It
is also the only 'tool' that most people have for
doing all the necessary work of everyday life. For
Freud, therefore, a dream of an injury to a hand had
obvious sexual significance.

Hands can also symbolise construction and
creation, healing and prayer. Clasped hands can be
the sign of completion of a task, or agreement with
another. Hands held in the praying position may
signify a desire for fulfilment, or submission.
Alternatively, the dreamer may be too 'heavy
handed' in relations with others, or about to be
caught – 'red handed' – in the act of doing
something immoral.

(See also: Finger)

Hat Another dream symbol with a variety of
meanings. A hat covers one's head, and so it not
only conceals one's mind ('keep it under your hat')
but it can change one's whole appearance. For this
reason, the type of hat can represent the personality
that the dreamer would prefer to present to the
world. However, a hat can be put on and taken off at
will, and may symbolise a specific event or activity.

Freud, on the other hand, stated – 'with certainty'
– that a hat symbolised the sexual organs. Did the
dreamer put on a special hat for a special occasion?
Or was it lost? Or did the wind blow it away?

(See also: Cap; Uniform)

*Thetis dipping the infant Achilles in the River Styx to render him
invulnerable. She succeeded but for the heel by which she held
him. An arrow wound to this one weak spot claimed his life.*

Head A symbol of the dreamer's conscious intellect, and consequently of 'hardheadedness' – we speak of someone acting 'rather from the head than from the heart'. Dreaming of injuries to the head, therefore, can signify the frustration of some practical plan, perhaps in favour of something more satisfying to the emotions.

Heart The opposite of the head, the heart is traditionally the seat of love and romance, as well as the driving force of life itself. Sometimes, in sleep, the sound of one's own heart is magnified, and may be represented as a drum beating regularly, or even as blows falling on an empty container.

In the pack of cards, the heart is believed to be derived from the symbol of the Holy Grail, and it still has the form of a goblet in the Tarot pack. In this sense, a dream of the suit of hearts may symbolise the search for spiritual fulfilment; on a more mundane level it represents the home and family.

(See also: Box; Drum; Emptiness; and Ace; King; Knave; Queen)

Heel The heel is a vulnerable part of the body. In Greek myth, it was the one place in which the hero Achilles could be injured; and the tendon named after him can be ruptured by accident. A dream of pain in the heel may be an omen that one is liable to attack by an enemy.

The heel is also a means of exerting pressure with the weight of the body – we speak of being 'under the heel' of an oppressive person. As part of a shoe, the heel is equally significant: the dreamer may be 'down at heel', with a part of his or her life needing urgent attention. Finally, a low-down, despicable person is called a 'heel', and the dream may represent someone of this kind.

(See also: Foot; Shoe and boot)

Helmet See Armour; Cap; Hat

Hood See Cloak; Mask; Veil

Identity Was the dreamer being asked to establish his or her identity? Perhaps they were asked for a passport, a driving licence or a credit card, and could not produce it. What followed was a confusing sense that they were unsure who they were. This dream symbolises a lack of self-confidence, the feeling that one is not fully accepted into society. Finding the identity document is a reassuring sign that the individual will regain self-respect.

a dream of immobility can symbolise their immovable attitude to the problems they face, or conflicting emotions that make it impossible to reach a decision.

Jaw In medieval illustrations, the entrance to the underworld was often represented as a pair of gaping jaws. This dream symbol, therefore, if it is frightening, can represent a fear of exploring the hidden depths of the unconscious self. As Jung wrote: 'The dread and resistance which every natural human being experiences when it comes to delving too deeply into himself is, at bottom, the fear of the journey to Hades.'

Kiss See Lips

Illness The connection between physical illness and the mental state remains a subject of much discussion among physicians and psychologists. Nevertheless, there is considerable evidence that the experience of sickness in the dream state can reflect an imbalance of some kind in the emotions. The principal part of the body affected may provide a clue to what is causing trouble in the mind.

On the other hand, as in other related dreams, the feeling can be a warning of some physical trouble that is not yet sufficiently developed to be detected medically.

Immobility During the REM stage of sleep, the motor cortex (the area of the brain that controls movement) becomes disconnected from most of the body's muscles, with the exception of those controlling the vital functions and the eyes. This is a natural phase, but some people suffer from a disorder known as sleep paralysis, in which they become completely immobile immediately before entering sleep or on waking up. For others,

Leg The leg is a symbol of one's position in society, one's 'standing'. An injury to a leg can therefore symbolise a loss of status or reputation. Similarly, we say of someone who cannot make a case in an argument that 'they haven't a leg to stand on'.

In Freudian terms the leg, like other limbs, has a phallic connotation. For a man to dream of injuring or losing a leg, therefore, reflects the basic fear of castration.
(See also: Foot)

Lips As well as their actual appearance, with the promise of a loving kiss, lips can also symbolise the female sex and the vagina. They are also one of the most expressive parts of the face, and may have a message to communicate.
(See also: Face; Mouth)

Mask A mask is used to conceal the identity – was the dreamer putting it on, or taking it off? The mask may be worn by a reveller at a carnival, by a thief during a robbery, or by a fictional 'masked avenger' like the Lone Ranger or Batman. In which role did the dreamer see himself or herself?

(See also: Carnival; Cloak; Cosmetics; Robbery)

Medicine Giving or taking medicine can be a symbol of spiritual problems – known or unknown – that are being taken care of by the healing power of sleep. Alternatively, the dreamer may be aware that, in a situation in waking life, he or she will have to 'take their own medicine' – that is, face up to the implications of their actions, and accept the consequences.

Mouth As one of the principal openings of the body, the mouth has an obvious sexual symbolism. In a more general sense, the mouth is both receiving and demanding, suggesting some deep need of the individual. It is also the main means of communication and, even if in the dream it did not speak, its expression may contain a message.

(See also: Lips; Teeth)

Navel A sign of the infant's separation from its mother; but also, in many ancient cultures, it is the omphalos – the 'navel of the world', which is the centre of the cosmos. We speak of someone 'contemplating their navel' when they are withdrawn from everyday matters, and deep in philosophical thought.

Neck Like the back, the neck is a vulnerable part of the body. We speak of 'getting it in the neck', and one is warned 'not to stick one's neck out'. This dream can be a warning not to take part in something for which the dreamer could be condemned.

On the other hand, this may be a punning reference to a romantic situation – 'necking'.

(See also: Back; Shoulder)

Nose For Freudians, the nose is an obvious symbol for the penis, but the nose in dreams can have a variety of other meanings. As the organ of smelling, it represents intuition, but also investigation: we say someone has 'a nose for news', or is a bit nosey– perhaps an acquaintance is being too inquisitive. Or is the dreamer being 'led by the nose' into some doubtful undertaking?

Through our noses, we take in the 'breath of life'. Did the dreamer seem to suffer from a blocked nose? This may be due to no more than obstruction by the bedclothes, but it can also be a sign that the dreamer is not taking enough from waking life. Dreaming of losing one's nose can represent the fundamental male fear of castration – but remember the saying 'cutting off one's nose to spite one's face': the dreamer may be about to do something in a fit of temper, which will cause only him or her harm.

(See also: Senses)

Nudity Everybody, at some time or another, has dreamt of being naked – or (at least) discovered in their underclothes. The state of their feelings in such a dream will generally reflect their attitude to nakedness in waking life – but bear in mind that dreams can sometimes go by opposites.

For some people, nudity is 'dirty'. Finding themselves naked – often, in the dream, in the company of others who are fully dressed – provokes feelings of embarrassment, shame, even guilt. If they also consider sex 'dirty', there is likely to be a sexual connotation; but the dream may reflect, instead, their feelings about an embarrassing or shameful situation in waking life. Possibly they fear exposure over some misdeed.

Even those who are at ease with nakedness may well connect it with sex. On the other hand, the dream may represent a desire to be more open, to reveal the 'bare facts' and the 'naked truth'.

Alternatively, the dream may represent a wish to attract attention, even to shock, in some waking situation. The dream may be a warning not to go too far.

(See also: Abdomen; Bathing)

Ointment See Medicine

Pocket This may well be a sexual symbol, but it can also represent the possessive, secretive aspects of the dreamer's personality. A hole in the pocket may be connected with fears that money, or some valued object or belief, is being lost.

Senses The senses symbolise four qualities of mind. Sight represents the intellect; smell represents intuition; hearing represents emotion; and taste and touch represent sensation.

Shoe and boot The first function of a shoe or boot is to protect the foot, and this dream symbol may have just that significance. But shoes and boots are also designed to be decorative, and in this way they have a distinct sexual connotation. A dream of wearing old shoes suggests that the dreamer is doubtful about his or her attractiveness. According to Wilhelm Stekel in *The Interpretation of Dreams* (1943), a dream of lacing up shoes is 'a well-known symbol of death'.

(See also: Foot)

Shoulder Dreaming of pains in the shoulders, when there is no physical cause, is a sign that the dreamer is taking on too much in waking life.

(See also: Back; Neck)

Skin The outer covering of the body, the skin is the part of the individual that is seen by others, and in many ways equivalent to clothing. Dreaming of blemishes on the skin, therefore, represents a fear of

how other people see one, and possibly even a shameful secret that one had hoped to keep hidden. Hard or coarse skin can signify that the individual is strongly resistant to criticism – 'thick skinned'.

(See also: Cosmetics; Disfigurement)

Skirt In a man's dream, a skirt can symbolise a woman. For a woman, dreaming of buying a new skirt can be a portent of enjoyable times to come; frustration at being unable to find a suitable skirt can suggest that those times will not materialise. Scots, however, can wear a kilt in a dream without further significance!

(See also: Dress)

Stocking For both men and women this can be a sexual symbol, particularly if it encases a shapely leg. If a woman dreams that her stockings are wrinkled or laddered, it is a sign that she is losing her self-esteem. On the other hand, the dream may be of a Christmas stocking, filled with the promise of good things.

(See also: Leg)

Stomach The seat of repressed emotions, which may be symbolised by the dreamer's sensations concerning his or her stomach. Alternatively, dreams involving discomfort in the stomach may be a sign that the dreamer has lost his or her appetite for a relationship or a task – they cannot 'stomach' it.

(See also: Abdomen)

Suit Regarded as a formal way of dressing, a suit may symbolise the dreamer's need to impress someone in waking life. On the other hand, this may be an example of the mind's punning: perhaps the dreamer is involved in a legal action, or contemplating a marriage. Or was it a reference to a pack of cards?

Teeth There are two periods in an individual's life when he or she tends to lose teeth. The first occurs in childhood, when the milk teeth are replaced by adult teeth; the second is towards the end of life. A dream of losing teeth, therefore, can have two interpretations, and other circumstances in the dream may be a help to understanding its meaning. It may represent the taking on of responsibility, or a fear of waning powers.

A visit to the dentist generally involves the removal of decayed material, and its replacement with something new and healthy. Such a dream may well symbolise a situation in either the dreamer's spiritual existence, or his or her waking life.
(See also: Jaw; Mouth)

Tongue Even more than the nose, the tongue can be a powerful phallic symbol. At the same time, it is closely connected with speech, and particularly with indiscretion – we speak of 'wagging tongues' and the need to 'hold one's tongue'. Dreaming of a tongue may well be a

reference to such a situation in waking life.
(See also: Mouth; Senses)

Underclothes See Nudity

Uniform The purpose of a uniform is to distinguish an individual from the crowd; but at the same time it imposes a uniformity with others dressed identically. Much will depend upon other circumstances in the dream. If the dreamer was the only one in uniform – and he or she could be a member of the armed forces or police, a nurse or medical orderly, a parking meter attendant, or even a Scout or Guide – it signifies a desire to be different from the 'common herd', and to have some measure of control over others.

On the other hand, if the dreamer was one of a group, all in the same uniform, it is a sign of his or her wish to suppress individuality, to conform to society's conventions, and even to abandon responsibility by slavishly following orders.
(see also: Armour; Army; Cap; Cloak; Policeman; Soldier)

Urine According to many psychologists, urine represents latent sexuality, and the desire to pour out one's emotions upon a loved one.

Veil A dream of a woman in a veil is a symbol of some part of the individual's personality that they tend to conceal, or are only partially aware of.
(See also: Nun)

Zip The ease with which a zip fastener can be opened (and some of the places in garments where zips are generally found) gives this symbol an obvious sexual connotation. A zip that breaks, or opens inadvertently, can represent both insecurity and embarrassment.
(See also: Button; Nudity)

PEOPLE

There are very few dreams that do not have other people in them – even if their presence is only felt, rather than seen. Their symbolism can take a variety of forms: they can represent (even though they may not physically resemble) those that the dreamer knows in waking life; they can be idealised symbols of specific concepts; or they may be aspects of the archetypes proposed by Jung. But, whatever form they take, and however distanced from the dreamer they seem to be, it is still often likely that they represent the individual, himself or herself, or at least certain elements of his or her personality.

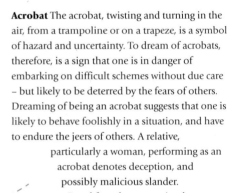

Acrobat The acrobat, twisting and turning in the air, from a trampoline or on a trapeze, is a symbol of hazard and uncertainty. To dream of acrobats, therefore, is a sign that one is in danger of embarking on difficult schemes without due care – but likely to be deterred by the fears of others. Dreaming of being an acrobat suggests that one is likely to behave foolishly in a situation, and have to endure the jeers of others. A relative, particularly a woman, performing as an acrobat denotes deception, and possibly malicious slander.

Freud found a connection between acrobats and sex. He wrote that the pleasure the observer gets from seeing acrobats 'is a memory-image, often unconscious, of an observation of sexual intercourse, whether between humans or animals'.

Angel Heavenly messengers play a part in all the world's religions, and represent a very deep-rooted human symbol. Dreaming of angels is indicative of coming changes, whether spiritual or material. If the dream is particularly pleasant, it foretells success in love, or an inheritance to come. For those who lead a good life, the dream will portend recognition of their virtue; for the sinner, it warns of the need for repentance.

Army An army, by definition, moves as a single body of undifferentiated individuals, determined to overcome all opposition. The individuals need not be human: we speak, for example, of an 'army' of ants. But an army, by its nature, is destructive.

To dream of being in an army, therefore, can symbolise a number of different things. It may represent subjugation of one's own individuality to the discipline of the community; it may be a sign of one's desire to seek the assistance of others to overcome difficulties; or it may be a realisation of one's suppressed aggression. To see an army fighting is an omen, generally, of domestic discord; while to be a member of a

defeated army denotes many troubles ahead. *(See also: Officer and official; Uniform; War)*

Baby See Child

Band See Orchestra and band

Barber See Hair

Beggar This is another dream symbol that can go by opposites. It can represent good fortune, particularly if the dreamer gives money to the beggar; on the other hand, to refuse to give money is a bad omen. If the beggar is very old and decrepit, it signifies that the dreamer should try to economise.

The dreamer may be the beggar in the dream – but even if this is not so, the figure can still

represent him- or herself. It can symbolise that something is lacking in their life, something that they are subconsciously begging for.

Bishop See Clergy

Blacksmith In former times, the blacksmith was an important man: he worked with fire and knew the secret of making iron, and it can be said that his skills led to the development of modern civilisation. In some mythologies, he was equated with the creator of the physical world.

For the present-day dreamer, the blacksmith is likely to be unfamiliar; but

Dwarfs have figured in the mythology of nearly every race, and are not normally considered harmful to people, though they can be mischievous. They are also believed to be skillful, as can be seen here.

his appearance in a dream may be a resurfacing of an ancient atavistic symbol. On the other hand, the dream may reflect a memory that the blacksmith of Gretna Green, the first village over the border from England into Scotland, was traditionally permitted to perform marriage ceremonies.

(See also: Fire; Horseshoe; Iron)

Butcher A dream symbol that must be interpreted with care. Because of his activities, the butcher is, first of all, associated with blood and – for meat-eaters and vegetarians alike – a degree of brutality. Was the dreamer the butcher, revealing the aggressive, even destructive, aspects of his or her personality? Or was the butcher a friendly person, a provider of essential nourishment? The meat itself represents the carnal instincts. What kind of meat was involved?

(See also: Animal Kingdom; Knife; Meat)

Child For both men and women, a dream of a child may be simply a representation of the desire for a family. Alternatively, the child can represent some immature part of the dreamer's personality, or even an idea that needs encouragement and development.

Clergy For many people a member of the clergy – whether a minister, bishop or the Pope – represents a father figure. The dream may be a sign that the dreamer is in need of well considered advice. Alternatively, in Jungian theory, the figure can represent the Self as the Wise Old Man; and, for a woman, it can be the Animus.

(See also: Abbey; Altar; Baptism; Church)

Clown The tragedy that lies behind the painted face of the clown is a well known dramatic concept. As the humpbacked clown Tonio sings, in Leoncavallo's opera *I Pagliacci*: 'Laugh, Punchinello … laugh, for the pain that is eating thy heart!'

To dream that one is a clown, therefore, can signify that one is putting on a brave face to hide a deep sorrow; and seeing a clown can have much the same meaning. Of course, the symbolism need not be so tragic. The dreamer may feel that he or she has been 'clowning around', when a more serious attitude to life was appropriate. Nevertheless, the paint that disguises the face is a sign that something is being hidden from the world.

(See also: Acting; Circus; Cosmetics)

Conjurer Like the acrobat, a conjurer is a symbol of uncertainty; but there is more to it, because he is deliberately producing an illusion. To dream of watching a conjurer is a warning that things are not what they seem. But if the dreamer is the conjurer, it can be a sign that they have been 'up to tricks', and the nature of the trick can indicate the element of the dreamer's life concerned.

(See also: Acrobat; Rabbit)

Dentist See Teeth

Devil The significance that the dreamer attaches to the Devil will obviously depend upon their beliefs, or what they learnt in childhood. Even someone who does not believe in the Devil will recognise that his appearance in a dream can symbolise wickedness and punishment. Perhaps they feel a subconscious guilt about something.

However, devils can also represent intelligence and cunning – 'you clever devil!' – and even sexuality. Among Jungian archetypes, the Devil is the Shadow, the part of the individual that has not been allowed to develop fully. Quite possibly, the dreamer envies someone who is cleverer than they are or more successful in sexual relations.

Doctor Doctors symbolise healing, and the individual who

A 19th-century print of fairies from William Shakespeare's A Midsummer Night's Dream.

dreams of being treated by a doctor is subconsciously aware that something in his or her physical or spiritual state is in need of treatment. For many people doctors represent authority, and may even symbolise the archetypal Self.

(See also: Examination; Hospital; Medicine; Nurse)

Dwarf In folklore, dwarfs possess a knowledge of magic and divination. Perhaps the dwarf has something to tell the dreamer. But a dwarf also can have a sinister look, and represent a threat.

For the dreamer to feel that he or she is a dwarf may be no more than a recollection from childhood; or it may mean that they feel inferior to others.

Enemy Enmity in a dream may reflect a situation in waking life, or it may reveal feelings about someone of which the dreamer is not consciously aware. At the same time, it must be remembered that it is the dreamer's mind that constructs the dream, the dreamer who has created the image of an enemy. This enemy may well be the dreamer, and represent elements of their personality that they would like to be rid of.

Engineer See Machinery

Fairy Traditionally, fairies can represent wishes, and in folklore they are credited with the ability to grant them. The dream may therefore refer to some childhood desire that was never fulfilled, or it may be a sign that the dreamer hankers after the freedom and beauty that the fairy

childhood, when all adults loomed high overhead. It may represent a daunting obstacle that the dreamer doubts can be overcome. Or it may have sexual significance, particularly if the giant is threatening with a huge club.

(See also: Club; Dwarf)

Grandparent Very often in childhood one's grandparents seem kinder and more forgiving than one's parents. They are symbols of wisdom and sound advice, and the circumstances of the dream may suggest that this advice is well worth taking.

Guest Is the dreamer the guest, and perhaps an unwanted one? This is a suggestion that they are interfering too much in other people's lives. Receiving an unwelcome guest can be a similar symbol in the opposite sense, but greeting guests in one's home can be a sign that one is ready to accept new projects and interests.

symbolises. But he or she should beware: fairies are mischievous, and there is often a hidden condition to the wishes they grant.

On the other hand, the 'fairy' may have some connection with homosexuality.

(See also: Dwarf)

Ghost A symbol of something that is no longer attainable: we speak of people not having 'a ghost of a chance'. Alternatively, the dreamer may be 'haunted' by a sad or unpleasant memory.

If the dream is of the individual's own ghost, it can be a sign that they are not taking proper care of themselves. On the other hand, they may be expressing a desire to explore another person's life without being detected.

(See also: Double; Invisibility)

Giant A dream of a giant can have a number of different meanings. It may be a memory from

Gypsy Gypsies are traditionally credited with the ability to tell the future. Other circumstances in the dream can give a clue to what is being predicted. On the other hand, the 'gypsy life' is one of roaming free from responsibilities. Perhaps this dream expresses the longing to be rid of one's cares and 'throw fortune to the winds'.

Housekeeper The first 'housekeeper' that a child encounters is its mother, or somebody with an equivalent position in the household. This figure – viewed generally with a mixture of affection and awe – insists on cleanliness, tidiness and good behaviour. In adult life, a housekeeper has similar attributes. She (it is usually a she) must be strict, to keep the establishment running smoothly, but often this strictness becomes domineering, and inspires fear rather than respect. Even the sound of her jangling keys can be sufficient warning of unpleasant scenes to come.

In dreams, therefore, the appearance of a housekeeper can represent the mother figure, or some other person who exerts a controlling influence in the dreamer's life. It may be a suggestion – particularly when it is remembered that the house can symbolise the dreamer's person – to 'put one's house in order'.

(See also: House; Key)

Intruder A burglar, an unwelcome salesman, a pestering tramp, even an alien being – the intruder can take many forms; in a man's dream he represents the Jungian Shadow, and in a woman's dream the Animus.

In most cases, the dreamer makes strenuous efforts to keep the intruder out; but sometimes the dream changes, and the intruder proves to be helpful. This is a sign that the dreamer needs to recognise something in him- or herself that will lead to further understanding.

(See also: Beggar; Robbery)

Judge See Court; Jury

Jury Historically, a jury is intended to exert a balance against the unilateral power of the judge and his court. The jury hears all the arguments, listens to the judge's advice on the law, and finally reaches a considered opinion about the guilt or innocence of the accused. As a dream symbol, therefore, a jury represents the dreamer's concern with the opinion of others, and possibly his or her desire to be absolved of feelings of guilt.

(See also: Court; Lawyer)

King Was it the dreamer who was king – the wielder of power, the ultimate judge or, at the least, the leader in his particular field? Or was it someone whose position had to be looked up to – but who, perhaps, was raised to an eminence that they did not truly deserve? In many cases, the king can represent either the father figure or the employer.

If the dream was of a playing card, the king of clubs symbolises an honest and generous man; the king of spades, a man whose ambition overrides everything; of diamonds, an angry and vengeful man; and of hearts, a well-meaning man whose advice cannot be relied upon.

Knave If the dream concerns a pack of playing cards, the knave of hearts symbolises a dear friend, but possibly a long-lost one; the knave of clubs, a sincere but impatient friend; the knave of spades, an envious and untrustworthy person; and the knave of diamonds, a selfish or jealous relative.

Lawyer For most people, consulting a lawyer is something done only as a last resort, after all other means have failed, or as an annoying necessity to fulfil legal requirements. In popular thought, lawyers are notorious for demanding too much money, and wasting too much time.

The symbolism of a dream of this kind, then, can be rather complex. The dream lawyer can represent someone of a completely different profession, but one who affects the dreamer's life in a similar way. On the other hand, it may be the dreamer who is the lawyer. Perhaps this is an indication that he or she is aware of some transgression – whether of their own or by someone else – that must be accounted for. Or did they simply enjoy their performance in court?
(See also: Acting; Court; Jury)

Locksmith A skilled person who can open the door for someone who is locked out; this may represent an acquaintance who could get the dreamer out of a difficulty, or even a psychotherapist. On the other hand, the dream may be an amusing example of the mind's word play: remember the saying 'love laughs at locksmiths'.
(See also: Door; Key)

Madonna A symbol of the archetypal mother figure, but – rather illogically – with specific connotations of purity and virginity. If the dreamer is a man, this contradictory aspect may be a valuable clue to his attitude towards women in general, and his sexual partner in particular: does he place her 'on a pedestal', and feel that he should 'worship' her? This is not a healthy attitude because it frequently conflicts with his sexual desires, provoking frustration and guilt.
(See also: Blue; Statue)

Mechanic See Garage; Machinery

Mermaid Half fish and half woman – but essentially a virgin – the legendary mermaid was notorious for luring unwary seamen to a watery grave. Even if the dream does not refer directly to a seductive, but dangerous, woman, the predominance of water symbols shows that it is very much concerned with emotional matters.
(See also: Fish; Ocean; Water)

Minister See Clergy; Government; Parliament.

Monk For most people, a monk is a quiet – sometimes compulsorily silent – man who has vowed to spend his life in spiritual discipline and asceticism. Dreaming of a monk is, for them, likely to be a reflection of their own beliefs, and possibly a sign that they are achieving inner peace.

But, for some, a monk – clad from head to foot in a hooded habit – is a sinister individual, with esoteric knowledge that he is prepared to impart only to those who accept his beliefs; a threatening symbol. Such a dream probably does not refer to spiritual matters, but to a secretive person, possibly untrustworthy, in waking life.

Alternatively, there may be a reference to the idea of chastity and the denial of sex.
(See also: Abbey; Monastery; Nun)

Nun Although a nun is, in principle, the female equivalent of a monk, she is likely to be a more ambiguous symbol. In fact, the nun in a dream may be no more than a representation of the dreamer's sister, or someone who is seen as playing a sisterly role. For a man, the nun can be a perverse sexual symbol, or represent the repression of sexual desire. A woman's dream –

whether she sees or meets a nun, or dreams that she herself is one – is also generally connected with sex and its denial, although it may reflect a desire to cut herself off from everyday problems and find peace and rest.

(See also: Hair; Monk; Nunnery)

Nurse A nurse symbolises care and healing; a dream of one can signify that the dreamer is in need of this, or that the healing process – physical or spiritual – is already taking place. Alternatively, the dream may be an erotic

resurfacing of games of 'doctors and nurses' played as a child.

(See also: Doctor; Hospital; Medicine)

Officer and official Symbols of authority, and possibly also of obstruction. If the dreamer was one of those in authority, it may be a comment on the way in which he or she exercises their powers. On the other hand, having to deal with officers or officials can reflect the dreamer's attitude to experiences in waking life. In either case, the role of the authority – whether he or she was a member of the armed forces or police, a Customs officer or a nit-picking petty official – can give further clues to the meaning of the dream.

(See also: Army; Identity; Policeman; Uniform)

Orchestra and band Was the dreamer listening to the music, or performing? In the former case, the dream is a suggestion that the dreamer is devoting too much time to idle pleasure, following the crowd and not striking out on his or her own.

Playing in a band or orchestra, on the

other hand, is a symbol of working together with a group of like-minded people. It demands discipline, and the need to subjugate one's individual intentions to the common plan. However, at the same time it is a creative activity – and there comes the glorious moment when one is allowed self-expression in a solo. But was the solo a success?

(See also: Drum; Guitar; Trumpet; Violin)

Orphan A symbol of loneliness and rejection. If it was the dreamer who was the orphan, it can be a reflection of childhood days, when 'no-one seemed to understand', or an expression of the need for greater affection and sympathy in adult life. Meeting – and perhaps caring – for an orphan can represent the dreamer's desire to look after another person.

(See also: Child)

Pirate A bold, swaggering adventurer who robs on the high seas. Was the dreamer the pirate? (There have been women pirates as well as men.) Was it the freebooting life on the ocean, the fight with another ship, or the carousing that followed, that was the dominant aspect of the dream? In a more general sense, 'piracy' means the theft of other people's ideas; perhaps this was the significance of the dream.

(See also: Ocean; Robbery; Ship; Skeleton and skull)

Policeman Much can depend upon the dreamer's personal attitude to the police. Their function is to see that the laws – and, within the dream, the conventions – of society are upheld. As figures of authority, they can represent more dominant individuals in the dreamer's waking life. And, in the same way, they can be oppressive, obstructive and demanding.

At the same time, the policeman can be a friend. Calling the police can represent an appeal for control over one's reckless impulses. The circumstances of the dream – a burglary, a traffic accident, a domestic drama – will give a clue to further meanings.

(See also: Accident; Intruder; Officer and official; Robbery)

Postman Someone who brings a message. Was it a letter, with welcome or unwelcome news? Or a long awaited parcel containing good things? What the postman brought may be the most significant aspect of the dream – or was he attacked by a dog and driven away before he could deliver?

(See also: Envelope; Letter; Parcel)

Prince and princess These dream symbols can represent the male dreamer and his sister or, in an archetypal sense, the Hero and Princess whom he must rescue.

On the other hand, the dream may signify that the dreamer has an elevated opinion of him- or herself, and can be a warning not to get 'above one's station'.

(See also: Dragon; King; Queen)

Professor The dream professor may have been wise and authoritative, or eccentric – the popular 'mad professor'. If the dreamer was the professor, it is a sign that he or she has valuable information to impart; similarly, another person can represent someone with this information. But perhaps the dreamer felt at the mercy of a clever, but unpredictable, individual.

(See also: School; University)

Prostitute In former times, the 'sacred prostitutes' played an important role in the temple, and were regarded as the earthly representatives of the female gods. There may be

some atavistic memory here. On the other hand, a man's dream of prostitutes may reveal his attitude to women in general.

Alternatively, the dream may merely reflect the feeling that the dreamer is not fully appreciated in his or her waking life, and is 'prostituting' his or her talents.

Queen A queen can be a ruler in her own right, or only the necessary consort of a king. A woman's dream of being a queen, therefore, can reflect the way she sees her position in waking life. Alternatively, the queen can symbolise the Jungian Mother.

If the dream was of cards from a pack, the queen of hearts symbolises a gentle, loving woman; the queen of clubs, a temperamental one; of spades, a treacherous woman or a widow; and of diamonds, an interfering woman fond of scandal.

(See also: King)

Referee Someone whose function is to oversee a conflict, and make sure the rules are adhered to. Whether the dreamer was the referee, or one of those subject to his rulings, will reflect some situation in waking life.

(See also: Game)

Schoolteacher A symbolic authority figure: he or she may be a memory from the dreamer's schooldays, but is likely to represent a more contemporary individual, such as an employer.

(See also: Examination; School)

Scientist A word that can cover a wide variety of professions; but in general terms it involves the concept of experiments being carried out in a laboratory. Perhaps the nature of the experiments is the key to such a dream; or it may suggest that the dreamer should get out of a rut, and try a new approach in waking life.

The scientist, who may or not be a university

teacher, is a symbol of innovation and invention – but also of absentmindedness and eccentricity. *(See also: Laboratory; Professor)*

Shepherd As one who has charge of a flock of sheep, a shepherd is a symbol of control over others. Was the dreamer the shepherd, and did he or she successfully manage the flock? Or did they escape and scatter? Or, indeed, was the dreamer one of the sheep? *(See also: Sheep)*

Soldier In a dream, soldiers – a group of people moving under orders, frequently with violent intentions – can symbolise the dreamer's suppressed obsessions. A single soldier, on the other hand, represents the archetypal Hero, while a wounded soldier signifies that the dreamer's intentions are threatened. *(See also: Army; Officer and official; Uniform; War)*

Stranger Most psychologists agree that a stranger represents a side of the dreamer's personality of which he or she is largely ignorant, or would rather deny. Alternatively, the stranger may be an unexpected aspect of someone the dreamer knows. Jung equated the stranger with the Shadow or, if the figure was awesome, with the Self.

Tramp The tramp may be an intruder, an unwelcome vagrant at the kitchen door; or he may represent the dreamer, content to drift along without commitment, or anxious to escape from present responsibilities. *(See also: Beggar, Gypsy; Intruder)*

Twin Dreaming of a twin who does not exist in waking life can symbolise two sides of the dreamer's personality. He or she may be successfully combining them, or they may be in conflict. Alternatively, the 'twin' may represent another person who is 'two faced'.

Virgin The virginity need not be physical; the symbolism is just as likely to refer to intellectual, emotional or spiritual innocence. *(See also: Madonna; Nun)*

Waiter In a dream, a waiter can symbolise a friend or acquaintance who is able to offer helpful advice or material assistance. On the other hand, an aggressive or careless waiter can represent someone who is causing trouble in waking life, or some slipshod act on the part of the dreamer.

The dream may be a suggestion that the dreamer should not be so submissive to the orders of others. But remember, as John Milton wrote: 'they also serve who only stand and wait'.

So perhaps this was one of the mind's word games, and the dreamer is waiting, expectantly or impatiently, for some event or item of news. *(See also: Restaurant)*

Witch The witch, along with the giant, the dragon and other monsters, is an element in the Collective Unconscious of Jung, and plays an important part in childhood fears and folktales. In adult dreams, she is more likely to represent an unpleasant acquaintance, or some aspect of the dreamer's personality with which he or she is unhappy. *(See also; Dragon; Dwarf; Giant)*

Youth The youthful figure can represent the less mature aspects of the dreamer's personality, or a desire to recapture the hope, virility and freedom from care of earlier years. Some experts believe that a dream of one's original innocence is a sign that the self and psyche are being stimulated and renewed.

OBJECTS

The individual objects that appear in a dream are the most easily recognisable of dream symbols, because they have a specific identity. Although they are often unusual, out of context or apparently irrelevant, there is seldom any doubt as to what they are, and their particular significance is relatively easily interpreted. The environment in which they are seen in the dream is, of course, also important.

Ace Playing cards are frequently used in prediction, and in dreams the aces of each suit can have a particular significance. Traditionally, the ace of diamonds portends quarrels; the ace of clubs, money; of hearts, bad luck; and of spades, good news.

(See also: individual symbols; King; Knave; Queen)

Altar A powerful symbol, and one that can have many meanings, depending upon the circumstances of the dream. It is a warning against making mistakes, or a sign that mistakes have been made and must be repented of.

Traditionally, to dream of being married at the altar is not a good sign: it foretells many minor difficulties. To see someone else being married foretells the sorrow of friends, possibly the death of a near one. And the sight of a priest at the altar is a sign that deceit will bring about difficulties in business and in the home.

On the other hand, the subconscious mind can play word games during dreams. Maybe there is no religious element in this dream: it is a pun, reminding the dreamer that it is time to 'alter' something.

(See also: Abbey, Church; Clergy; Marriage; Wedding)

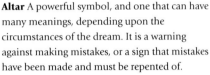

Amber In modern-day life, an amber-coloured light is often used as a warning, and it has much the same traditional significance in dreams. In particular, it is a warning against pride; and

173

dreaming of possessing something made of amber is traditionally held to be a sign of obstacles between oneself and a loved one.

Amethyst The name of this semi-precious stone comes from the Greek, and means the absence of drunkenness: the Greeks often drank their wine from amethyst cups, in the hope that this would protect them from excess. Dreaming of an amethyst, therefore, is a sign of sober contentment, both in life and in business.
(See also: Jewel)

Ammonia Whether as a pungent gas, or in its more familiar form as an equally pungent solution in water, ammonia is an unpleasant dream symbol. Traditionally, it can signify quarrels, lost friends, misfortune in love, even a dangerous accident to come. For those who associate its smell with a stable and horses, however, it may prove to be a good omen. And if the dreamer regularly uses ammonia for domestic purposes, it could be a sign of the need to 'clean up' an unpleasant situation.
(See also: Cleaning; Horse; Senses)

Anchor Traditionally, the anchor, which for the sailor can mean the reaching of a safe haven, is a symbol of hope and salvation. But when a ship's anchor is raised, and she sails away, the sailor's loved ones are left behind. So, while a dream of an anchor is a fortunate sign, it can also portend separation: moving home, travel, and being at a distance from one's family and friends.

Arrow See Archery

Ashes Ashes are grey, bitter and cold, all that is left when a fire has burnt out. In a religious context they represent the confession of sins, and the phrase 'sackcloth and ashes' comes from the ancient Jewish custom of wearing sackcloth and sprinkling ashes in the hair to signify mourning or penitence.

In a dream, therefore, ashes can denote loss, a decline in spiritual powers, or the consciousness that one has done wrong and must be humiliated for it. But there is still hope: if the ashes are raked, a tiny spark may survive and can be coaxed into flame.
(See also: Fire; Fireplace)

Axe Someone holding an axe is in a position of power. In ancient Crete, the double-headed axe was the most important religious symbol; in the Middle Ages, the executioner represented the ultimate control of a ruler over his subjects; and, in modern times, the fasces – an axe bound about with staves that was the symbol of Roman legal authority – gave its name to Mussolini's Fascists.

In a dream, therefore, an axe can have ambivalent significance. To own an axe, and not use it, is a sign of confidence. But if the dreamer is cutting down trees or chopping wood, he (it is usually a male dream) may be clearing away obstacles, or deliberately destroying something to express his aggressive instincts.

If someone else holds the axe, the circumstances of the dream are important. A friend working with an axe is a sign of good-fellowship; but if the person seems threatening, this can foretell the loss of a job.

Badge See Medal and badge

Bag and baggage The bag is a symbol of possession: what is possessed may be material objects, knowledge and learning, or spiritual strength. To dream of putting objects into a bag can signify storing these possessions for future use – or it can represent putting things out of sight, in an attempt to ignore them.

Dreams of missing baggage are common: they may derive from a waking experience, but they represent the fear that something important may be lost by carelessness. Finding the missing baggage is a reassuring sign: the feeling of relief can be almost overwhelming, and it means that there is sure to be a way round present difficulties.

The baggage represents what one accumulates during one's lifetime. In this connection, it is interesting that dreams of baggage can be symbols of the married condition.

On the other hand, the unconscious mind may once again be playing its word games. Could the 'bag' represent an annoying old woman? Or the 'baggage' a bothersome young one?

(See also: Basket)

Ball This symbol has an obvious sexual connotation, which can be either male or female (representing in the latter case the woman's breast or belly). Many games involving two or more players, however, are played with balls, and – although this, too, may have a sexual significance – the particular game being played in the dream can be important.

Traditionally, a dream of the game of billiards can portend good news, as can one of baseball or cricket; football is a sign of unease; while tennis foretells the birth of a child.

(See also: Game)

Balloon A balloon represents creative ideas, but it is difficult to restrain, and can easily escape, rising into the air out of reach. To dream of being in the basket of a balloon is a sign that one's ideas will meet with success; perversely, dreams of ascending in a balloon portend misfortune

during a journey, while descending in a balloon can be a sign of failure and a coming loss of income.

(See also: Descent; Flying)

Basket A basket is a more intricate symbol than a bag. It also has a fixed shape. It may be wide and welcoming, or it may be woven with a narrow neck, making it easy to put things in, but difficult to get them out. What the basket contains is equally significant, and both the basket and its contents can represent the dreamer – has he or she been 'putting all their eggs in one basket' and so risking everything on a single undertaking?

A full basket can be a symbol of success, but it also warns that care is necessary. An empty basket represents a lack, whether of possessions or ideas, but it is also ready to be filled. A number of baskets can reveal that the dreamer is deeply uncertain about what to do next.

(See also: Bag and baggage)

Bed The dream may reflect no more than the state of the bed in which one is sleeping, in which case it is most likely to occur just before waking. However, a bed can also have a similar

significance to a bath, and symbolise the desire to escape from everyday cares. It can represent marriage or other sexual activity; or it can denote projects that have to be 'put to bed'. In this context, to dream of getting out of bed can represent 'getting on one's feet' and pursuing projects successfully – but not if one immediately slips over!

To dream of being in bed with someone else need not have sexual connotations. The bedfellow may represent a partner in some enterprise; or, depending on the circumstances, an unwelcome problem that cannot be resolved.
(See also: Bathing)

Bell Bells are connected with a wide variety of signals. The doorbell and (in many countries) the telephone bell – as well as the old-time town crier's bell – announce the arrival of people and news; while the alarm bell sounds as a warning. Church bells can ring out a peal for a joyous occasion, or toll for someone's death.

So the kind of bell that rings, what it means to the dreamer in waking life, and the circumstances of the dream can all affect the interpretation. If the dreamer is ringing the bell, it may mean that he or she has something important to impart, or needs to attract attention. A warning bell can represent something troubling the conscience, or merely – in dreams just before waking – that it is time to get up.

It is also important to remember how dreams can go by opposites. A single tolling bell may portend bad news; but, depending on other circumstances in the dream, it can equally foretell the arrival of someone with good news.

Bone See Skeleton and skull

Book Books in a dream can symbolise knowledge and learning; similarly, they can represent the sum of the dreamer's experience. Old and dusty books may be a part of that experience that has been subconsciously forgotten or neglected. A closed book represents a problem that seems impossible to solve: opening the book may reveal words or symbols that hold the key to solving the problem.
(See also: Library)

Bottle With its narrow neck and roomy body, a bottle is a strong symbol for the womb, and dreaming of trying to fill it – whether with a liquid or some solid material – has clear sexual significance. An empty bottle can be interpreted in a similar way.

Pandora, an archetypal negative anima, was empowered by the gods to bring about the ruin of man. From her jar – later Pandora's box – flew forth all the evils that afflict the world.

But the bottle can also be a container. Perhaps the dreamer is 'bottling up' his or her emotions; or, alternatively, storing up experience for later use.

Bow See Archery

Box A box can be identified with a coffin, and so represent either death or death wishes. Freud suggested that it symbolised the womb – although this was in part due to the fact that the two words can be somewhat similar in German: *Schachtel* and *Schoss*, respectively.

To dream of being confined in a box, a terrifying experience, can therefore relate to a struggle to return to normal existence, or to the similar struggle at the moment of birth.

An empty box can symbolise the absence of ambition, or material disappointment. A closed box is a temptation – what can be inside it? It may turn out to be like Pandora's box, full of troubles. But remember, when all the troubles had escaped from the box into the world, hope remained at the bottom.

(See also: Burial; Death)

Bubble In most cases, bubbles represent pleasure and lightheartedness. But the pleasure is shortlived, because the bubbles soon burst. There is also a darker, and more sinister, aspect to be considered: bubbles rise to the surface of water when a person is drowning, or because something is rotting below.

(See also: Balloon; Champagne)

Buoy A guide to navigation, and a signal marking a safe channel between hazards, a buoy is a symbol of hope and the successful outcome of a project.

Cage Something in a cage is being held captive there. If it is a bird, it symbolises that aspirations and spiritual feelings are not being allowed their freedom. On the other hand, if it is a fierce animal, it can indicate that the dreamer is successfully keeping their more destructive instincts under control.

To dream of being in a cage, however, is a sure sign of the feeling that circumstances are restricting one's activities.

(See also: Animal Kingdom; Zoo)

Camera In dreams, the camera usually represents the self, observing others in a detached manner, yet at the same time trying to uncover some part of their personality – some primitive peoples refuse to have their photographs taken, fearful that the camera will capture their souls. If the camera fails, it may mean that the dreamer is trying to avoid an important issue.

(See also: Photography)

Candle A candle can be an obvious phallic symbol, but it can also represent wisdom and understanding – the light in the darkness. For a man, a flame burning brightly, or otherwise sadly guttering, can symbolise his feelings about his potency. Alternatively, the candle flame can have religious significance, and represent questions of faith or morality.

Numerous lit candles symbolise a common purpose or cause, as in a church service or a vigil. Extinguishing candles is a sign that a problem will be solved, and that the dreamer will no longer continue to 'burn the candle at both ends'. *(See also: Church; Fire; Lamp; Light)*

Card See Ace; King; Knave; Queen; also Club; Diamond; Heart; Spade; Game

Carpet The significance of this dream can depend very much upon the dreamer's experiences. If they have travelled in the Near East, they may well associate it with the eager salesmen who lay out carpets to be walked on in the bazaars. As W.B. Yeats wrote:

I have spread my dreams under your feet,
Tread softly because you tread on my dreams.

More generally carpets, their patterns and colours are said to symbolise women. We say of someone who is about to face a rebuke that they are 'on the carpet': perhaps the dreamer fears justified criticism from a female friend or colleague.

(See also: individual colours)

Chair A chair can be the seat of authority and judgment, or something that offers rest and relaxation. If the dreamer has chosen the chair, it may be necessary to take time off, perhaps to consider a new direction. If the chair was offered by another, it is a sign that it is worth paying attention to any advice that is given. Seeing an empty chair can denote that news of an absent friend will be received.

Clay Ancient myths describe how the first humans were fashioned from clay. A person who dreams of making something from clay may be trying to give a new form to his or her personality.

Clock and watch Clocks in dreams can be oppressive symbols – large and threatening (or strangely distorted) clocks frequently appeared in the paintings of the Surrealists. They show the way in which time is passing, most usually terrifyingly fast; but there are dreams of anxiety in which, as in waking life, the hands of the clock do not seem to move.

Because it marks off every second of our lives, a ticking clock can symboize the human heart. And it reminds us, inexorably, that time is running out.

Club This is a word with very different meanings, and the appearance of any form of club in a dream may be an example of the mind's word games and symbolise another meaning. A club, a gathering of like-minded people, represents social relationships and the desire for identity within the community; the kind of club is therefore significant. Is it a sports club, a club for card players (a further pun), a theatre club, or an association of people who are dedicated to collecting a specific object?

Another kind of club, a weapon, is a symbol of aggression – unless it is a golf club, in which case it may again be a two-sided pun.

In divination with a pack of cards, clubs represent money matters, and may have a similar significance in dreams. *(See also: Game; Theatre)*

Coal In the north of England and in Scotland, the 'first footer', the first person to cross the threshold of the house at New Year, traditionally brings a piece of coal, to symbolise comfort during the coming 12 months. Therefore coal, a valuable mineral dug from the earth by hard work, can represent, despite its blackness, good fortune.

Coffin See Box; Burial

Compass A compass is a circle on which directions are indicated; it is also the drawing instrument that can make a circle. If the dreamer is using a compass to steer a steady course, the omens are good. But if the compass needle is wavering, it can be a sign of the dreamer's

uncertainty, and an indication that a new direction should be decided upon.
(See also: Circle; Directions)

Cord See Rope, cord and string

Cork In films, the symbol of a cork popping from a bottle – particularly a champagne bottle, with the wine bursting forth – has often been used to represent successful sexual climax. But a cork firmly in place can suggest that the dreamer is 'bottling up' feelings.
(See also: Bottle; Champagne)

Cradle All dreams concerning young children can be related to creativity, to new ideas that need to be developed. The cradle itself is a symbol of care and comfort; but, if it is upset, it is a sign of problems ahead.

A woman who dreams of tending a child in a cradle should remember the saying that 'the hand that rocks the cradle rules the world'. The dream may be a comment on her importance within the family or at work.
(See also: Child)

Crown The symbol of a ruler, the crown can represent wholeness and unity. If the dreamer is wearing, or is given, a crown, it is a sign of being asked to fill a position of responsibility and power. Alternatively, the crown can represent an important secret.
(See also: Chair; King; Queen)

Cupboard and closet A symbol of something that is being hidden, and not brought out into the light – we speak of 'a skeleton in the closet', and, recently, of people 'coming out of the closet'.

(See also: Skeleton and Skull)

Curtain Drawing the curtains, being behind them, or even making them, is a sign that the dreamer has something to conceal. Equally, if the curtains are being opened, it symbolises that something is about to be revealed. But if the dreamer is taking a bow at the 'final curtain', it may mean that they have come to a point where they must give up a rather pretentious way of life, and return to the mundane.

(See also: Acting; Swan; Theatre)

Crutch Dreaming of being a cripple, walking with a crutch, is often a sign that the dreamer needs support and encouragement in some part of their waking life. Other circumstances of the dream are important: perhaps the crutch signifies that the dreamer is not in need of support, but feels he or she is being called upon unduly to support others.

(See also: Limping)

Crystal Some people believe that crystal can store up a particular kind of healing power. The word comes from the Greek meaning 'ice', because of its transparency and hardness, but crystal is not ephemeral like ice. Like precious stones, it is a symbol of the combination of intellect and spirit: the way in which a crystal can be cut to catch the light may represent the many different facets of the individual.

(See also: Diamond; Ice; Jewel)

Diamond The dream symbol may be seen as the precious stone itself, or as the simple four-sided figure. In either case, it represents the whole Jungian Self: the proper combination of the male and female principles in the personality.

To dream of buying diamonds may represent a desire for material wealth; or, alternatively, the intention to make a proposal of marriage. Being given a diamond may signify that one's abilities will be recognised; or it can reflect a need to strengthen one's emotional relationships.

(See also: Jewel; and Ace; King; Knave; Queen)

Dice See Betting

Dish In the symbolism of the Tarot cards, the golden disc (or coin, which has become the diamond of the modern pack) is believed by some to represent one of the 'Grail Hallows', the dish used in the Last Supper. A dish may therefore have a specific mystical meaning for the dreamer, or it may be something far more mundane. Is the dreamer asking for more, like Oliver Twist in Dickens's novel?

If the dream is of washing dishes, it can represent either domestic harmony, or a more generalised feeling of tedious labour. By extension, smashing dishes can symbolise the dreamer's desire to break free from domestic or other emotional restraints. On the other hand, like the plates or glasses that are broken in some wedding ceremonies, it may symbolise forthcoming married bliss.

Doll A doll can signify childhood, and indicate immaturity; it can also represent undesired aspects of adulthood. Even children who take good care of their dolls will sometimes express their frustration with adults by attacking, and even dismembering, a favourite doll. The significance of a dream of this kind is clear.

In mature life, a doll can be used to represent another person: in witchcraft, sticking pins into such a doll was a way of causing a particular individual harm. Some dolls can be sinister and menacing. In the

film *Dead of Night*, for example, a ventriloquist's doll gradually takes over his owner's life, and drives him mad. All these aspects of dolls can occur in dreams.

(See also: Ventriloquism)

Drawer A drawer is a place of storage, somewhere things are put away, or hidden. A set of drawers can also represent one's inner state: if the contents are in disarray, this can indicate mental or emotional disorder.

Alternatively, this may be another case of the mind playing word games. Maybe the drawers are a suggestion of a pair of drawers, something that

the dreamer is using to hide his or her sexuality.
(See also: Nudity)

Drum 'Beating one's own drum' is a way of drawing attention to oneself, and expressing the true personality. The sound of the drum can be an omen, whether it foretells pleasure or disaster to come. Playing drums in a band or orchestra is a symbol of being a valuable member of a group, but one playing a supporting part, rather than a leading role. Drums are also an important part of ritual dance.
(See also: Dancing; Orchestra and band)

Emerald One of the rarest of gems, the emerald is in fact a richly green diamond. It has the same general significance as the diamond, but its colour relates it to vitality and hope.
(See also; Diamond; Green; Jewel)

Envelope Envelopes usually contain something: a letter with news, important papers, or a week's wages. The dreamer is undoubtedly expecting something, almost certainly of a welcome nature. If the envelope is not opened, or if it is empty, it can be a sign that the dreamer has missed an opportunity; but if an eagerly awaited envelope arrives, it is an portent of a happy event in waking life.
(See also: Postman)

Fan A fan may be used for cooling off, or for 'fanning the flames' to make them burn brighter. This makes the dream symbol difficult to interpret, particularly taking into consideration the fact that dreams may go by opposites. The circumstances in which the fan is being used may be a clue.

On the other hand, this may be one of the puns that the mind makes. Perhaps the dream refers to someone who is a 'fan' of the dreamer.
(See also: Fire; Heat)

Feather Feathers can stand for birds; they also symbolise lightness or, in connection with cushions and beds, warmth and comfort. To the ancient Egyptians, the feather was a symbol of righteousness, and they believed that the heart of a dead person would be weighed in the balance against the feather of Maat, the goddess of truth. The native Americans of the Plains added a feather to their headdresses for each enemy they killed.

The feather, therefore, is a complex symbol. In general terms, it can represent the spirit or personality of the dreamer. Some birds, such as the peacock, have splendidly ostentatious feathers: perhaps the dreamer has been 'showing off', or would like to be more attractive – 'fine feathers make fine birds'. Feathers being plucked from birds will reveal the naked truth beneath. And a feather-filled quilt can be a sign that the dreamer is in search of a security that they may be in danger of losing.
(See also: Bird)

Flag A flag on its pole can be a phallic symbol; and whether flying proudly or drooping limply it can be an indication of the individual's feelings about their sexual abilities.
(See also: Pole)

Fur A dream symbol that can represent warmth and luxury; perhaps it is a gift signifying love or achievement. Many people, however, are fiercely opposed to the wearing of animal fur. If they dream of it, this can signify a feeling that, while they have been rewarded for something, they do not really deserve it.

Gallows How did this image come into the dreamer's mind? It is not something he or she would have seen in real terms: it is most likely to have come from an illustration or a film. It is nonetheless real within the dream and usually represents a desire for punishment, either of another or of the dreamer – but not necessarily for any major wrongdoing.

There is a related image that will be known to those who are familiar with the Tarot pack: the 'Hanged Man'. Opinions vary greatly on the symbolism of this card, but most probably it represents Judas. The

gallows, then, may signify betrayal, or the dishonest acceptance of payment.

(See also: Execution)

Glass Glass is a transparent material, but it is solid. A dreamer looking through the glass of a window is separated from all the activities of the world going on outside. Glass is also easily broken. Traditionally, glasses from which a solemn toast has been drunk are smashed, so that they cannot be used for a more profane purpose; glasses are also broken in certain wedding ceremonies to ward off any misfortune.

Breaking glass in a dream can therefore have a number of meanings. If the dreamer is smashing a window, it can be a sign of a desire to become more involved in life. On the other hand, the glass may represent the dreamer's ideals or faith, which are insufficiently strong. If glass is being broken in a rage, it perhaps reflects the dreamer's feelings about previously held beliefs, or the state of their marriage.

(See also: Curtain; Mirror; Window)

Glue Glue is a substance used to fix pieces together, and can symbolise the successful joining up of the various parts of a problem. However, if the dreamer got glue all

over his or her fingers, it could be a warning that the solution to the problem may cause them embarrassment or shame.

Gold Of the seven metals known to the ancients, gold was the most magical, since it was incorruptible: it did not tarnish or decay in any way. Because of its colour, it was associated with the sun.

A dream suffused with golden colour is a delightful and warming experience: it is an omen of a bright future. Handling objects made of gold can be a promise of rewards to come – or may symbolise only the dreamer's desires, and not necessarily their fulfilment.

Guitar The shape of a guitar has often been likened to that of a woman. A man who dreams of playing a guitar is likely to be revealing a desire for sexual fulfilment; while a woman playing may be lacking the true expression of her female nature.

Traditionally, hearing the plaintive sound of a guitar is a warning against flattery and seduction.
(See also: Orchestra and band; Violin)

Gun A potent phallic symbol, and a very aggressive one. At whom was the dreamer pointing it? Or was it aimed at them? Did it fire, and did the bullet hit the target?

Alternatively, the gun may have been intended for self-protection, indicating that the dreamer is apprehensive of some danger.

Hammer Most usually, a hammer is a symbol of male power, but it can also suggest the intention to forge new ideas. It can be destructive, smashing anything that gets in the way; but it may also symbolise the desire to win an argument, 'hammering home one's point'.
(See also: Blacksmith)

Hive See Bee

Horn If it is an animal's horn, this can be an obvious phallic symbol. Even if it is a musical instrument (and among musicians all brass instruments are frequently referred to as 'horns'), it can still have this connotation. Alternatively, it may be a reference to the concept of 'blowing one's own trumpet' – it may be the dreamer trying to draw attention to their exploits, or another person with a similar aim.

If the dreamer is Jewish, the horn may be a reminder of the shofar, the ram's horn that is blown in the synagogue at New Year and on the Day of Atonement, as a call to repentance and sacrifice.

There are other possible connotations: the horns of the Devil; the horn of the huntsman, maintaining discipline over his pack of hounds; the 'horns of Elfinland faintly blowing'; or even the ancient gesture indicating that a man's wife has betrayed him. Finally, it should not be forgotten that we speak of someone being 'on the horns of a dilemma'.
(See also: Orchestra and band; Trumpet)

Horseshoe A horseshoe is a traditional symbol of good fortune. Some people maintain that, if it is upside down, the luck will drain out of it. It is also considered a female sexual symbol.
(See also: Blacksmith; Horse; Nail)

Iron Iron is strong and can symbolise willpower and the aggressive instincts; but if it is neglected it will rust away. A dream of a domestic iron can signify the desire to 'iron out' difficulties – but if the result of ironing is poor, with creases in the wrong places, maybe even a burnt patch, the omens are not good.

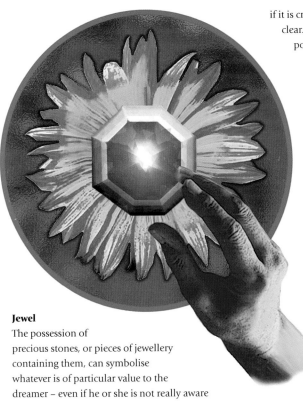

if it is cracked or broken, the implication is clear. A jug also holds liquid that can be poured out. Possibly the dreamer is ready to give a major element of his or her emotions to another person – and this, too, can have sexual connotations.

(See also: individual liquids)

Kaleidoscope The mirrors of a kaleidoscope reflect tiny coloured fragments, forming them into attractive patterns that are constantly changing. This dream can symbolise the dreamer's difficulty in putting together a number of scattered thoughts into a meaningful whole: every movement of the kaleidoscope produces a possible solution, but each may seem equally appealing.

Key Primarily, this is a powerful phallic symbol: for a woman, the image of unlocking can have an obvious meaning; while a man who dreams of unlocking one room after another may be thinking of several concurrent love affairs.

The key can have other meanings, however. Locking something up is a symbol of secrecy, or of suppressing one's feelings. Alternatively, the key can represent the solution to a problem; and losing it signifies the frustration of failure.

(See also: Locksmith)

Kite A kite is a symbol of soaring inspiration, but controlled by the strings of reason and wisdom.

Jewel

The possession of precious stones, or pieces of jewellery containing them, can symbolise whatever is of particular value to the dreamer – even if he or she is not really aware of its worth: individual integrity, spiritual wholeness, incorruptibility. Reaching out to grasp jewels, but failing, can therefore suggest that the dreamer is setting personal standards that are too high.

A jewel can have other dream meanings. It can stand for a loved one; while a woman wearing jewels is displaying her genitalia. And the sight of a jewel lying in a flower is a symbol of the union of opposites: male and female, carnal and spiritual.

(See also: individual jewels; Gold; Silver)

Jug Traditionally, the jug is a symbol of virginity:

In certain circumstances, it can have a similar meaning to a bird.

(See also: Bird)

Knife For Freud, a knife was a phallic symbol, and one with violent connotations. Was the dreamer threatening another person, or was that person threatening the dreamer?

On the other hand, a knife can be a useful tool for cutting. Perhaps the dreamer wishes to cut something out of his or her life – a lover, an associate, an unattractive aspect of the personality, or a bad habit.

(See also: Back; Butcher; Killing; Sword)

Knot Dreaming of trying to untie a knot, and the frustration involved, is a sign that the dreamer is subject to restriction of thoughts, emotions or actions. There is a 'knotty' problem that must be unravelled; if the knot comes undone this is an encouraging omen.

Alternatively, the knot may symbolise anxiety about a coming marriage.

(See also: Rope, cord and string)

Ladder A ladder is a means of climbing, slowly but steadily, upwards. In a dream it can symbolise developments in the dreamer's career or social status, or it may represent a rise to a new level of spiritual understanding.

But one can also climb down a ladder. It may be with the satisfaction of having successfully completed a job of construction. It may be to bring a stored treasure from the attic of the memory. Or it may be a descent into the lower depths of the unconscious.

On the other hand, as with so many dream symbols, Freud found a sexual connotation in the ladder – and, in this connection, it must be asked: did the dreamer climb the ladder with success, or fall off?

(See also: Climbing; Descent; Stairs)

Lamp The lamp that lights the night, the lamp left burning in a window to guide the traveller home, the lamp held in the rescuer's hand – all

these are symbols of guidance, hope and recovery. The colour of the lamplight may be significant: all over the world, green is the encouragement to go forward, amber is a warning, and red is an instruction to stop. If the lamp goes out, it can mean that hopes will not be fulfilled.

(See also: Light)

Lead One of the seven metals known to antiquity, lead was associated with the planet Saturn: it is grey and heavy, and matched the serious, cautious, pessimistic – saturnine – character. At the same time, lead is soft and pliable – but it is also poisonous.

The circumstances in which lead appears in a dream are therefore important. The most likely is that the lead is being used as a weight: perhaps at the end of a fishing line, or in greater quantity for a diver. The amount of lead can correspond to the seriousness of the dreamer's intentions. Since the water represents the unconscious, is he or she making a rather idle exploration – 'fishing for ideas' – or prepared to descend deep into the unknown?

(See also: Fishing; Descent; Diving)

Letter A letter contains information, and so can symbolise the acquiring of knowledge, which may be practical or spiritual. Alternatively, it may be a portent of news to be received.

In Freudian terms, an unopened letter represents virginity – and opening it has an obvious connotation.

(See also: Envelope; Postman)

Lock See Key; Locksmith

Machinery A complex dream symbol with a variety of interpretations. The human body is often described in mechanical terms, and the

circumstances in which the machinery was situated, and what happened to it, may reflect the physical condition of the dreamer. For example, the movements of the machinery can have obvious sexual connotations, while a steam engine is said to represent the stomach.

On the other hand, the machine may suggest that the dreamer is functioning 'mechanically', and that he or she needs to improve their attitude to life, or their social relationships.

Similarly, a dream of watching or studying the workings of a machine can symbolise an examination of the individual's inner motives.

(See also: Factory; Tool; Workshop)

Magnet A symbol for the mysterious power that seems to draw two individuals together – 'personal magnetism' – or the attraction of an unusual concept. It may alternatively represent the need to pull ideas together to examine them.

(See also: Compass)

Map A dream symbol that suggests that the dreamer is in search of the best way to go forward. Reading the map correctly may be a sign that all will be well.

Maypole A symbol with more than one sexual connection, not only in Freudian psychology but in traditional folklore – which is why use of the maypole was forbidden during the Puritan period in English history; at the same time, the maypole represents popular fun and enjoyment. Perhaps it is a suggestion that the dreamer should take greater pleasure in sex.

(See also: Carnival; Pole)

Medal and badge Symbols of achievement and social service. Perhaps the dreamer has recently accomplished something worthy of recognition. If someone else was receiving a medal, the dreamer may have felt that they deserved it, or that they were being honoured unfairly. A badge can also be a sign of good integration in society.

Mirror A mirror reflects, and in this sense it can symbolise the need to give greater thought to plans before carrying them out. A cracked or cloudy mirror may well be a portent that the individual's plans are likely to be frustrated.

However, what the mirror reflects is likely to be more important, and generally this will be the dreamer. The mirror image can be the representation of how others see him or her; alternatively, because it reflects left as right, it may present the opposite of what the conscious mind is aware of, and suggest that the dreamer is guilty of wishful thinking.

A mirror can also represent egotism, vanity and self-obsession. Fortunately, being aware of the meaning of such a dream can lead to a greater knowledge of the self.

(See also: Glass)

Money In dreams, money can represent anything that the dreamer values, whether it is time, energy, inner spiritual resources, or – most likely of all - love. Was the dreamer being generous or miserly, possessive or extravagant? Or was he or she investing, in the hope of greater returns in the future?

(See also: Bank; Bankruptcy; Debt)

Nail Possibly a straightforward phallic symbol, in the same way that the horseshoe is considered a female sexual symbol. At the same time, nails are used to fix other things, and can symbolise the bringing together of two or more concepts. There is a sense of very positive thinking here – 'hitting the nail on the head'.

(See also: Blacksmith; Horseshoe)

Needle A probable phallic symbol, particularly when its power of penetration is taken into consideration. On the other hand, the use of a needle in sewing suggests that there are aspects of the dreamer's waking or spiritual life that need mending or bringing together.

Alternatively, the dreamer, or someone of his or her acquaintance, may be 'getting the needle' about some matter in waking life.

(See also: Sewing)

Net A net is used to trap something, and the dreamer may feel trapped in some waking situation. There are other possible allusions: using a fishing net, or catching a butterfly, can suggest that there are ideas – or aspects of the unconscious – that the dreamer is trying to grasp; while being inside a mosquito net, or behind net curtains, implies a desire to hide away and protect oneself from some impending misfortune.

(See also: Butterfly; Curtain; Entanglement; Fish; Fishing; Hunting)

Newspaper Like a letter, a newspaper conveys information. If the dreamer feels anxiety about the newspaper's content, it is likely to represent his or her concern about their reputation. Dramatic headlines – generally without any sense of the accompanying text – may be a portent of some future event.

(See also: Letter; Postman)

Nut and bolt The phrase 'nuts and bolts' is often used to describe the down-to-earth facts of a situation. Dreaming of screwing a nut on to a bolt is a symbol of putting matters together in a practical way.

(See also: Machinery)

Oar See Boat

Oil A symbol of riches and comfort – whether in the sense of 'striking oil', oil that is used for heating or massage, or the holy oil that is used in consecration or the anointing of people who are very sick. There may also be a reference to 'pouring oil on troubled waters' – calming an emotional situation.

(See also: Massage)

Paper A clean sheet of white paper can be a symbol of youthful innocence, or represent a new beginning in spiritual or waking life. At the same time, things made of paper are notoriously insubstantial and this dream may be a reference to an ill-judged plan or a fleeting love affair.

Parcel Dreaming of receiving a parcel and opening it can represent the start of a new phase of self-discovery – what was in the parcel? Wrapping up a parcel implies the successful completion of a project – unless the paper and string kept coming apart.

(See also: Box; Packing)

Pearl The pearl is associated with the feminine principle, the moon, and water – all connected with the unconscious – and a common phrase is 'pearls of wisdom'. The roundness of the pearl and the way it is formed inside the body of a mollusc symbolise the wholeness of the individual's psyche. Perhaps the dreamer has had his or her most intimate beliefs scorned by others, and they feel they have been 'casting pearls before swine'?

(See also: Jewel; Oyster)

Pen and pencil Two obvious phallic symbols, particularly if the pen is a fountain pen, or the pencil is being sharpened. On the other hand, using the pen or pencil for writing can suggest that the dreamer is making use of someone else; or, if another person was using the implement, the converse may be true.

(See also: Letter; Paper)

Photograph See Camera; Photography

Pipe For many people who remember old tobacco advertisements, a pipe is still a symbol of masculinity, and an image of a contented father offering protection to his family. A 'pipe of peace' may represent the successful resolution of a disagreement. On the other hand, the action of sucking is related to that of the child at the breast, and denotes a feeling of insecurity, and possibly a desire for more affection.

Alternatively, the pipe may be a drainpipe, representing an escape into the unconscious; or part of a pipeline, a symbol of communication.

Plough Since ancient times, ploughing has been a masculine sexual symbol, while the furrow represents the female genitalia. A dream of a plough can therefore refer to the male sex drive, and the related concept of planting and raising crops may reflect a desire to have children.

Ploughing can also represent the development of new ideas and plans. However, it is also hard and exhausting work, and there may be a suggestion that the dreamer is in a rut – 'ploughing on'.
(See also: Digging; Farm)

Pole An unambiguous phallic symbol, and one that frequently turns up in popular speech. However, the mind may be playing word games:

the dream symbol may represent, not only someone of Polish descent (and more so if he or she is tall and thin), but even, perhaps, the result of an election.
(See also: Election; Flag; Maypole; Tent)

Puzzle What kind of puzzle was it? A crossword puzzle, in which the answers to the clues related to one another, and in which the words themselves seemed to have a particular significance? A jigsaw – probably with pieces that could not be fitted in, or even missing, so that the complete picture could not be seen? Or a three-dimensional puzzle of some kind, impossible to complete? All these can symbolise problems facing the dreamer that appear insoluble.

Quilt A patchwork quilt is put together with love and ingenuity, and can symbolise the many

different aspects of the dreamer's life that contribute to his or her domestic comfort. Perhaps the dream was a suggestion to relax, and take more pleasure from married life.

(See also: Bed)

Radio A common object in nearly every home, the radio often becomes no more than a background of sound – increasingly heard also in shops and the workplace. But, in addition, it communicates information: possibly the dream is a warning to pay closer attention to what is being said.

Ring A symbol of commitment and dedication – and this need not be only in marriage: the reference may be to business, emotional or spiritual matters. As a circle, a ring also signifies completeness.

(See also: Circle)

Rock A rock can symbolise stability and permanence; in this sense, it has a connection with the earth, and so with the Jungian Mother. On the other hand, the immovable solidity of the rock can suggest that the youthful enthusiasm of the dreamer has ended in disillusionment and depression: we speak of 'having reached rock bottom' emotionally.

Rope, cord and string All these things are symbols of attachment, and quite possibly of love: we speak of 'the cords that bind', and of 'fluttering heart strings'. However, each can have other significance.

A rope can be used to restrain an animal, but at the same time allow it to graze freely – perhaps the dreamer has been giving him- or herself 'too much rope' in exercising his or her animal instincts? A rope can also be used to

moor a boat, which may represent the dreamer's sexual activity.

A cord can represent a pun by the mind: the dreamer may be trying to seize on an idea or a memory, and thinking 'that strikes a chord' – or there may be a musical reference.

String is easily tangled and knotted: a dream of trying to disentangle it may represent a 'knotty' problem that must be solved. There is also a suggestion of manipulation, either of the dreamer or of another person: we speak of 'a puppet on a string', or 'stringing someone along'.

(See also: Boat; Entanglement; Knot; Orchestra and band)

Ruby The rich red colour of the ruby symbolises passion, virility and riches. The deeper the colour of the stone, the greater its importance and value.

(See also: Jewel; Red)

Sapphire Like the emerald, the sapphire is a rare form of diamond, of a bright blue colour, and the symbol of fidelity, cool intellectual reason, and spiritual energy.

(See also: Blue; Diamond; Jewel)

Scales Perhaps the dreamer is faced with making a decision, and is weighing the pros and cons of the matter. Or he or she may have been a shopkeeper, weighing and selling food.

In astrology, the sign of Libra, the Scales, is associated with the kidneys and bladder: a dream of scales may indicate some underlying state of ill health in this region.

(See also: Food & Drink; Shop)

Silver As a dream symbol, a silver object has an intrinsic beauty, and reflects simple and honest wealth. There is also a symbolic connection between silver and the moon.

(See also: Gold; Moon)

forgotten? Was it a problem to be solved, or one that the dreamer was trying to ignore? A spade can also be a symbol of facing up to reality, as in the expression 'calling a spade a spade'. In this connection it is significant that, in using a pack of cards for fortune-telling, the spade represents bad news, difficulties in personal relationships, and other problems that must be dealt with resolutely.

(See also: Digging)

Skeleton and skull Traditional symbols of mortality and danger – remember the skull and crossbones of the pirate flag. A skull has also often been used to suggest the importance of looking into the 'meaning of life'; while a skeleton may be a reminder of someone, now dead, whom the dreamer used to know.

A skeleton is made up of bones: perhaps the dreamer is considering a problem and needs to get down to 'the bones of the matter'; or perhaps it is a reference to a 'bone of contention'. On the other hand, the dreamer may be harbouring a guilty secret – 'a skeleton in the closet'.

(See also: Cupboard and closet; Pirate)

Spade An implement used for digging, a spade has connotations of searching and uncovering – or burying. Was it a pleasant memory being sought, or an unpleasant one that was best

Spear A well known phallic symbol, with strong connotations of aggression. At the same time it is a weapon of defence, and may symbolise a feeling of insecurity and danger on the part of the dreamer.

(See also: Gun)

Sponge A sponge is absorbent, soaking up liquids. This symbol can be a warning that the dreamer is too easygoing, absorbing experiences without reacting to them. We speak of a 'sponger', someone who is always seeking favours or material loans – perhaps this represents someone in the dreamer's waking life? Or a heavy drinker?

Statue If the dream represented someone known to the dreamer as a statue, it can signify that the person is inflexible and that there is no way of communicating with them. Similarly, if the dreamer was the statue, it is a sign that he or she has become distanced from reality.

On the other hand, statues are erected to honour people. Perhaps the symbol represents someone the dreamer admires too deeply, and whom they have 'placed on a pedestal'.

Stone See Jewel; Rock

String See Rope, cord and string

Sword This is a phallic symbol, but also one of superior power. In Greek mythology, the peasant Gordius was elected king of Phrygia, and tied up his wagon with a knot that no-one could undo. Told that whoever untied it 'would reign over the whole East', Alexander the Great cut it free with one blow of his sword.

The phrase 'a sword hanging over one's head' – signifying imminent danger – also comes from Greek mythology. Damocles was allowed to sit on the throne of the ruler of Sicily, but found a sword suspended by a horsehair above it, and hastily removed himself.

(See also: Knife; Knot)

Tap A constantly dripping tap suggests that the dreamer is being drained of emotion by a situation in waking life, but a tap that can be turned on and off at will signifies that the dreamer has matters under control. There is also a possible sexual symbolism.

(See also: Water)

Telephone A symbol of communication, but with a variety of implications. If the dreamer did not answer the telephone, was cut off, or put the receiver down, it is a sign that messages from the unconscious are being ignored, or interrupted by material preoccupations.

(See also: Bell)

Tool A traditional euphemism for the penis. But what kind of tool was it? A screwdriver has obvious sexual symbolism, as does an awl and, most probably, a spanner. A hammer, however, while it is a symbol of power, can also represent the concept of 'driving a point home' in an argument. A carpenter's plane, which is used for making wood smooth, can symbolise the re-establishment of a friendly relationship after a quarrel; and a file, with its punning connotations, may be a reference to conditions at work, or to dealings with authorities.

(See also: Machinery; Workshop)

Top A spinning top remains stable as long as it continues moving, but sooner or later it topples over. This can be a warning that the dreamer is being far too active in waking life, and that exhaustion is about to set in. On the other hand, it may be a punning symbol: the dreamer is feeling 'on top of things'.

Trumpet A showy brass instrument, very expressive but generally rather loud. Perhaps the dreamer wants to draw attention to him- or herself. Or is the attention undeserved, and they are 'blowing their own trumpet'?

(See also: Horn; Orchestra and band)

Umbrella A shield against the water of the unconscious, but a fragile one that can be blown inside-out by the 'winds of change'. An umbrella can also be used in dreams like a parachute – as in the film *Mary Poppins* – easing descent and preventing a fall.

(See also: Descent; Falling; Rain; Water; Wind)

Dick van Dyke and Julie Andrews in Walt Disney's Mary
Poppins. *The children's nanny with the magic touch, Mary
Poppins is often seen with her umbrella. On one occasion she even
uses it as a parachute to float safely to the ground.*

Watch See Clock and
watch

Wheel A widespread
symbol of the cycle of
history and nature, and so
of eternity. Possibly the
dreamer needs to consider
his or her place in society
– are they a 'big wheel', or
a small one?
*(See also: Circle; Machinery;
Mandala)*

Whip A symbol of
authority, but also of
punishment. Was the
dreamer wielding the
whip, or was he or she
guilty of some bad action?
Perhaps they felt the need
to 'whip up' their energies,
or express themselves
forcibly in a waking
situation. There is also the
possibility of sexual
symbolism.

On the other hand, this
may be yet another example of the mind's word
games. Was the dreamer responsible for
collecting money from friends or colleagues – a
'whip round'?

Violin Like the guitar, the violin – and other
members of the same family of instruments – has
the symbolic shape of a woman. Was the dreamer
producing beautiful sounds with his or her bow,
or did the strings break?
(See also: Guitar; Orchestra and band)

Wreath Generally a symbol of sympathy,
following the death of someone. Perhaps this
dream is a sign that the dreamer is feeling self-
pity, or mourning the loss of a relationship. A
laurel wreath, however, is a symbol of success.
(See also: Laurel)

HAPPENINGS & EXPERIENCES

Whatever the dream, it comprises events and experiences, and the dreamer's feelings about what took place. Many of the events will seem commonplace, even banal, although the sequence in which they occur will often be unusual or apparently unconnected. Other events, however, can be bizarre, and even completely outside the waking experience of the dreamer. These are most likely to be the surfacing of atavistic impulses, drawn from Jung's Collective Unconscious. On the other hand, those who believe in reincarnation will identify them with one or more of the dreamer's previous lives.

Abduction True to the belief that many dreams go by opposites, to dream of abduction is traditionally a sign of good things to come. Whether it is a man or a woman who is being carried off by force, the dream portends that plans will come to fruition. If it is a child who is being abducted, a mystery will be solved.

Accident It might be thought that a dream of an accident is a clear warning to take care and avoid any unnecessary activity, but this is not always so. A dream of an accident in the air, for instance, is held traditionally to be a sign of a vigorous mind; an accident in a car can mean that riches are on the way. Minor accidents involving the head, hands or feet have a specific significance. An accident to the head portends danger to oneself or one's father; to the right foot, danger to one's brother or sister; to the left foot, danger to an employee; to the right hand, danger to one's mother; and to the left hand, danger to one's children.

Acting Those who play a part on stage are not themselves, they are pretending to be someone else. Dreams of acting must be regarded with caution: plans are likely to come to nothing,

friends will prove unreliable. And a dream of being introduced to an actor is a sure warning of hurtful gossip.

Traditionally, watching an actress on stage can mean that a letter containing good news is on the way; but being introduced to an actress is a sign of troubles in the home.

(See also: Audition; Cinema; Platform, Rehearsal)

Archery The bow is a symbol of power, and the arrow is the object that utilises this power to make sure of finding its target. In Greek mythology, the bow and arrow of Apollo stood for the energy of the sun, its rays, and their fertilising and purifying abilities. There is also Cupid's arrow, which awakens love in the desired one.

To dream of hitting a target with an arrow, therefore, is an omen of success, whether in one's career or in love; missing the target is a sign of failure. A similar interpretation must be given to a broken bowstring or arrow. Having many arrows is a sign of uncertainty; and if other people have the bows and arrows, there is danger of betrayal by friends.

In astrology, the bow and arrow is carried by Sagittarius the centaur, half man and half horse. Sagittarius is considered to govern the hips and thighs, and the dreamer may be subconsciously aware of trouble in this area.

(See also: Horse)

Audition The dream that one is attending an audition – most usually for a role as an actor or dancer on stage, although it may also be as a singer or musician – is a relatively modern image, but the concept goes back to antiquity in the idea of being tested before a panel of judges. It signifies doubt in one's abilities to attain a specific goal. Fortunately, few auditions end with a brusque dismissal. Either the candidate is accepted, or at least put on a short list; or they are told, encouragingly, to practise harder, and to try for another role at a later date. So, even if the dream audition ends badly, it contains a message to persevere.

(See also: Examination; Rehearsal)

Bankruptcy For many people, bankruptcy is a shameful state that must be avoided at all costs; for others, it is a convenient way out of present difficulties. But these may be only conscious attitudes: deep down in the unconscious, those who think that bankruptcy is degrading may in fact regard it as a welcome relief; while those who cheerfully exploit it may be repressing their embarrassment.

For these reasons, great care must be taken in interpreting a dream that one is bankrupt. The bankruptcy is more likely to be one of ideas than of money. The dreamer may believe that he or she is truly unable to find a way out of present difficulties, while still subconsciously aware that a solution exists, if only they can summon the initiative to deal with the situation.

(See also: Debt)

Baptism For most people, baptism no longer has the great significance that it had in earlier

Christianity: the saving of a new baby from the state of original sin in which it was born. Nowadays it is more a pleasant social ritual, welcoming the child into the religious community and confirming the names it has been given. Nevertheless, it still represents a new beginning, an escape from past difficulties, and an introduction to a different way of life.

To dream that one is present at a baptism, perhaps one of the godparents, signifies that one is about to encourage a new enterprise; but at the same time it warns that one will have to take on considerable responsibility. If the person to be baptised is oneself, it means that one's selfish instincts will have to be suppressed for the common good.

(See also: Church; Water)

Bathing Several dream images may be combined in this experience. First, there is water, an archetypal symbol for the unconscious or the Mother. Then there is the concept of cleansing and purification: it may be that the dreamer wants to be rid of something distasteful in waking life. The temperature of the water must be taken into account: was it warm and comforting, fresh and invigorating, or cold and dispiriting?

Also, there is the question of what the dreamer was – or was not – wearing. If they were taking a bath, it was likely to be in private, and they would be naked. If they were at a lakeside or on the beach, they may have been under the impression that they were in swimwear, only to discover that they were wearing nothing. This is a common type of dream, and many people experience intense embarrassment at this point, whether or not there are others present. However, if they are at ease with nakedness in their waking life, they may feel nothing but an interested curiosity.

Interpreting this kind of dream, therefore,

requires a careful consideration of each separate element.

(See also: Nudity; Water)

Beheading This is not a dream that occurs very often, and it is likely to have been triggered by something the reader has read or seen in a film or on television. However, if there appears to be no influence of this kind, the dream can have a considerable significance. Perhaps it literally represents 'losing one's head': either in a panicky situation, or in letting one's bodily instincts overrule the mind's logic. Equally, for a man, it can reflect the deep Freudian fear of castration.

(See also: Execution)

Betting To dream of betting on a horse race is a warning not to place too much reliance on one's own opinion; this is very different from the predictive dream of seeing or hearing about the winning horse. If one wins, it may be a sign that one is over-confident; conversely, losing the bet indicates a lack of confidence.

Birth Everybody has experienced the shock of their birth; and many – perhaps all – people retain some subconscious memory of it. Various dream images may reflect this experience: crawling out of, or into, narrow caves; travelling along tunnels or canals; even leaving or entering the sea. Nador Fodor, the author of *New Approaches to Dream Interpretation* (1951), gathered confirmatory evidence of this. He took details of particularly striking dreams of this kind, and was able to have the circumstances of the actual birth verified by the subjects' mothers.

Dreams of giving birth are not confined exclusively to women. The 'birth' may be that of a new idea or invention produced by the unconscious mind. A dream of being present at a birth, or of assisting, can be a subconscious suggestion that someone else's ideas are worth encouraging.

(See also: Cave; Death; Mine; Tunnel; Water)

Bomb We live in a violent world, and a dream of a bomb explosion may prove to be a prediction of a terrorist attack somewhere. Equally, it can be an omen of a serious disaster that is shortly to affect the dreamer.

At the same time, the explosion – or perhaps the frantic attempts of the dreamer to disarm the bomb, or escape from the vicinity – can represent the dreamer's awareness of an 'explosive' situation, and the need to tread carefully. Perhaps they themselves are so emotionally wound up that they feel 'I could explode'.

Break Many different forms of dream can involve the breaking of something. It can be deliberate: a violent rampage, or perhaps a coldly satisfying smash-up. Or it can be accidental: the destruction of an object of value, whose loss will be the cause of sorrow; or the almost casual breaking of something that the world will be better without.

Generally, dreams of this kind reflect social or emotional relationships in the dreamer's waking life. Breaking glass or china, in particular, can symbolise something fragile that the dreamer finds it difficult to hold on to: beliefs, ideals, marriage. In this context, it is significant that the traditional

breaking of a glass or plate at a wedding is a symbolic gesture, intended to ward off any misfortune in the marriage.

Burglary See Intruder

Burial To dream of seeing a burial does not necessarily have anything to do with death: it can be a sign that the dreamer is about to break away from old habits, circumstances or relationships.

Dreams of being buried alive are quite common. They may be due to no more than the fact that the bedclothes have covered the sleeper's face; but they can also be a recollection of the struggles during birth. By extension, they may represent troubles with a possessive mother in adult life.
(See also: Birth; Box; Cemetery)

Cannibalism This can be a very disturbing dream, particularly when it is recollected on waking, because cannibalism is a forbidden act; however, its symbolic significance is less specific. Among primitive peoples, cannibalism was a ritual way of assimilating the power of the other person: in dreams it can represent the desire to take over another's ideas or duties, or be an image of living off another's abilities or money.

Carnival In many parts of the Christian world, carnival is the last wild orgy before the weeks of self-denial that precede Easter, and similar celebrations occur in other religions. So a dream of this kind may occur in the nights before a new and major undertaking, one that will take up all the dreamer's attention, leaving no time for relaxation.

On the other hand, the dream may be a message that 'things can be fun'. So, a sexually inhibited person may dream of someone making advances to them during the abandon of a

carnival. But, if the dreamer feels left out, taking no part in the enjoyment, it is a sign that life is passing them by.

(See also: Fairground)

Chase Is the dreamer being chased, or chasing someone else? In the first case, the dreamer is likely to be trying to escape from an oppressive situation – although, if the chaser is of the opposite sex, it can signify a longing to be wooed and loved. Seeing someone else being chased can signify the dreamer's aggression towards that person. However, it is important to bear in mind that the dreamer may have projected their own personality on to the chaser, in which case the chase is likely to be of a loved one.

Being chased by fierce animals can symbolise the dreamer's desire to shake off his or her aggressive instincts.

(See also: Hunting)

Cleaning Some people are obsessed with cleanliness during their waking lives; this is frequently an expression of some deeply suppressed feelings of guilt. A dream of this type – while it is not socially disturbing – is likely to represent feelings of the same kind.

(See also: Dirtiness)

Climbing One climbs from something below to something above: up a ladder, a rope, a staircase, a steep hill path – they are often all very much the same symbol. Other circumstances of the dream are therefore important to its interpretation. If the dreamer is principally conscious of getting away from below, it implies that they feel their present situation to be a lowly one – and they may find the struggle to rise too difficult. They can, of course, be escaping from some threatening event; but in many dreams of this kind the climb seems to go on for ever.

Dreamers who regard the climb as a way of moving upwards, however, are expressing their ambitions, or their satisfaction at having already completed a demanding task in their waking life. *(See also: Cliff; Escaping; Ladder; Mountain)*

Conspiracy Was the dreamer one of the conspirators, or does he or she feel that other people are plotting against them? In either case, the dream may be a clear warning. *(See also: Spying)*

Dancing Since the earliest times, dance has been an important form of ritual. A man and a woman dancing together can be seen as a prelude to love-making, and may portend marriage. Dancing in a group is a social activity: it can represent a desire for something, necessary to the group, to happen, or it can be a celebration that the event has occurred.

Dreaming of dancing alone, however, is rather different. It can signify a solitary triumph; it may reflect the fact that, in waking life, one is unable to express one's personality freely; or it may be akin to appearing on stage, playing a part that does not reflect one's true nature. *(See also: Acting; Circle)*

Debt To dream that one is unable to pay one's debts can be a sign of underlying anxiety, and it need have nothing to do with money. It can reflect the feeling that too much is being demanded of one in waking life, or that one is 'in someone's debt' for a favour given. Similarly, if the debts are owed by other people, the dreamer may be expecting too much of them.

In more general terms, the dream may signify that there is something in the dreamer's life that needs 'balancing up'. *(See also: Bankruptcy)*

Demolition Is it the dreamer who is demolishing a building, or are they watching a demolition gang at work? The kind of building is important. If the dreamer is doing the work, it can reflect an aggressive attitude to what the building represents. Alternatively, the demolition can represent the break-up of a situation or a relationship, either one that is desired, or one that comes as an unwelcome surprise.

Demonstration There is something in the dreamer's life that he or she should speak out about, but which they have so far kept to themselves. At the same time, there is an element of the crowd mentality about a demonstration: was the dreamer there principally to show solidarity with others?

If the demonstration was led by somebody else, it may be that the dreamer is aware that this person – it could well be a husband, wife or partner – has not been allowed an adequate say in domestic or business matters.

Descent Dreams of going down – on a stairway, in an elevator, into the earth, through water, or even through the air by parachute – are a sign of a decline in physical or spiritual energy, or perhaps a decline in social status. They can symbolise the descent into the unconscious to bring hidden aspects of one's personality to light. And if the descent is followed by ascent, the omens are good.
(See also: Abyss; Cave; Cellar; Falling)

Digging This is a dream symbol with a rather obvious meaning, although it may have rather more implications than appear at first sight. What is being dug for? It can be a long-buried memory, or the root of an emotional problem. Or perhaps the dreamer is searching for facts to confound an opponent, or 'digging the dirt' on someone.

On the other hand, the dreamer may be digging a hole to bury something, an unpleasant experience or a bad deed they want to forget.
(See also: Ditch; Plough; Spade)

Dirtiness Children, say their parents, enjoy getting dirty; and they are often chided and sometimes punished for it. A dream of being dirty may therefore be a sign of a desire to return to the innocence of childhood, or it may be connected with guilt about a recent action. In addition, the dream may have sexual implications, and the dreamer's reactions to the dirt can be an indication of his or her feelings about sex.
(See also: Cleaning)

Disgrace Being 'in disgrace' is a common childhood experience, and a dream of this kind can represent either a resurfacing of some infant episode, or the awareness of having committed a wrong – the subconscious frequently magnifies something that is no more than an indiscretion into a major sin. If the dreamer feels that the disgrace is unjustified, it may be a sign that he or she is insufficiently assertive, and should stand up for their rights or beliefs.

Diving In Freudian terms, diving into water can symbolise sexual intercourse. The diver may be wearing a tight scuba suit; perhaps this represents a feeling of restriction in sexual relations – or the tightness and the material may have fetishistic connotations.

Water can also represent the unconscious; diving in symbolises an exploration of the deeper recesses of the mind. But the water may be deep and dangerous; the dream can be seen as a warning.
(See also: Swimming pool; Water)

Dream within a dream When someone dreams that they are dreaming, it is a sign that they are trying to put aside the symbolic significance of the primary images – making them 'only a dream'. They want to ignore what the mind is trying to communicate.

At the same time, this may be a way in which the mind attempts to overcome the resistance of the dreamer, presenting otherwise unpalatable facts as a dream within a dream.

Drowning A large body of water can represent the unconscious; it can also have a sexual connotation, and symbolise the dreamer's relationship with a mother figure. A dream of drowning can therefore signify being overwhelmed by repressed ideas, or by emotional stress. On the other hand, it can indicate the end of one stage of spiritual development, followed by the resurgence of a newly washed personality.
(See also: Swimming pool; Water)

Eaten A dream of being eaten alive symbolises the jaws of death. This may refer, not to physical death, but to the suppression or extinction of the personality in some sense. But there is hope: like Jonah in the belly of the whale, the dreamer may subsequently be brought back to life.

This dream is also reminiscent of the initiatory trance experiences of a shaman. *(See also Disfigurement)*

Election An election is the moment at which one makes a choice. The dream is most likely to reflect the dreamer's waking life. If he or she is the candidate for election, it is probably a reference to a hoped-for promotion, or some other improvement in material conditions. If the election is of someone else, the dreamer is faced with making an important decision.

But elections can also be exciting, even rowdy, events, and sometimes there is a suggestion of malpractice, or the dreamer's favoured candidate is not elected. Is the dreamer involved in disputes at work or in the home?
(See also: Parliament)

Emptiness Opening a box and finding it empty or seeing an empty container are obvious omens of disappointment to come. Alternatively, it may be the dreamer's life that lacks something; this is more likely to be emotional than material.

Entanglement A dream of being entangled – among thorny bushes, creepers, the coils of a serpent, or the arms of an octopus, for example – is a sign that the dreamer wishes to escape from an overwhelming problem. This may be related to something material, but it is more likely to be emotional; in particular, it can refer to an over-possessive mother or lover.
(See also: Octopus)

Escaping Dreams of trying to escape are said to be the commonest of all. Few people can claim a life that is so contented and balanced that there is nothing from which they would prefer to escape. The first question to be asked is: what was the dreamer trying to escape from and what did it symbolise? Secondly: did this symbol represent an external threat, or some aspect of the dreamer's character that he or she would like to deny?

Did the dreamer manage to escape? Depending upon the nature of the dream, this may or may not be a good sign. Equally, if caught, was this frightening or a relief, even an eventual pleasure? It could be like a young people's party game, in which players pretend to flee, but are at last happy to be caught and given a kiss.

Examination The dreamer may be attempting to answer written or oral questions in a school test, giving evidence in court, or being examined by a doctor. In each case, although there is the possibility that the dreamer is being called to account for something done or undone, it is most likely that he or she is in fact the examiner. They are questioning themselves. The apprehension or confidence they experience will reflect what they feel in waking life. If the examination is a medical one, it may be a sign of some physical trouble of which they are not yet consciously aware.

(See also: Court; Doctor; Hospital; Schoolteacher; University)

Execution The images in this dream will, in most cases, depend upon what the dreamer has read, or seen in illustrations or in films. Of these the commonest are likely to be of a beheading, either by the axe on a sixteenth- or seventeenth-

century scaffold, or by guillotine in the time after the French Revolution.

Was the dreamer watching an execution, or about to be executed? In either case, they should probably be identified with the victim. They may feel guilt or disgust at something they have done, and consider themselves worthy of punishment. Or there may be some aspect of their life that they feel should be ruthlessly cut off.

It should be remembered, however, that the word 'execution' can also mean the successful completion of a task.

(See also: Beheading; Cart)

A French print depicting the execution, by guillotine, of Marie Antoinette at the Place de la Revolution.

Explosion See Bomb; Volcano

Failure Some dreams are suffused with the depressing feeling that one has failed, without any details being apparent. Others can be more specific, and often relate to anxiety about some coming event. However, even an unspecific sense of failure generally arises from some event in waking life. The only solution is to determine what the problem is, and try to recover self-confidence by recalling past successes.

Falling Dreams of falling from a height are common, and frequently occur during the first stage of sleep. They may also be related to dreams of failure, or the feeling that one has 'fallen from grace'.
(See also: Abyss; Cliff; Descent; Flying)

Fighting It is quite common to dream of fighting, and the dreamer often awakes while dealing a physical blow. This is a reference

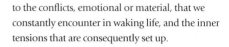

to the conflicts, emotional or material, that we constantly encounter in waking life, and the inner tensions that are consequently set up.

Fishing Traditionally, fish represent the thoughts swimming in the water of the mind. Trying to catch a fish, therefore, can symbolise the attempt to seize on a particular concept. In a more general sense, it can represent an exploration – but perhaps rather trivial – of the inner depths.

On the other hand, if the dreamer is an angler, the activity may be associated with peaceful relaxation; alternatively, it may reflect the exhilarating contest with a fighting fish. Losing the fish could be an omen of disappointments to come.

Floating Is the dreamer floating in the air, a free spirit, or in water, drifting through the unconscious?
(See also Flying; Swimming pool; Umbrella; Water)

Flying This is a rather common dream. Freud (naturally) identified flying with sex, while Jung, more generally, thought it symbolised the desire to break free from all kinds of restrictions.

Flying in a dream can take many different forms. The dreamer may be soaring high, and possibly even identify with a bird (and here the species of bird may be significant), or swoop low over the ground. The flight may be free, or aboard an aircraft.

If the dreamer is looking down at the landscape below, he or she may be surveying the whole of their life. In this context, the influential Austrian psychologist Alfred Adler thought that flying symbolised the desire to dominate others. The nature of the landscape can also be important to understanding the dream's significance.

The overwhelming sensation may be one of unfettered freedom, or it may be touched with a fear of falling. It is said that older people dream more often of flying, and this may reflect their consciousness of the many responsibilities that keep them 'down to earth', and their desire to be free of them.

(See also: Aeroplane; Balloon; Bird; Falling)

Game Even in their most informal aspect, games have a ritual nature, and may represent a ceremony of a more serious kind. The type of game is also significant: did it involve athletic skills on the open field; was it an indoor sport such as table tennis or billiards; or was it a table game? And in its Freudian implications, a game can frequently represent sexual activity.

(See also: Ball; Club)

Giving A dream that one is making a gift to someone can have a rather perverse significance. The gift often represents something that the dreamer wishes to give, but not something that the other person needs or wants; it may even be something they actively dislike. This dream arises from difficulties that the dreamer has with the other person, and the nature of the gift can reveal the cause of the conflict.

Government To dream of being a member of the government is a sign that one's life is firmly under control. At the same time, it is important to pay attention to the wishes of the opposition – a sudden change in fortune could find them in one's place.

(See also: Election; Parliament)

Grinding To dream of grinding spices, or the zest of a lemon, can be a pleasant experience, with both the smell and the suggestion of preparing good food. In a more general sense, however, it may signify the dreamer's sense of hard and unrewarded work; or perhaps some burden is like 'a millstone round the neck'?

(See also: Lemon; Machinery; Mill; Spice)

Gymnastics If the dreamer was performing gymnastic exercises, possibly in a gym, it can signify physical wellbeing or success at work. Or was this a punning dream about someone named Jim?

Seeing others performing difficult gymnastics can be a symbol of uncertainty about the outcome of one's plans.

(See also: Acrobat)

Hunting If the dreamer is searching for something, it is a sign that they are seeking fulfilment, either spiritual or physical.

On the other hand, if the dreamer is taking part in a hunt, it can indicate that he or she is trying to catch up, either with a person (perhaps to get the better of them) or with an elusive idea. Many people, in waking life, abhor the hunting of animals, whether with a gun or on horseback. If they are enjoying the dream hunt, this can symbolise the repression of their more animal instincts. If they are themselves being hunted, the species of animal they feel they represent can be significant.

(See also: Animal Kingdom; Chase; Searching)

Infidelity A dream of sexual infidelity may be no more than a piece of wish-fulfilment, but it is just as likely to represent a feeling of guilt about current relationships. On the other hand, it can be a symbol of losing one's religious faith, or denying some other long-held spiritual beliefs.

Initiation A solemn ceremony in which the dreamer is inducted into a sect, a secret society, or perhaps a primitive tribe. It symbolises some important advance that is about to take place in the dreamer's life: possibly something as mundane as a new job, but more likely a development in the personality or spiritual understanding.

Invisibility Children often long to be invisible – usually to enable them to spy on activities from which they are excluded, but sometimes to escape punishment. Dreaming that one is invisible may well be a resurfacing of this desire. In a similar sense, it can reflect a wish to escape from a coming confrontation in waking life, or to attract less attention.

If it is other people in the dream who are invisible, but whose presence is detected, they can symbolise something unattainable, probably spiritual.

(See also: Ghost; Spying)

Joke Often, a dreamer hears or makes a joke, and wakes laughing – but, on recollection, the joke seems quite unfunny. This can reflect a feeling that the dreamer is excluded from a particular social circle, or from some kind of esoteric knowledge.

Juggling See Acrobat; Clown; Conjurer

Jumping Dreams of taking great leaps, clearing hurdles, walls, even sailing clear over mountains, are all propitious omens. But if the dreamer was jumping up and down in one place it suggests that he or she was unable to develop the motivation to go forwards.

(See also: Falling; Flying)

Killing A dream of killing, usually by the dreamer of someone else, does not have

necessarily a negative, violent significance. It can frequently be a symbol of the need for the dreamer to 'kill off' some aspect of life or personality that is no longer required.

If the dreamer was killing an animal, it is important that the significance of the specific animal should be considered.

(See also: Animal Kingdom; Butcher; Hunting)

Kiss A kiss can have several different meanings. It can be romantic, and represent a fulfilment of the dreamer's desire. It can be the kiss of peace. Or it can be the kiss of betrayal. Whether the dreamer was giving the kiss or receiving it, the circumstances, and the dreamer's feelings about the gesture – all these have to be considered carefully before the symbolism becomes clear.

Knock A symbol of arrival, or an announcement of some kind – 'Fate knocks at the door'. Was the dreamer knocking on a door, desperate to get in or out? Possibly they were knocking on a table at a meeting, to maintain order, or to attract attention.
(See also: Door; Entrance; Platform)

Laughter See Joke

Leak A dream of a liquid leaking from a container of some kind can have a sexual connotation, but there are other interpretations. It may be a sign that someone in waking life has been indiscreet; or that money has unaccountably disappeared.

Limping It may be the dreamer who is limping, or an injured animal. In the first case, the dream symbolises a fear of being humiliated or degraded in some way. In the second, the nature of the animal will give a clue to the meaning of the dream.
(See also: Animal Kingdom)

Loneliness Particularly in waking dreams, the dreamer returns to consciousness with a sense of desolation and loss. This may refer to events of an earlier dream, as the dreamer realises that those events are unlikely to be recovered, or that another day of unrewarding labour must be faced.

Marriage Fundamentally, marriage represents the commitment of one person to another. Obviously, a dream of a marriage may be a matter of wish-fulfilment, or a reflection of envy – or relief – that someone else is about to commit themselves. On the other hand, it may signify taking up responsibility of a different kind.
(See also: Wedding)

Massage In the contemporary world, 'massage' has a clear sexual connotation. Whatever the circumstances, it remains an intensely sensual experience. A dream that one is being massaged, therefore, signifies that one feels the need for physical comfort and release.

Melting The change from a solid, rigid condition to a fluid, flexible state. Thawing snow and ice in springtime denote the arrival of the season of new growth. A dream of this kind can reflect the development of the personality from coldness to warmth, from fixed conventionality to new creativity.
(See also: Cold; Ice)

Operation If the dreamer was undergoing some kind of surgical procedure, it can be a sign that something in their life needs to be cut out or repaired. This may be a harmful aspect of their own personality, or a relationship with someone else. However, if the dreamer was the surgeon, the implication is that they are aware of subconscious problems and are working on them.
(See also: Doctor; Hospital)

Packing Packing a case for a journey, or preparing for a move to a new home, symbolises a major change in the dreamer's life.
(See also: Bag and baggage; Parcel)

Painting This dream can take two different forms. Painting a picture in oils or watercolours – if it is not one of the dreamer's usual activities – can signify the desire to make a major change in one's way of life: the picture may represent the very different situation that one hopes for. Painting as redecoration – of a room, of a piece of furniture, or some other object – can equally symbolise a wish for change, but it can alternatively represent the need to wipe out some unpleasant memory.

Paralysis See Immobility

Photography Although 'the camera cannot lie', a photograph is only a representation of a single moment of reality. Taking a photograph may represent the wish to fix a particular memory. On the other hand, because a photograph is not 'real', the implication may be that the dreamer is the victim of deception, either of him- or herself or at the instigation of an associate.

(See also: Camera)

Pregnancy Although this is predominantly a female dream, it is not uncommon for a man to dream that he is pregnant. For either sex, it can represent the gradual development of a concept that is not yet ready for expression. On the other hand, the dream may be due to no more than a heavy meal before bedtime.

Procession The procession may contain symbols that represent the course of the dreamer's life, or it may be a parade to celebrate an achievement – possibly of the dreamer's own. On the other hand, the dreamer may be merely a passive observer, seeing the life of others pass by, without being able to take part.

Protest See Demonstration

Puncture A symbol of deflation, possibly post-coital – and was there some concern about contraception? Alternatively, perhaps the dreamer feels 'let down' by somebody.

Punishment Whatever the punishment, and whatever its cause, this reflects feelings of guilt or shame. This is so even if it was someone else who was being punished, because they can usually be identified as a projection of the dreamer's self.

Pushing A complex symbol that can be interpreted in a variety of ways. The simplest explanation is that this represents a comforting sensation, a childhood memory of being pushed in a pram or on a swing. A rather more sophisticated interpretation relates directly to experience in waking life: the feeling that the dreamer is being subjected to pressures that he or she would like to resist, but cannot – they are being 'pushed around'. Finally, there is the possibility that the dreamer is 'pushed' for money.

(See also: Swinging)

Quarrel In a dream, a quarrel – no matter with whom – usually signifies an inner conflict, rather than a disagreement in waking life. The circumstances of the quarrel, and the arguments used to settle it, can provide guidance on how to resolve the problem.

Raid Was it a police raid, a raid by bandits, or an air raid? Or was the dreamer a member of the raiding party? In either case, the raid represents a sudden and unexpected event. If it was the dreamer suffering the raid, did he or she have something to hide? Or perhaps they were fearful of an attack on something they valued. On the other hand, if the dreamer was one of the raiders, the dream could symbolise an intention to use any possible means to get hold of something – an idea or a material advantage – that was important to them.

(See also: Pirate; Rape; Robbery)

Rape This is a very disturbing dream event that most commonly occurs among women, but is perhaps no less devastating when experienced by a man. In a few cases, it can be a perverse reflection of wish-fulfilment but, apart from any sexual connotations, it will represent a fear of a violent attack on the dreamer's beliefs, emotions or material wellbeing.

(See also: Robbery)

Rebirth and resurrection A dream of being born again, or raised from the dead, can symbolise the individual's desire to leave more material preoccupations behind, and enter a new phase of spiritual development.

(See also: Birth; Burial; Death)

Rescue Was the dreamer being rescued by someone else – in which case the identity of the rescuer is of prime importance – or were they the rescuer? Was the rescue from a pursuing animal – another important symbol – or from a different kind of danger? Remembering that the dreamer frequently identifies with the other person, this dream can represent the need to

extricate oneself from a potentially hazardous situation in waking life.

(See also: Animal Kingdom; Chase)

Robbery Was the dreamer robbed in the street, or at home? The circumstances are as significant as the robbery itself. In general, this dream is a sign that the dreamer is facing an identity crisis, or a loss of some kind in his or her life, such as a divorce or a serious illness.

(See also: Intruder; Raid)

Running A common dream event – but was the dreamer running from something, or towards a particular goal? The feeling of struggling ever onwards, and getting nowhere, probably reflects the conditions of the dreamer's waking life. Perhaps he or she should try to slow down.

(See also: Chase; Hunting)

Sailing Was it all 'plain sailing' for the dreamer, or a battle with stormy seas? The details of the dream may depend upon the dreamer's acquaintance with sailing boats. The dream may represent a desire to be more adventurous in life, a reflection of quiet pleasure, or a battle against overwhelming influences. In the latter context, the connection between water symbols and the archetypal Mother may be significant.
(See also: Boat; Ship; Water)

Sale A shop sale offers bargains that are not always what they seem to be. Was the dreamer satisfied with his or her purchases? Or did they turn out to be trash? The articles can represent ideas or beliefs t too easily acquired, and worth relatively little.

Alternatively, perhaps it was an auction sale. Did the dreamer feel that his or her beliefs and ideals were being 'knocked down' at less than their true value, and taken up by others who were insensitive to their worth? Or did he or she manage to obtain a real bargain, signifying that careful negotiation and knowledge would bring them success in a waking transaction?

On the other hand, it may be the dreamer who was selling – possibly getting rid of something that was no longer needed: a stage in his or her career, an outmoded belief, or even a partner. Or were they aware that they were selling themselves too cheaply in some waking situation?
(See also: Shop)

Searching A common dream event. It may, of course, merely reflect the dreamer's anxiety about something that has been lost or misplaced in waking life – even if the object being sought is different in the dream. On the other hand, the dream can refer to something that is lacking in the dreamer's emotional or spiritual life – maybe it is a matter of 'soul searching'.

Seesaw This may well be an example of the mind's word games, referring to something that appeared and then vanished – 'now you see it, now you don't'. On the other hand, it can be a reference to the perceived ups and downs of fortune.
(See also: Swinging)

Sewing If the dreamer was repairing clothing, this is a sign that something in waking life needs mending. Making clothes or other fabric articles is a creative act, and the symbolism of what was being sewn is important. Embroidery, in particular, is itself full of symbols, and may have the same significance as painting a picture.

For Freudians, however, the needle is an obvious sexual symbol.
(See also: individual articles of clothing; Needle; Painting)

Shooting See Arrow; Gun

Singing Although singing is customarily associated with joy, there are both happy songs and sad songs, lullabies and dirges. The kind of song may give a clue to the meaning of the dream, but it must be remembered that dreams sometimes go by opposites. Perhaps the dreamer was singing in a choir: if he or she was out of tune, it is a sign that they feel out of place in a particular waking situation.

Skating Flying across the ice, the skater experiences a freedom that is close to that of a bird in the air. But perhaps he or she was also skating over difficulties, paying them insufficient attention – possibly, even, 'skating on thin ice'. The ice itself, hard and cold, suggests that the dreamer has built an emotional barrier against matters that should be dealt with, in order to enjoy his or her freedom – and, in this context, the water below the ice can represent both the unconscious and the Jungian Mother.

(See; Bird; Ice; Water)

Smell The sense of smelling something in a dream is usually triggered by a real smell. Often, the smell will evoke memories of people or places; conversely, dreams that derive from these memories may conjure up the appropriate imaginary smell.

(See also: Senses)

Speechmaking See Election; Parliament; Platform

Spinning Not many people in the modern world dream of working a spinning-wheel, but this was a potent symbol in previous centuries. In ancient Greek mythology, the three Fates determined the course of human existence: Clotho spun the thread, Lachesis wove the web of the individual's life, and Atropos cut the thread to end it.

Nowadays, the dream is more likely to be of another type of spinning wheel, such as is used in table games or at a casino, perhaps of a spinning top, or even of the dreamer spinning round and round. This is a symbol of uncertainty, possibly about a task that must be undertaken. Or perhaps the dreamer has been 'spinning a yarn'.

(See also: Spider; Top)

Spying Was it the dreamer who was the spy, or did he or she feel that someone was spying on them? The dream may, of course, refer to something that the dreamer has recently read, or seen in a film, and much can depend upon how he or she felt about the hero or villain of the piece. On the other hand, this may be a direct reference to a situation in waking life.

Sting Something in the dreamer's waking life has caused, or is about to cause, a sudden and unforeseen hurt.

Strangulation Dreaming, and then waking, with the feeling that one was being strangled is a sure sign that something is preventing full expression of the true self. These may be powerful external forces, but they are just as likely to be repressive influences in the dreamer's own makeup. Even if the dream is of strangling someone else, this is one of those cases where the dreamer should identify with the other person.

Strike See Demonstration

Sucking One of the actions that the newborn child performs instinctively. In an adult dream, it suggests a feeling of insecurity and a desire for greater affection.

Swimming See Race; Swimming pool

Swinging A dream generally imbued with a sense of enjoyment, but also some degree of insecurity. Freud regarded this as a sexual symbol – particularly if the dreamer was being pushed by someone else. In this context, the modern use of the word 'swinger' to denote someone who engages freely in sex can be significant.

(See also: Fairground; Pushing; Seesaw)

Taste Most usually a waking sensation, but generally deriving from some deeper dream experience. Whether the taste was sweet, bitter, salt or acid, or just unpleasant, will relate to what has gone before.

(See also: Senses)

Tattoo A word with two very different meanings: a design pricked into the skin, or a dramatic military performance.

Historically, a tattooed design was a sign of initiation: it may represent a new development in the dreamer's life – and the design itself may have a significant symbolism. At the same time, the tattoo is something that is very difficult to remove. Is the dreamer aware of some ingrained habit that he or she is willing to give up, but is finding the task hard?

A military tattoo is an impressive event, often performed at night, with marching bands and sweeping lights. It can symbolise the desire to show off or, if the dreamer was a passive spectator, a sense that life is more enjoyable for others.

(See also: Initiation; Procession)

Tennis See Ball

Thirst A feeling of thirst in a dream can be due merely to physical causes. On the other hand, it may represent a desire for greater emotional or spiritual fulfilment.

Throwing What was the dreamer throwing? Or did someone else do the throwing? Was an object being thrown at a target, or was it being thrown away? This dream may symbolise the desire to get rid of a person, or some unwanted element, from one's life.

(See also: Ball)

Ventriloquism A symbol of alienation: by means of the dummy, the dreamer may be voicing thoughts and opinions that he or she is unaware of, or that they would not dare express openly. The dummy may seem to be uncontrollable, even sinister in its refusal to obey the dreamer's wishes:

this can be a sign that the dreamer is subconsciously affected by emotions that conflict with his or her practical desires.

(See also: Conjurer; Doll)

Visit See Guest

Voting See Election; Government; Parliament

War Even for those who have never fought, images of warfare are familiar from films and television. The conflict is likely to be within the dreamer's personality, or reflects a situation in waking life.

(See also: Army; Soldier; Uniform)

Wedding This dream may be a memory of past experience, a case of wish-fulfilment, or the anticipation of a coming event. However, a wedding can also represent the successful marriage of two different aspects of the dreamer's personality. The figures who played a part in the ceremony are also significant.

(See also: Altar; Church; Clergy; Marriage)

Wrestling In its simplest connotation, this dream can be sexual. On the other hand, it may concern a problem that the dreamer has to 'wrestle with'.

Or perhaps the dreamer was at a professional wrestling match. It is common knowledge that many (if not all) of these matches are carefully plotted, with a foregone conclusion. There is pleasure for many people in watching the performance, but the events – the cries of agony, the displays of temper, the eventual triumph of one wrestler over the other – are all faked. Was the dreamer subconsciously aware that, in waking life, a display of strength was being made to impress him or her, but that it was all show?

(See also: Fighting)

FOOD & DRINK

Whether they involve actual consumption, or merely the sight of food and drink, dreams of this kind can have a variety of meanings. They can be triggered by real hunger or thirst: the dreamer may have missed a meal or drunk nothing for some hours before going to bed, or he or she may be on a restrictive diet that evokes cravings for forbidden foods.

On the other hand, there is a distinct sexual connotation, particularly in dreams of food. This can be the result of the dreamer converting sexual desire, which he or she possibly finds embarrassing, into a different physical appetite. In waking life, preparing food often expresses love for someone, and this can carry over into dreams.

Finally, both food and drink can represent spiritual nourishment.

Many of the individual ingredients of food – specific fruit and vegetables and animals used for food – will be found in the Plant Kingdom and Animal Kingdom respectively.

Acid There are many different acids, and not all are dangerous. Hydrochloric acid, for example, is an essential constituent of the digestive juices of the stomach; citric acid is found in lemon juice; and acetic acid is the principal constituent of vinegar. However, all these – and others – have the typical acid taste, and to dream of drinking anything notably acidic is a sign of coming troubles. For a woman, this can mean compromising situations or even ill health.
(See also: Bitterness; Senses)

Bacon Traditionally, a dream of eating bacon is a good sign, particularly if the dreamer is with another person; and frying bacon is a portent of receiving an unexpected gift.

Baking This remains a powerful symbol for women, and it is undoubtedly connected with conception. Detailed market research has revealed

that women are more likely to buy cake-mix shortly before menstruation – and it is no coincidence that pregnancy is popularly described as having 'a bun in the oven'.

(See also: Cooking; Kitchen)

Banquet See Feast

Bitterness Tasting something bitter represents the necessity to undertake an unpleasant task. It can also suggest that resolving a difficulty will require an immoral act, giving way to compulsive feelings, or quarrels with others.

(See also: Acid; Ammonia; Senses)

Bread A universal symbol of nourishment, whether physical or spiritual. Stale or mouldy bread, therefore, signifies disappointment of one's expectations. Giving bread is an ancient symbol of hospitality.

(See also: Baking)

Butter The rich, creamy taste of butter makes it seem a luxury food, and sometimes it can be 'too much of a good thing'. Was the dreamer buttering bread, making it even more palatable? Were they put off by the sight of a dish swimming in too much butter?

Or were they aware of the necessity to 'butter someone up'?

Cake A symbol with a variety of different associations. Cakes are luxuries, traditionally produced on occasions of celebration. They are a reward for effort, yet that effort does not always seem so very great: we say that a task soon accomplished is 'a piece of cake'.

A cake can symbolise wealth: the saying 'you cannot have your cake and eat it' means that you cannot keep your money if you spend it. Sharing a cake with others can represent generosity. But a cake can also symbolise a promiscuous woman (a 'tart'); while a woman who dreams of baking a cake is possibly thinking of pregnancy.

(See also: Baking)

Champagne Dreaming of drinking champagne may be a sign that one needs more pleasure in life. On the other hand, it may be a warning that one is devoting too much time to enjoyment, perhaps being over-indulgent.

(See also: Bubble)

Cheese For centuries, eating cheese shortly before bedtime has been believed to result in night-mares –

achievements properly recognised, or it may be a warning against too much attention to selfish comforts. In ancient Mexico, chocolate had a religious significance, and it has also been considered an aphrodisiac. There may be sexual connotations, in which the colour of chocolate may also be important.

(See also: Brown)

Cooking A symbol of creativity. But the creativity may not be the dreamer's own: 'what's cooking?' we sometimes ask. If a woman dreams she is preparing a dish, and the result is a failure, it may be that she is questioning her maternal abilities.

(See also: Baking; Cake; Kitchen)

Drink The first source of human nourishment is the mother's breast or the baby's bottle, and so drinking may signify a desire to return to childhood. Water can represent the unconscious, and a thirst for water a desire to draw on what the unconscious has to offer – we speak of people having 'a thirst for knowledge'. Drinking alcohol can be a symbol of a thirst for pleasure, or of a desire to escape the cares of the world. Red wine is often a symbol for blood.

(See also: Blood; Milk; Water; Wine)

although in fact cheese, being already partly digested protein, is unlikely to be the cause. Dreaming of cheese, therefore, may be the prelude to a more unpleasant dream – which accords with the traditional interpretation.

There are other meanings to be considered, however: popular speech often describes an important person as a 'big cheese', while a minor disappointment that must be endured is known as 'hard cheese'. The dreamer should look to his or her waking life to discover what is referred to.

Chocolate For most people, chocolate is an indulgence and a reward. In a dream it may therefore represent the desire to have one's

Egg An egg can symbolise a number of different concepts. It can represent wholeness, and even the universe – the 'cosmic egg'. It can be a symbol of fertility, birth – and rebirth, which is its significance at Easter; and Freud considered the egg a male sexual symbol.

But for all its wholeness, an egg is easily broken. What emerges may still be fertile, it may even be a newly hatched chick, or it may be spilt upon the ground and wasted.

(See also: Basket; Bird; Nest)

Feast A feast is more than a big meal; it is a special occasion to bring people together to celebrate an important event. Was the dreamer helping to prepare the feast, laying the products of his or her creative abilities before the public? Or was he or she one of those attending, meeting old friends, making new ones: enjoying a cheerful social occasion that signifies a well-balanced position in the community? The special event being celebrated will also be significant.

At the same time, people tend to eat and drink too much at a feast. This dream may be a sign that the dreamer is too self-indulgent, demanding attention and comfort from family and friends.

(See also: Meal)

Honey Among the sweetest of all sweet things, honey has been a symbol of pleasure for thousands of years; while, as something that has to be stolen from the bees' nest, it can represent reward for achievement. However, many people find honey too sweet: perhaps there is someone whom the dreamer finds too attentive, or whose affection is cloying?

(See also: Bee)

Hunger The dream may be no more than the realisation

that one has not eaten well before retiring to bed, but it can also indicate a need for greater affection, and the importance of expressing one's emotions more openly.

Jam Like honey, jam is very sweet, and it can have a similar connotation. A dream of making jam may have a connection with the specific fruit being used, or it may be a more precise aspect of cooking in general.

Alternatively, a dream about jam may be an example of the mind's ability to produce punning symbols. Perhaps the dreamer is in a difficult situation – a 'jam' – in waking life, or worrying about some appliance that has jammed.

(See also: individual fruits; Cooking; Honey)

Jelly Jelly is principally a childhood food, and this dream may reflect a desire to escape present-day cares and return to the happier days of infancy. On the other hand, jelly is an amorphous substance, which assumes the shape of the mould in which it is made. Could it suggest that the dreamer – or an acquaintance – is too ready to adopt the opinions and beliefs of others? In this context, too, jelly is wobbly, and easily broken up: in a situation they are unable to control, people often speak of being 'turned to jelly'.

Juice The essential extract of a fruit or vegetable. In this sense, juice will usually have a sexual symbolism. It may be leaking, perhaps staining something; it may be being extracted by squeezing; or it may be drunk – that is, taken into the body.

(See also: individual fruits; Drink; Leak)

Meal Sharing a meal with one other person is said to represent the desire to have sexual relations with them. Those who have seen the 1963 film *Tom Jones* will remember the intense sexual excitement built up during the scene in which the hero shares a meal with the woman he is seducing.

(See also: Feast)

Meat In dreams, meat symbolises the carnal instincts. The kind of meat being eaten reflects the attributes of the animal from which it comes – beef, for instance, is said to represent strength and sexual aggression, while chicken represents timidity.

(See also: Animal Kingdom; Butcher; Meal)

Menu Scanning the menu in a dream restaurant need not represent the intention to have a meal. The list of dishes may symbolise the attitudes and plans of the dreamer, and some of them may be found to be 'off'. The relative cost of the dishes may also be significant.

(See also: Meal; Restaurant)

Milk As the only nourishment given to a baby in its early days, milk can symbolise a desire to return to infancy. For a woman, it often represents the maternal instinct: pouring a glass of milk for someone can be a symbol of the strength and support she can give them.

On the other hand, Freudians identify milk with semen. A man drinking milk, therefore, signifies his need to maintain his masculinity.

(See also: Drink)

Pasta Pasta comes in a very wide variety of forms, and it is most likely the specific shape that has symbolic significance. Spaghetti, for example, may evoke the image of worms – while the difficulty of disentangling it can represent emotional problems, or a host of minor problems in waking life.

(See also: Entanglement; Worm)

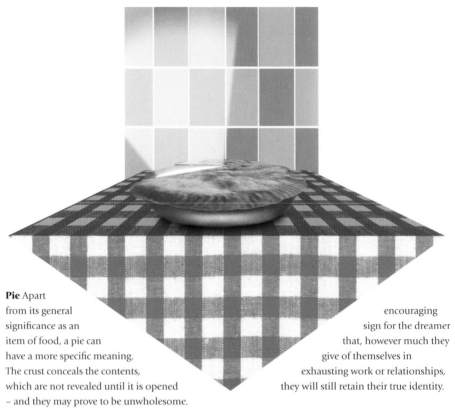

Pie Apart from its general significance as an item of food, a pie can have a more specific meaning. The crust conceals the contents, which are not revealed until it is opened – and they may prove to be unwholesome. This may be a warning that waking events may not be all that they seem: 'pie in the sky' is a promise of good things that never arrive.

Pudding The description 'pudding' is sometimes applied to people who are too plump. Perhaps the dreamer is conscious of this – and dreaming of eating a pudding will almost certainly reinforce this feeling. Finding money or trinkets hidden in a pudding is a portent of unexpected good things to come.

Rock A stick of seaside rock is an obvious phallic symbol. But it could have another meaning: however much is bitten away, the name remains still legible inside the stick. Perhaps this is an encouraging sign for the dreamer that, however much they give of themselves in exhausting work or relationships, they will still retain their true identity.

Salt Salt enhances the flavour and piquancy of food, but too much will make it unpalatable: it can symbolise the pleasure to be had from everyday life, but warn against over-indulgence. In alchemy, salt represented fixity and solidity, and the dream symbol may represent someone who is 'the salt of the earth' – steadfast and reliable. On the other hand, the dreamer may be reminded of 'rubbing salt in the wound'.

Spice Spices add flavour and excitement to food – perhaps this dream is a reference to 'the spice of life'? But too much spice – particularly pepper or curry powder – can be unpleasant, and this may be a warning to go easy in matters of enjoyment. *(See also: Grinding)*

Stew A stew is a relatively simple dish to make – and useful, in that it can combine a number of ingredients that are individually in short supply. Possibly the dreamer is aware that he or she has a number of skills that – although insufficiently developed to be employed each on their own – combine to make them successful in their profession. Or was the dreamer 'in a stew' about an irritating problem in waking life?

Sugar See Honey

Tea In many communities, the act of serving tea has the status of a social ritual. Particularly in Britain, a cup of tea is regarded as the outstanding symbol of refreshment. Was the dreamer taking a well-earned break, restoring his or her energies before going back to work? Or was the dream of a tea party, where everybody was expected to be on their best behaviour? This dream can have something to say about the way the individual regards his or her position in society.

Alternatively, the dream may be a reference to minor problems that will soon be resolved – a 'storm in a teacup'.

Wine Red wine is a widespread symbol for blood and sacrifice. Alternatively, dreaming of drinking wine can mean that one is gaining valuable emotional experience in waking life. Bottles of wine can represent people whom the dreamer regards as more mature, and who can give him or her knowledgeable advice.
(See also: Blood; Drink; Red)

On the eve of his crucifixion, Christ and his apostles partook of one last meal together – the Last Supper, one of the most powerful and resonant images to link wine with blood sacrifice.

TRAVEL & VEHICLES

The view of an individual's career as a journey through life is a common one, and it is not surprising that many dream symbols represent a part of that journey. Most of these will refer to past or present events, but some will reflect hopes and desires for the future – or even events that are to come. And, as Robert Louis Stevenson wrote: 'to travel hopefully is a better thing than to arrive.'

Abroad To dream that one is abroad is common enough, particularly given the number of people who take holidays in foreign countries, and it may be no more than the anticipation or memory of such a holiday. However, in the absence of such an influence, a dream of going abroad may mean that there is going to be a change in the place of work, or at the very least that the dreamer will shortly take a pleasant journey with friends.

On the other hand, to dream of being abroad signifies that matters are unsettled; returning from abroad means that present conditions will shortly change.

Aeroplane The aeroplane provides a relatively quick and easy way of moving from one culture to another, and a dream of an air journey may signify the desire to reach the conclusion of some matter, without having to pay attention to details on the way there. The flight itself can symbolise a wish to escape from down-to-earth ideas, and give the imagination a free rein.

(See also: Accident; Balloon; Flying)

Bicycle See Riding

Boat A boat floats on water, the symbol of the archetypal Mother; it is also hollow, and so represents a woman – and yet, in the way it pushes through the water, it can equally represent the penis. The interpretation of a dream involving a boat is therefore complex, and attention must be paid to surrounding circumstances.

A voyage in a boat reflects the dreamer's journey through life, and the water may be calm or stormy. Setting off on a voyage represents a break with family, and coming ashore symbolises the end of an ordeal. Being becalmed or stranded is a sign of idleness or laziness, and can prove more dangerous even than a violent storm. If the boat is leaking, there is likely to be a relationship that needs 'patching up'.

(See also: Sailing; Ship; Water)

Bus A journey in a bus represents a relatively short phase of the dreamer's life. It may, for instance, symbolise the necessity to 'get along' with other people. Alternatively, the bus can be merely a stage between two other dreams, without a particular significance of its own.

Missing the bus has an obvious meaning. The dreamer may be over-tired, unable to keep up. Or perhaps they are unable to fit their plans to the demanding schedules of waking life. Getting on the wrong bus is a sign of conflicting desires.

Being unable to pay the fare suggests that the dreamer is paying

insufficient attention to the practical, apparently trivial, aspects of everyday life.

(See also: Car)

Car Although cars are driven equally by men and women, they are still thought of as a 'man's toy'. In male dreams, a car frequently symbolises a woman, and represents the man's desire to exercise his sexual drive.

If there is something wrong with the car, the dreamer – man or woman – may be suffering from physical illness or mental worry. If the brakes or steering fail, it is a sign of lack of control in some waking situation, and an overloaded car means that the dreamer has taken on more responsibilities than he or she can manage.

Traffic accidents and violations can also symbolise lack of control, often with a sexual significance. A woman who dreams of being run down by a car is fearful of sex, possibly of rape.

(See also: Garage; Horse; Motorcycle; Truck)

Cart The cart may be a farm cart – perhaps a recollection of happy times in childhood, or a

realisation of heavy labour to come. Or it may be a symbol of threatening disaster, like the tumbril that carried doomed aristocrats to the guillotine after the French Revolution. People who are in trouble, and destined for punishment, are said to be 'in the cart'.

(See also: Execution)

Cruise A cruise ship is intended to be a floating palace of pleasure. As a dream symbol, a cruise represents the dreamer's desire for rest and relaxation, leaving the work and navigation to others and drifting comfortably through the warm seas – and minor storms – of life.

(See also: Ocean; Ship; Storm)

Engine Biologists often compare the living body to a machine, and the engine is its driving force: the energy of physical vitality and sexual impulses. The condition of an engine in a dream can therefore be a sign of the dreamer's physical state. If it is running smoothly, all is well; but perhaps it needs servicing – by sessions at a gym, a visit to a medical practitioner, or more regular sex. If the engine will not start, it is a sign that the dreamer is reluctant to embark on a new project or emotional commitment.

(See also: Car; Garage; Machinery)

Ferryboat There are two very different connotations in this dream symbol. In most cases, it is likely to be seen as only a very temporary journey across water between one piece of dry land and another. So, in this sense, it can represent an important change in the circumstances of one's life.

However, the Greek and Roman concept of the ferryman Charon, who carried the dead across the river Styx to the underworld, must also be borne in mind. This can symbolise death, but also a journey into the depths of one's soul in search of spiritual truth.

(See also: Boat; Death; Ship; Water)

Flight See Aeroplane; Flying

Journey Some dreams seem to last for ever, and going on a long journey can represent a review of the dreamer's life, particular incidents along the

way symbolising key episodes in it. Alternatively, the dream may represent a specific undertaking, intellectual or spiritual, that the dreamer is contemplating. Was the destination in sight, perhaps even reached? If so, this is obviously an excellent omen. But if the way was set with obstacles, which the dreamer despaired of overcoming, it is a sign that he or she is not yet ready for the project.

The individual events that occur during the journey each have a specific symbolism and should be considered carefully in turn.

Lorry See Truck

Journeys often represent new beginnings. It is fitting, then, that Christianity itself began with the journey of the Magi, who travelled to bestow gifts on the newborn Saviour.

Luggage See Bag and baggage

Motorcycle Even in waking life, the motorcycle is considered a phallic symbol. As a powerful means of transport that needs care and control, it can be thought of as the modern equivalent of the horse, but it also represents exhibitionism and danger.

(See also: Horse; Riding)

Overtaking A symbol of the dreamer 'getting ahead' and 'taking over' control of his or her position in life. Being overtaken by another driver, however, represents the reverse.

Passport An important – and often essential – statement of the identity of the individual. Examination of the passport at a frontier can symbolise the questions that the dreamer is asking himself or herself in moving from one stage of life to the next.

(See also: Identity)

Railway See Line; Railway station; Train; Tunnel

Riding A dream symbol that almost always has the connotation of sexual intercourse – whether it was a horse or other animal, a bicycle or a motorcycle that was ridden. Riding implies control and mastery, and the harness or the handlebars can represent the exertion of the conscious will.

At the same time, a bicycle, in particular, can be a symbol of adolescent sexuality, and some writers identify riding with masturbation.

(See also: Horse; Motorcycle)

Ship Although it has many of the connotations of a boat, a ship is very much larger, and the passengers have no control over its navigation, which they must leave to others. A voyage aboard ship may represent the whole of an individual's life, or only a part of it: it may be a journey from one place to another, or a cruise that eventually returns to the port of departure.

The events of the voyage – calm seas, storms, even shipwreck – can reflect the conditions of the dreamer's waking life; and 'going off to sea' may represent a break with the family or a change of employment.

(See also: Boat; Cruise; Ferryboat; Storm; Water)

Train The train, driving powerfully ahead along its determined track, is a symbol of vigour and confident ambition in the dreamer. In this context, a dream train may also be an example of the mind's word play, suggesting that the dreamer should 'train' – either physically, in order to be fit to continue his or her career, or to gain further experience for the job in hand.

Events affecting the train – such as derailment, being held up at signals or switched to another track – can mirror developments in the dreamer's waking life.

(See also: Bridge; Lamp; Line; Railway station; Tunnel)

Truck A dream symbol that is related to the car, but implies a greater degree of skill and responsibility. The contents of the truck will also have a specific significance.

On the other hand, this may be one of the mind's word games: could it be that the dreamer wants to 'have no truck' with some annoying individual?

(See also: Car; Garage)

Wagon A dream symbol that probably has the same connotation as a cart – although it may be a suggestion that the dreamer should be 'on the wagon'.

(See also: Cart)

ANIMAL KINGDOM

For Jung and his followers, dreams of animals were directly connected with the 'animal vitality' of the dreamer, whether the sexual instincts of the body, or the lower, 'bestial', aspects of the unconscious. Taming or harnessing animals, for instance, is regarded as an attempt on the part of the dreamer to control his or her instincts, making them usefully constructive. Killing an animal, on the other hand, is destructive, representing an unhealthy repression of instincts. And trying to find a refuge from animals signifies a struggle with one's instincts.

Albatross In Samuel Taylor Coleridge's *Rime of the Ancient Mariner*, it was the shooting of an albatross that brought misfortune on a ship's crew:

> *Instead of the Cross, the Albatross*
> *About my neck was hung.*

According to traditional dream dictionaries, however, the shooting of an albatross is a sign that the dreamer – like, indeed, the Ancient Mariner – will eventually escape from present peril. To see an albatross can be a sign that good news will be received from a stranger – but it can also be a warning not to lend money to others.

Alligator or crocodile Traditionally, this is a symbol of great danger ahead. It is a sign that the dreamer is surrounded by enemies, and even the closest friends may deceive him or her. The creature must be killed, but even then it is necessary to proceed with caution. However, a dream of wearing the skin, as a jacket, shoes, or even a handbag, is a sign that the difficulties will be overcome.

Bat Bats are traditionally associated with evil; most people find them ugly – and terrifying. A dream of a bat is not a good omen, and even less so if there are many of them. They represent

troubles and sorrows, and, traditionally, the extraordinary sight of a white bat can portend the sickness, and possible death, of a child.

Bear For many centuries, particularly among the Celtic peoples, the bear was the symbol of a great military leader. At the same time, the female bear can represent the mother – one who 'bears' children and guards them jealously. Traditionally, therefore, the dream of a bear can be a sign of domination that must be struggled against.

On the other hand, the mind may be playing

word games here. Possibly the animal symbolises burdens that are 'hard to bear'; or does it indicate something that must be exposed – 'laid bare'?

Bee Busy from dawn to dusk, bees are a symbol of industriousness and organised activity. However, they may also be a sign that the dreamer is devoting too much time to matters that are not as important as they seem – we speak of having 'a bee in one's bonnet'.

But bees, with their painful sting, can also be dangerous, particularly when they are swarming. Traditionally, to dream of a swarm of bees is a warning that fire could break out in the home.
(See also: Insect; Sting)

Beetle See Insect

Bird The Romans placed great importance on the behaviour of birds in flight: People called auspicers were appointed to divine the omens of the birds' movements – and it is from this that we get the word 'auspicious'. With their freedom to move in all directions through the air, birds can represent the imagination – the 'flights of fancy' – as well as aspiration and the spiritual soul.

The type of bird is, of course, significant, and so is its behaviour. Some birds are menacing; others are domestic and comforting; some are outstandingly beautiful, but aloof. Was it a single bird, or a flock? Was the dreamer being attacked? Did the birds seem oblivious of human presence; or were they in full flight, wheeling high in the sky?

Where was the bird, and what was its condition? A caged bird frequently represents the dreamer or a close companion. On the other hand, a bird enjoying its full freedom may reveal that the dreamer is envious of that ability.
(See also: individual birds)

Blackbird Traditionally, the blackbird is a symbol of misfortune; and the sound of blackbirds singing is a sign of more than one marriage to come.

Boar In many of the ancient myths of life and death, a god was killed by a wild boar, and his body thrown into a river; in due course, he was resurrected. This myth represented the cycle of the seasons. A dream of a wild boar, therefore, may be a surfacing of this atavistic symbol.

On the other hand, the boar can reflect archetypal masculinity: the phallus, brute strength and unthinking destructiveness – and in this context the mind may also be playing one of its word games, and signifying 'boor'. For a woman to dream of a boar is a sign of the negative aspect of the Animus. She may be trying to avoid confrontation with an important problem that must be faced.
(See also: Pig)

Bull This is a powerful symbol, but a confusing one. At the more obvious level, the bull represents male sexual passion and creative power, or, in its negative aspects, obstinacy and brute rage. However, the earliest pictorial representations of bulls are found in the cave paintings of Paleolithic times; and some researchers have suggested that here they symbolise the Animus in the female, the male element being represented by horses.

The significance of a bull in a dream must therefore be considered with care. Is it a sign of creativity, of 'bullheadedness', or 'bullish' confidence? Or, particularly in the case of a woman's dream, is it a surfacing of one of the earliest of archetypal symbols? Some traditional dream dictionaries say that for a woman to dream of a bull means that 'she will have an offer of marriage, but, by declining this offer, she will better her fortune'.

Was the bull dangerous and frightening, and did it chase the dreamer? Or was it untypically gentle? Both of these aspects can have obvious sexual significance, but they can equally relate to circumstances in the dreamer's relationships with superiors at work.

In astrology, the sign of Taurus the bull is associated with the throat. It is possible that the dreamer is about to suffer, or is recovering from, an attack of laryngitis, or some similar infection. *(See also: Cow; Horse; Ox)*

Butterfly Butterflies are beautiful and, like birds, free to move at will through the air – and their movements, indeed, are lighter even than birds'. They can represent the fleeting nature of thought, and the difficulty of pinning it down. Butterflies can also symbolise frivolity: perhaps the dreamer is being too trivial or flirtatious. And the metamorphosis of a slow-moving and unattractive caterpillar, through an apparently lifeless chrysalis, to a thing of beauty, can suggest that the dreamer should throw off old habits, and set the spirit free. *(See also: Bird; Insect)*

Chicken Chickens are kept for a practical purpose: birds that do not fly, they can represent the submission of the imagination to useful ends. Their eggs can symbolise concepts that must be nurtured in the hope of future development.

Alternatively, there may be a reference to some situation that the dreamer has 'chickened out of'. *(See also: Cock; Egg; Farm)*

Cock The cock is the bird that greets the first rays of dawn and, like a bell, it may be a symbol that occurs just before the dreamer wakes. In much the same way, it can also signify that the individual

should 'wake up' to their potential. Alternatively, it may portend the arrival of news.

In other connotations, the cock is an obvious sexual symbol. So, in a related sense, it may signify an over-confident, 'cocky', young man.

On the other hand, in Chinese astrology, the cock is associated with critical tendencies and efficiency, but also tactlessness.

Cow Since very ancient times, the cow has been a symbol of maternal care and nourishment. In Egyptian mythology, Nut the goddess of heaven,

the female half of the pair who created the cosmos, was often referred to as the 'holy cow'. For reasons such as this, the cow should not be thought of as the opposite of the bull, but rather as representing gentler aspects of the same attributes.

All the same, a cow in a dream may stand for the dreamer's mother. On a more abstract level, it can represent the fertility and richness of the dreamer's emotional life; and a grazing herd of contented cows portends prosperity and wellbeing.

(See also: Bull; Farm; Ox)

Crab A strange and disturbing dream symbol. With its hard shell and menacing claws, the crab can be a threat that is difficult to deal with. As it scuttles sideways, shifting its ground, it is like an adversary in an argument who cannot be pinned down.

In astrology, Cancer the crab is associated with stomach troubles and 'watery' diseases such as pleurisy and dropsy. Perhaps the dreamer is subconsciously aware of a disorder of this kind that has not yet developed.

Crocodile See Alligator

Crow and raven Like many other bird and animal dream symbols, crows and ravens can have a number of different meanings. These black birds may be considered harbingers of doom and death, but they can also represent good fortune. At the Tower of London, for example, it is said that, as long as ravens stay in the grounds, the city will remain standing.

Both types of bird have been credited with wisdom and understanding, and of being in touch with the gods. The Scandinavian god Odin had two pet ravens, which brought him details of what

was going on in the world. They were identified with thought and memory, and represented the mind's ability to gather information, as in a dream or a trance.

(See also: Bird)

Cuckoo In folklore, the call of the cuckoo is a signal of deceit in marriage. In popular speech, someone who is concerned with ideas that do not seem to make sense is often said to be 'cuckoo'. Either of these concepts may be signified in the dream.

Alternatively, the cuckoo may be a sign that the dreamer is intruding in an unwelcome way on other people – 'a cuckoo in the nest'.

Deer Deer are graceful creatures, fleet of foot, and able to clear many obstacles in their path. They may represent the dreamer's aspirations, free to roam at will, but perhaps constantly escaping out of reach. At the same time, deer are symbols of gentleness, and this may be an example of the word games played by the mind, recalling someone who is 'dear' to the dreamer.

(See also: Stag)

Dog 'Man's best friend' can be a dream symbol full of different meanings. Like all animals, the dog can represent the dreamer's animal nature, but it can also be affected by their feelings about dogs in particular. In popular speech, the dog can suffer, or enjoy, a wide variety of treatments. One can be 'dog tired', suffer 'a dog's life', or 'go to the dogs'. One can be 'top dog', or 'run with the pack'; persistence is called 'doggedness', and one can be 'faithful as a dog'. Any one, or more than one, of these meanings can be reflected in a dream.

Then, too, there are guard dogs, including those that traditionally guard the underworld. Is the animal fierce or friendly? Rarely, the individual may dream that he or she is actually a dog. This is likely to say more about their personal attitude to dogs, but the dream can also reflect their feelings about the way in which others treat them.

For those familiar with Chinese astrology, the years of the dog are associated with open-mindedness and a desire for justice.

Dolphin The dolphin is believed to be one of the most intelligent of mammals. It is considered a friend to humans, and is credited with saving the lives of drowning people. In this sense it may represent a rescuer.

As aquatic mammals, dolphins may symbolise the interaction between air and water, representing our conscious and unconscious selves. They may be carriers of messages between these two halves of the self; or, in their connection with water, they may have something to communicate about sexuality.

(See also: Water; Whale)

Dove The dove is an international symbol of peace and love; it can also represent the human spirit – more particularly, for Jungians, the Anima. The sound of a dove can signify contentment, but it can also be mournful, and portend the death of a loved one. Flying doves can have the same meaning as other birds, and represent freedom of thoughts and feelings.

(See also: Bird)

Dragon An ancient and potent symbol, and one that has very different connotations in the West from those in the East. In the West, a dragon has similar meaning to a serpent: it is fierce and devouring, guarding treasure or a beautiful maiden, who must be saved by a bold rescuer, symbolising the struggle between the noble and ignoble aspects of the self. On a more mundane level, a dragon could represent an interfering mother-in-law!

In the East, dragons are also guardians, of the cardinal points of the compass, but they are considered wise creatures of the air. If the dreamer is familiar with Chinese philosophy, this meaning may be the predominant one. And, in Chinese astrology, the dragon represents energy, passion and boldness.

(See also: Cave; Lizard; Snake)

Duck Ducks live on the water, and dive beneath it, searching this symbol of the unconscious for nourishment. A flight of ducks makes a 'V' in the sky, and this may be the mind's reminder of something beginning with this letter.

(See also: Bird)

Eagle For many centuries the eagle has been a symbol of power and leadership. Because it flies so high, it has been associated with the sun; and, like other birds of prey, it has excellent sight. These noble attributes may be combined, however, in the symbolism of a very commonplace dream – could the eagle represent a sharp-sighted and inquisitive superior at work?

Another ancient symbol is the eagle with a serpent in its claws. This can be read as the higher aspects of the mind struggling with – and, hopefully, subduing – the physical instincts.

(See also: Bird; Snake)

Elephant The elephant is characterised by its size, its immense strength, and by the popular belief that it 'never forgets'. For many centuries, particularly in the Far East, it has also been associated with princely power.

If the dreamer was riding the elephant, it is a sign of being in control, rising above material worries. But perhaps the animal was trampling down everything in its path, signifying that the rider was either exercising too much power, or had lost control.

Elephants seen in the wild can represent different aspects: the threatening bull, with his raised trunk (a phallic symbol), or the herd instinct and mothering care of the females. They can also be reminders of matters that must be remembered in waking life.

Fish Fish, seeming to flicker as they appear and disappear in the water, symbolise unconscious thoughts. They are also coldblooded and phallic in form, and may represent impotence – we refer to someone who does not relate readily to others as 'a cold fish', or 'a fish out of water'.

In astrology, the sign Pisces is said to govern the feet. A dream of fish may therefore refer to foot trouble – or perhaps even a foot fetish.

(See also: Fishing; Foot)

Fox A symbol of craftiness and cunning. Dreams of hunting a fox may reflect beliefs about hunting firmly held by the dreamer in waking life; but, since dreams can go by opposites, they may reveal some deeply repressed instinct.

(See also: Hunting)

Frog The frog's association with water can mean that it is a symbol of the unconscious. However, the way in which it metamorphoses from a swimming tadpole into a hopping land animal suggests transformation, either material or spiritual. In this context, a woman who dreams of a frog may be evoking memories of the story of the frog who turned into a prince, and predicting marriage or some change in her married state.

(See also: Toad)

Goat The appearance of a goat in a dream has a variety of meanings. It is traditionally a symbol of lechery, in its resemblance to the ancient god Pan (the giver of fertility). 'Separating the sheep from the goats' signifies making a clear distinction between two groups of people.

A goat is also famously nimble, able to climb to the top of the steepest mountain, and so represents the ability to overcome daunting obstacles. On the other hand, a tethered goat may be bait to lure a ferocious beast into a trap – perhaps the dreamer is being set up as the innocent victim in a conspiracy, a 'scapegoat'. Finally, the goat may be a sign of inner rage, as in 'getting one's goat'.

In astrology, Capricorn the sea-goat is said to govern the knees. Those born with the sun in this sign are thought to be subject to much ill health, and the dream may have something to say about leg troubles.

Goose A goose can be of two different kinds: the farmyard bird, or the free-flying wild species. In the first case, it can have the significance of other farm animals, or it may be a reminder that the dreamer has been 'a silly goose'. In the second case, it will be a symbol similar to other birds, but with the additional connotations of cold and ice.

Like ducks, geese also fly in a 'V' formation. So a dream of a skein of geese in flight can be a reminder of something beginning with this letter.

(See also: Bird; Duck; Farm)

Hare In many popular myths in different parts of the world, the hare is renowned as a 'trickster', a wily individual responsible for the misfortunes that can befall human beings. The hare is also famous for its 'mad' behaviour at springtime. A dream of a hare can be a sign that one would rather not take responsibility for events, and prefer to attribute them to the irrationality of fate.

On the other hand, the sight of a hare may be a punning reference to 'hair'.

(See also: Conjurer; Hair; Rabbit)

Hawk Hawks can have much the same symbolism as eagles, but they lack the eagles' majesty, and are seen as fast-moving, predatory birds, often chasing their quarry low over the ground and in among the trees. To dream of being threatened by a hawk can be a sign of unforeseen danger.

(See also: Eagle)

Hen See Chicken

Horse A symbol of virility, positive energy, power and noble actions. Someone riding a horse is in a position of dominance over others, and in control of his or her life. A winged horse, like the animal Pegasus ridden by the mythical hero Bellerophon, is a symbol of poetic inspiration; but a horse harnessed to a cart or wagon signifies that its energy is being exploited for mercenary or utilitarian purposes.

If the dreamer is familiar with Chinese astrology, the horse can represent popularity, adventurousness, and cheerful sociability.

(See also: Bull; Horseshoe; Riding)

Insect With only a few exceptions, insects are regarded as unpleasant, 'creepy' and even repulsive, destroyers and infecters of food, clothing and plants, and generally 'dirty'. They symbolise something that 'bugs' the dreamer, and insects that sting or bite may represent the prick of conscience.

(See also: individual insects; Sting)

Kangaroo The kangaroo bounds along, clearing quite high obstacles with ease; and even while doing this, the female carries her young one in

her pouch. This can be a symbol of the mother, who seemed able to solve all difficulties when the dreamer was a child.

Lamb Ever since humans began to domesticate animals, the first-born lamb of spring has been a symbol of life renewed and its victory over death.

The baby lamb also represents innocence and gentleness. But there is a dark side to this symbolism. It was customary for that first-born lamb to be sacrificed as a thanksgiving for the end of winter, and we still speak of innocent, well-meaning people being 'led like a lamb to the slaughter'.

(See also: Farm; Ram; Sheep)

Lion The lion is popularly known as the 'king of beasts', and symbolises strength and fierceness, voracious appetite and unrestrained instincts. In the dream, the lion may have been docile and friendly: this can signify that the dreamer has proper control over his or her animal nature; or the beast may represent some powerful person in waking life with whom the dreamer is on good terms. On the other hand, if the lion was menacing, the indications are contrary.

If the dreamer identified with the lion, it is a sign that he or she is aware of the animal part of their personality, and should take care to keep it under control.

In astrology, those born with the sun in Leo are said to suffer trouble with the back or heart. The dream may refer to future problems that have not

yet manifested themselves.
(See also: Back)

Lizard The lizard is a slippery beast:
try to catch it by the tail, and it
escapes, leaving the useless tail in
one's hand. Perhaps the lizard
represents some concept that the dreamer
is trying unsuccessfully to seize upon.

Monkey The characteristic that is popularly
associated with the monkey is
mischievousness. This animal symbolises
the childish side of the dreamer's
personality, and possibly even represents
arrested development in some area.

Similarly, for a dreamer familiar with
Chinese astrology, the years of the monkey
are associated with charm and cleverness,
but a tendency to deceive.

Moth See Butterfly

Mouse A symbol of shyness and timidity,
which may reflect an aspect of the dreamer's
personality. Some people are frightened by
mice, and this could be a sign that small
problems in the dreamer's life are evoking fears
that are out of all proportion to their importance.
If the mice were nibbling away at food in store, it
can be an indication that other people are
insidiously undermining the individual's self-
esteem.

Nest A symbol for the home, or for home-making
urges. If young birds were leaving the nest, it can
be a reflection of children leaving the family
circle. On the other hand, perhaps the dreamer
was thinking about money – 'feathering one's
nest' or accumulating a 'nest egg'.

Dreams of the nests of other animals, as well as
birds, will have the significance of the specific
animal.
(See also: Bird; Egg)

Octopus A creature that can use its many arms to
entangle the dreamer and prevent movement.
This can symbolise any kind of clinging
relationship: an over-possessive parent or partner,
or the dreamer's own attitude to another person.
(See also: Entanglement)

Ostrich In popular myth, the ostrich buries its
head in the sand in the belief that this makes it

invisible. This bird symbolises that the dreamer is ignoring reality, and that he or she is in danger because of their attitude. On the other hand, if the ostrich was strutting, holding its head high, it can be a warning of undue self-confidence, even smugness.

(See also: Invisibility)

Ox A castrated bull, the ox is a symbol of docility and patient hard work. In Chinese astrology, the years of the ox are associated with similar characteristics.

(See also: Bull; Cow; Farm)

Oyster A bivalve closely associated, in most people's minds, with sexual activity. But within its closed shell there may be a pearl – of beauty, value or wisdom.

(See also: Pearl)

Parrot Parrots can be taught to speak, but they repeat only the words of others, without meaning to themselves. Did this dream refer to the dreamer, or reflect upon someone else's expressed statement – perhaps that of an 'official spokesperson'?

(See also: Bird)

Pig Commonly a symbol of ignorance, selfishness and gluttony. In everyday speech, a 'pig' is a person who eats too much, who behaves badly, or who lives in squalor. Did this represent one of the dreamer's acquaintances? Or had the dreamer been behaving badly towards another?

On the other hand, in Chinese astrology, the pig represents physical passion, honesty and consideration towards others.

(See also: Boar; Farm)

Pigeon See Dove

Rabbit When we speak of 'breeding like rabbits', we are acknowledging the animals' extraordinary fertility and, as a dream symbol, a rabbit may have a strong sexual significance. At the same time, the rabbit, like the hare, has a long-established association with trickery – and we describe a surprise development as appearing 'like a rabbit out of a hat'. It is possible that the dream could signal an unforeseen pregnancy – or (remembering the belief that a rabbit's foot is lucky) an unexpected but welcome, change in fortune.

However, for a dreamer who is familiar with Chinese astrology, the rabbit can be a symbol of artistic sensitivity and a generous nature.

(See also: Conjurer; Hare)

Ram The ram is a symbol of energy and aggressiveness. As the first sign of the zodiac, Aries the Ram marks the beginning of spring. Dreaming of a ram, therefore, may be connected with the need to embark on a new project with enthusiasm. But the ram's tendency to charge at anything in its way should be a warning against impulsiveness, or overbearing behaviour – 'ramming things home'.

In astrology, Aries is considered to govern the head and brain, and those born with the sun in this sign are said to be highly strung, although fundamentally healthy.

(See also: Sheep)

Rat Rats are associated with disease – with considerable justification: remember the rat-borne plague that devastated Europe in the Middle Ages. In this context, they can infest a house, a symbol for the body. The dream may be a warning of some physical deterioration that is not yet medically detectable.

Rats are also treacherous: we speak of 'rats deserting a sinking ship' (aware of the danger before anyone else), and describe a deceitful person as a 'dirty rat'. The dreamer should consider carefully whether he or she could be so described. On the other hand, a dream in which a rat is successfully despatched reveals that the dreamer is able to deal with a threatening situation.

However, if the dreamer is familiar with Chinese astrology, he or she may be aware that the years of the rat are associated with gregariousness, ambition and thriftiness.

Raven See Crow and raven

Scorpion A symbol of secretiveness and treachery. In the fable, the scorpion begged the frog to carry him across a river, and the frog made him promise not to sting. In the middle of the river, the scorpion stung the frog. 'Why did you do that?' asked the frog before he died, so drowning the scorpion. 'I couldn't help it,' said the scorpion, 'it's my nature.'

The dream probably refers to someone of the dreamer's acquaintance, but he or she should ask themselves whether it could possibly refer to them.

Alternatively, there may be a reference to astrological belief. Those born with the sun in Scorpio are said to be generally healthy, but with a tendency to have trouble with the sexual organs, the bladder or the kidneys.

Sheep Sheep are generally passive creatures that tend to stay together and follow their leader – and so often go astray. As a dream symbol, a sheep may suggest that the dreamer is not exercising his or her individuality; there may also be a warning against following the crowd. And perhaps the dreamer is feeling 'sheepish' about some foolish action. Or was it 'a wolf in sheep's clothing'?

On the other hand, in Chinese astrology, those born in the years of the sheep are kind and sensitive, artistic and highly emotional.

(See also: Lamb; Ram; Wolf)

Snake A very ancient symbol, with widespread connotations of sexuality and fertility. At the same time, because it lives underground, the snake has been attributed with arcane wisdom and the power of healing – as in the common medical symbol of two snakes twined about a rod.

As a result, the interpretation of a dream about snakes is complex. A snake can be frightening, representing threats and temptation, or a timid attitude towards sex. A 'snake in the grass' symbolises untrustworthiness or envy. And a terrifying monster snake, its jaws agape, can signify the fear of a descent into the depths of the unconscious.

On the other hand, a snake that does not appear threatening may be a symbol of spiritual healing and – because it sloughs its skin and so appears to possess the secret of eternal youth – renewal. A snake with its tail in its mouth – the ouroboros of the alchemists – is a symbol of cosmic completeness.

Chinese astrology combines both aspects of the snake: it represents strong sexuality, but also mystery and wisdom.

(See also: Dragon)

Spider The symbolism of the spider has three distinct aspects. They are its aggressiveness; its creativeness in weaving the intricate web; and the shape of the web itself, a spiral winding a continuous way to the centre, where the spider sits waiting. This represents the centre of the world, and in India the spider is regarded as Maya, 'the eternal weaver of the web of illusion'.

Many people are afraid of spiders, and most treat them with, at least, suspicion: the dream may symbolise some fear in waking life. The fact that some female spiders devour their mates can give rise to the interpretation that a spider in a dream can represent a dominant and restrictive woman. Similarly the web can symbolise the clinging ties of home or a relationship; alternatively, it may represent a 'web of deceit' or

illusion, woven by the dreamer or wound about him or her by someone else.

(See also: Spinning; Web)

Stag A proud and aggressive male beast, and a symbol of masculinity – which is why an all-male occasion is known as a 'stag party'. If the stag was being hunted, a male dreamer may feel that his masculinity is threatened in some way; a female dreamer may be expressing her feeling of superiority to the male sex – or perhaps there is some particular man she would like to capture!

(See also: Deer; Horn)

Swallow Like all birds, a symbol of freedom and aspiration, and a sign that spring has arrived at last. Possibly it represented an ambition that the dreamer hoped to accomplish – but remember, 'one swallow does not make a summer'.

On the other hand, this may be an example of the word games played by the mind. Perhaps there is some humiliation in waking life that the dreamer must 'swallow' – or has he or she made some indiscreet remark, and wished they could 'swallow their words'?

(See also: Bird)

Swan The Ugly Duckling, in Hans Andersen's tale, grew into a swan, a symbol of beauty, grace and calm dignity. Is this how the dreamer sees himself or herself? The swan can also be a symbol of farewell, as it is said to sing its 'swan song' before death.

Older dreamers, in particular, may find a different significance. 'Swanning' is taking an unplanned trip, drifting idly from place to place without a specific destination.

(See also: Bird)

Tiger More so than the lion, the tiger is a symbol of ferocity and voracious appetite. In India, it is often known as a 'man eater' – a word also applied to some women. Perhaps the dreamer knows someone who could be described in this way?

For those with a knowledge of Chinese astrology, the years of the tiger represent good luck, a willingness to take risks, and an appetite to enjoy life to the full.

(See also: Lion)

Toad The toad has something in common with the frog, but it is generally regarded as the frog's ugly and slow-moving opposite, and can symbolise whatever the individual regards as ugly in his or her personality or behaviour. Alternatively, the animal may represent someone, known to the dreamer, who is outwardly unattractive but 'has a heart of gold' – in legend, there was a priceless jewel in the head of every toad.

(See also: Frog)

Unicorn A relatively rare dream symbol. This mythical beast represents some of the qualities of the horse, but in medieval times, when the unicorn was believed to be a real animal, it symbolised purity and holy grace. Legend said that it could be captured only by a virgin, in whose lap it would lay its head, and perhaps this has a specific significance for the dreamer.

(See also: Horn; Horse)

Whale Although the largest of the mammals, the whale in dreams can often be regarded as a huge fish. Living in the deep ocean, it can represent the unconscious or the archetypal Mother. Its immense size may symbolise a problem or undertaking that the dreamer feels unfit to tackle.

(See also: Dolphin; Fish; Water)

Wolf For most people, the wolf is a wily, dangerous creature, with voracious appetites. In a dream, it can represent vicious, sadistic fantasies. In folklore, the wolf's true nature is often disguised: think of a werewolf, a 'wolf in sheep's clothing', or the wolf in the story of Red Riding Hood, who dressed himself as the grandmother. In the latter, the wolf obviously represents seductive, evilly inclined masculinity.

On the other hand, Native Americans regarded the wolf as a teacher, guide and fount of sacred wisdom.

Worm Worms are considered lowly, despicable creatures – and the word is used to describe people of this kind. At the same time, worms can be insidiously destructive, and are connected with death. In dreams, worms are almost invariably loathsome, and regarded as dirty. Like a snake, a worm can be phallic, but is not likely to be threateningly so.

(See also: Snake)

PLANT KINGDOM

*Flowers and fruit, trees and vegetables – all these can have as great a significance
in dreams as animals.*

*Flowers are symbols of beauty, delicacy and attractiveness, with a natural, open appearance of
innocence. In bud, or opening, they can represent developing personality and consciousness, or a
new relationship. Fading or withering flowers can obviously have the contrary significance. And the
word 'deflower' means to destroy virginity. Traditionally, in the 'language of flowers', each species of
flower has a specific symbolic meaning. The colour of the flower may also be important.*

*The fruit follows the flower; it is a symbol of development and completion, perhaps representing a
more mature stage of the dreamer's life. At the same time, the shape of individual fruits can have a
more overt symbolic meaning.*

*Finally, it must be remembered that the names of many flowers are given to women, and their
appearance in a dream may represent someone known to the dreamer.*

Acacia In the 'language of flowers', the acacia symbolises the immortality of the soul. In the Bible, the book of Exodus describes how the Ark of the Covenant and the tabernacle fittings were made of acacia wood overlaid with gold; and, in Masonic ritual, a sprig of acacia blossom represents the bush that was planted on the tomb of the legendary Hiram, who, it is said, taught that 'one must know how to die in order to live again in eternity'.

Nevertheless, in dreams, the acacia can have conflicting traditional meanings. When it is flowering out of season, it foretells the realisation of one's desires; on the other hand, if flowering in season it signifies that great disappointments lie ahead.

Acorn The acorn, gathered by squirrels in the autumn for their winter store, is a symbol of well-deserved prosperity. Traditionally, dreaming of collecting acorns is a sign that a welcome and

unexpected sum of money is on the way.

If the acorns are still growing green on the oak tree, it denotes that matters will change for the better; but pulling them from the tree is a sign that one is likely to injure one's prospects by indiscreet haste. If the acorns are withered or decaying, on the tree or on the ground, this portends setbacks and disappointments.
(See also: Oak)

Almond The almond, concealed within its hard shell, is a symbol of the reality hidden by external appearances. Traditionally, it denotes that a short-term sorrow will be followed by good fortune. An almond tree in blossom is a sign of coming happiness, as is a tree bearing ripe fruit. Unripe fruit, however, denote troubles ahead.
(See also: Nut)

Apple The apple plays an important part in many ancient myths, in which it usually has a connection with sexuality. The Greeks believed that it had been created by the god of wine, Dionysus, as a gift for Aphrodite, the goddess of love. When Paris was asked to judge who was the most beautiful of three goddesses – Hera, Athene or Aphrodite – he offered an apple to Aphrodite, to the great displeasure of the other two. And the apple that Eve gave Adam – from the Tree of the Knowledge of Good and Evil – was the cause of their expulsion from Eden. The apple, therefore, can be a symbol of temptation and discord.

Jung pointed out that 'the theft of an apple is a

typical dream symbol that occurs in many different variations in numerous dreams.' In such a case, it implies that the dreamer fears that he or she will suffer at the hands of someone else: either by the frustration of their plans or, indeed, in a sexual connotation.

Apricot Apricots (and, similarly, peaches) are a symbol of temporary pleasure, as well as of hypocrisy and deception. Unlike nuts such as almonds, in which the tasty inner fruit is hidden within a hard shell, the apricot is attractively

Eve tempts Adam with an apple from the Tree of Knowledge and brings about the Fall of Man. As with Pandora in Greek mythology, the ills of the world are, once more, attributed to a woman.

Cabbage First, ask yourself what is the condition of the cabbage? If rotting and with an unpleasant odour, it can signify that the dreamer's life and emotions are stagnating. But a fresh cabbage is thought to be a cleanser for sickness and depression, and can therefore symbolise physical or spiritual refreshment. On the other hand, a cabbage can also represent a dull, unimaginative person.

Cactus Many cacti are obvious sexual symbols. They can have beautiful flowers, but, unfortunately, these fade very quickly: this can signify a fear of declining male potency. Cacti are also prickly, and painful to the touch. Particularly for a woman dreamer, this can indicate an aversion to sexual intimacy. Or perhaps the dream represents a 'prickly' character in the dreamer's waking life?

Carnation and pink These flowers are a symbol of marriage and true love. It was an old Flemish tradition that a bride should hide a pink about her person on her wedding day, and the groom should search her and find it. In many old paintings, newly weds are depicted holding a pink in their hands.

coloured and juicy on the outside, but inside is a large, hard and bitter stone.

To dream of apricots growing on the tree, therefore, can be a sign that the future, although it may appear rosy, will eventually bring bitterness and sorrow. In summary, dreams of apricots are a sign that one has been wasting time on trivial matters, and is likely to be disappointed or deceived.

Banana An unambiguous phallic symbol. The banana skin, on the other hand, is a common symbol of the misfortune that can befall the unwary.

Cherry This dream symbol can have more than one meaning. Traditionally, dreams of cherries generally denote coming good fortune – 'a bowl of cherries' – unless the cherries are bad. However, in American popular speech 'losing one's cherry' means a loss of virginity; and traditional dream dictionaries identify a man's dream of picking cherries with the likelihood that he will be deceived by a woman.

Clover With its three leaves in one, the clover has long been a symbol of the Christian Trinity, and so may have a specific religious significance. The relatively rare four-leaved form is a traditional sign of good luck.

Corn An ancient symbol of fruitfulness and wealth. It can also signify the state of the dreamer's emotional development. If it is unripe, it is a sign of immaturity and innocence; if golden, ripe and ready for harvest, it represents maturity and good fortune.

It must be remembered, however, that the word 'corny' is used to describe poor humour, or something that is trite or out of date.
(See also: Gold)

Daisy Daisies, with their rayed petals, can represent the sun, which is the light of active intelligence. They are also a symbol of innocence.
(See also: Sun)

Date The date palm was a sacred tree to the Babylonians, in the Bible it is a symbol of the just, and to the Arabs the shape of the fruit resembles the vulva, symbolising passion and sensuality. As in other cases, a dream of dates may be an example of the mind's ability to make puns, reminding the dreamer of an important anniversary, or perhaps referring to a new relationship.

Field This can be a symbol for one's 'field of interest', and its condition is important. It may be fallow and choked with weeds; or it may be filled with a ripening crop. A very different interpretation identifies a

ploughed field with the archetypal Mother, and an unploughed field with a virgin.
(See also: Corn; Farm; Grass)

Fig In his novel *Women in Love*, D.H. Lawrence has one of the characters explain in detail the sexual symbolism of the fig, and its resemblance to the female genitalia. A dream of eating figs can have a very obvious sexual connotation. The fig leaf, too, has a traditional association with sexuality.

Forest The dark, trackless forest was a fearful place to early humans, and it has remained so in

many folktales. In a dream, it represents the unknown, threatening to all those who do not know the ways through it. It is not surprising, therefore, that a forest can symbolise the pubic hair.

Grape Sweet and succulent, grapes can be a symbol of richness, but also of decadence. They can represent a fruitful harvest, and also the thanksgiving sacrifice that follows.

Grass Lush meadows are a sign of nature's bounty, and their colour is a symbol of vitality and vigour. Sweeping lawns suggest peace and tranquillity, while their smaller suburban equivalent signifies domesticity. But sometimes 'the grass is greener on the other side', indicating dissatisfaction.

On the other hand, the mind may be playing one of its punning games: in criminal slang, to 'grass' means to betray. Perhaps the dreamer is aware of having unwisely given away information, or suspects that someone else is retailing scandal.
(See also: Farm; Garden; Green)

Holly Holly, particularly when it is covered in red berries, is a familiar symbol of Christmas, and whatever associations that may have for the dreamer. But holly leaves are very prickly: perhaps the dream is connected with someone who is easily offended. In medieval Christian art, the holly oak was a symbol of the Passion.

Ivy The ivy, clinging tenaciously to a wall or other support, is a symbol of affectionate attachment – or, in a related way, of a woman in need of protection. At the same time, because it is evergreen and often flourishes in churchyards, it has been identified with death and immortality.

Laurel In ancient Greece and Rome, the laurel was a sacred plant, dedicated to Apollo. Roman generals returning from war in triumph wore a laurel wreath, and this custom has come down to modern times in the naming of Nobel prizewinners as 'laureates', and the English institution of poet laureate. In a dream, therefore, laurel is a symbol of honour and the recognition of achievement.
(See also: Wreath)

Leaf Leaves are a very clear indication of the season in a dream. The bursting buds of spring signify new ambitions, new ideas, new love; the lush green leaves of summer suggest contentment and maturing projects; and the fading and falling leaves of autumn can represent the end of one stage of life, and the storing up of experience. The shapes of the leaves may identify a specific plant, or have a symbolic significance of their own.

(See also: Clover; Fig; and Autumn; Spring; Summer)

Lemon A popular folksong says:

> *The lemon tree is pretty, and the lemon flower is sweet –*
> *But the fruit of the lemon is impossible to eat.*

The lemon has a related significance in dreams. The sight of a lemon tree in blossom, as with other trees, is a sign of new relationships or spiritual development, and the lemon is traditionally a symbol of fidelity. But dreaming of eating a lemon, with its acid juice that puckers up the mouth, is a portent that a relationship will turn sour, or that plans will be foiled.

(See also: Acid; Senses)

Lilac Because of its normal colour, the lilac has always been associated with death – in fact, it is a popular superstition that lilac flowers, of any colour, should not be taken into a hospital or even the house.

Lily The lily is the traditional symbol of purity and, in medieval art, a lily among thorns represents the Immaculate Conception. The colour of the flower can be significant: red lilies are a masculine symbol, and white lilies feminine. Dreaming of this flower is a sign of spiritual health.

Maple Possibly a dream symbol related to something connected with Canada, because the maple leaf is the national emblem. An interesting American belief is that carrying a newborn child beneath a maple tree will give it strength.

Melon Because of its shape, the melon – and particularly the watermelon – is a symbol of pregnancy. Alternatively, its spherical form, with a hard rind enclosing flesh rich in water, can represent the Jungian Self.

Mistletoe The mistletoe was the sacred plant of the Druids, but in modern times it has come to be connected with Christmas and, in particular, with kissing. As a dream symbol, it may evoke suggestions of seasonal jollity and innocent sexuality; but it can also be a warning against trifling with someone's affections.

Myrtle In Roman times the evergreen myrtle was a symbol of love, and sacred to Venus. The Old Testament prophet Zechariah had a strange dream in which he saw 'a man riding upon a red horse, and he stood among the myrtle trees that were in the bottom; and behind were there red horses, speckled, and white'. Zechariah interpreted this dream as symbolising the love of God for Jerusalem; modern psychologists would identify the horses as representing the divine power that would protect the Jews.

(See also: Horse)

Narcissus The Greek myth told of the youth Narcissus, who fell in love with his own reflection in a pool of water, and drowned trying to embrace it. The flower has long been a symbol of self-love, and so of selfishness and indifference. As with so many dreams, only the

Beware self-love. In Greek mythology, Narcissus so adored his own reflection in a fountain, mistaking it for the presiding nymph of the place, that he jumped in to reach it and drowned.

dreamer will know whether the narcissus represents another person, or him- or herself.
(See also: Echo)

Nettle Possibly a suggestion that the dreamer must 'grasp the nettle' – that is, act boldly in a waking situation, despite the pain that he or she must suffer in doing so.

Nut The nut is a symbol of inner truth concealed by outward appearances. It may represent someone the dreamer knows, who is 'a hard nut to crack', or who is driving him or her 'nuts'. Dreaming of cracking one or more nuts can symbolise the search for a solution to a problem.
(See also: Almond)

Oak The oak tree is a symbol of long-lasting stability and strength; like all trees, it embodies both male and female qualities. Most probably, for the dreamer, it represents someone (often the Mother) who can provide protection.
(See also: Acorn; Tree)

Olive A beautiful tree, with silvery green leaves, and the fruit is the source of a rich, fragrant oil. The olive branch borne by the dove is an international symbol of peace and reconciliation. Almost certainly, this dream is full of good omens.
(See also: Oil)

Orange The typical colour of the orange is a combination of yellow, representing spiritual health, and red, representing physical love; the fruit itself has a similar symbolism. At the same time, orange blossom has long been a symbol of chastity before marriage.

Orchid The orchid gets its name from the Greek for testicle, because of the shape of the tubers from which it grows. In this way, the exotic flower of an orchid in a dream can symbolise the full development of the feminine side of a man's personality.

Pansy 'Pansies, that's for thoughts,' says Ophelia in Shakespeare's *Hamlet*, and the flower's name comes from the Latin meaning to ponder. In a dream, the sight of pansies can be a reminder to the dreamer to give due consideration to a planned action.

Peach See Apricot

Poppy Because of the opium produced by certain species, the poppy has long been a symbol of sleep, and the dreams that follow. The red poppy that flowered so profusely in the broken earth of the World War I battlefields has been adopted as a symbol of remembrance of the dead, and so it also carries an implication of everlasting sleep.

(See also: Dream within a dream)

Potato As something that develops underground, the potato is a symbol of the unconscious. In everyday speech it can represent a person lacking in vitality and inclined to watch the passing show – the phrase 'couch potato' is well known. And, in the 'language of flowers', the potato signifies calm benevolence.

Pumpkin The pumpkin is famous in fairytale as the vegetable that was transformed into a coach to carry Cinderella to the ball. Its association with Hallowe'en, the night when witches were believed to be abroad, also suggests a symbolism connected with magical change. Like the melon that it resembles, the pumpkin denotes pregnancy but, as the last fruit of autumn, it signifies completion and contentment.

(See also: Autumn; Melon)

Raspberry Because of its thorny stems, the raspberry can symbolise entanglement, but the luscious fruit will promise pleasure to follow. On the other hand, a dream of raspberries may be an example of the mind's play on words: is someone mocking the dreamer's intentions, and 'blowing raspberries'?

(See also: Entanglement)

245

Rhubarb A symbol of taking the bitter with the sweet. The use of rhubarb as a purgative may also give it the meaning of ridding oneself of something, physical or spiritual, that is undesired. Yet another meaning is possible: 'rhubarb, rhubarb' is what actors are supposed to mutter in a crowd scene, when they have no specific lines to say. Are people in the dreamer's waking life making meaningless or unnecessary comments?

Rose For many centuries, the rose has been a symbol of womanhood, beauty and romance, and Jung concurred in this – it signified, he said, the beloved woman.

Roses can also have a deeper significance, and can represent both good and evil, life and death. Their colour can be important: white roses symbolise purity; pink roses, romance; red roses, passion; and a black rose represents death.

Strawberry The strawberry is the symbol of 'the righteous man whose fruits are good works'. In this connection, the coronet of an English duke is decorated with the representation of eight strawberry leaves. In dreams, therefore, strawberries can represent good deeds and nobility of spirit.

Tree A tree is considered a bisexual symbol; the trunk represents the masculine aspect, and the fruit-bearing branches the feminine. Dreaming of climbing a tree, or sitting among its branches, can have two opposite meanings. The dreamer may be taking refuge from everyday reality in a fake spirituality: it is time to get his or her 'feet back on the ground'. Alternatively, it can be a sign that the dreamer is exploring the unconscious, and has withdrawn to find spiritual renewal.

Trees – and particularly pine trees – can also be a phallic symbol.

(See also: Leaf)

Vine Like the ivy, the vine is a clinging plant, but it bears luscious grapes. Taken together these two symbols can represent the pleasure of a closely affectionate relationship, but warn that it may not last.

(See also: Grape; Ivy)

Violet The 'shy violet' is a symbol of modesty and self-effacement. Strangely, it is also regarded in some parts as a flower of ill omen. Traditionally, a dream of gathering violets is a portent of favourable times to come, and possibly of promotion at work.

SHAPES, COLOURS & NUMBERS

Throughout human history, shapes, colours and numbers have had specific occult significance, and this will often reveal itself in dreams.

Some people believe that they dream only in black and white – this may be due to a lack of imagination or to a depressive personality. On the other hand, research suggests that most dreams are in colour, but that it fades rapidly from the memory. Other (lucky?) people claim to have dreams in brilliant colour. When a dream changes from black and white, or dull, scarcely differentiated hues, to bright, vibrant colour, it is said to be a sign of spiritual development in progress.

The Russian painter Vasily Kandinsky believed that colours have 'a corresponding spiritual vibration', and experiments reported by several researchers have established that people react to colours in ways that match their traditional significance.

Black The colour black is associated with misfortune and sadness. A general sense of blackness represents ignorance. If the dreamer is groping in darkness, he or she is trying to find a way out of difficulty.

(See also: Blindness; Night)

Blue Blue is the colour of the heavens, and the symbolic colour of the Virgin Mary. It is therefore associated with spiritual inspiration, but also with intellectual understanding, cool reason and faithfulness.

To dream of buying or wearing blue clothes is therefore a good omen, representing a well-ordered life, both material and spiritual, and friendly relations with others.

Brown The colour brown is associated in the infant mind with the mystery of what takes place between feeding and excretion. Much of the food the child particularly enjoys, such as meat purée or chocolate, is brown; but so, also, is its ultimate product. If the infant is praised (often the case) for its successful excretion, the colour may later come to be associated with money. Brown is also the colour of earth.

Traditionally, the colour brown has similar significance. To dream of wearing brown clothes is a symbol of pleasure without profit; and the colour itself represents close friendship.

(See also: Excrement)

Circle Since the earliest times, the circle has had a magical significance, and the Greek mathematicians found it a potent symbol. The line that describes its circumference has a fixed length, although it cannot be calculated exactly, and at the same time it goes on for ever. Ancient peoples recognised that the seasons, and indeed all human life, moved in cycles, and the universe is commonly represented as a sphere – a circle in every dimensions.

In dream terms, the circle symbolises the Jungian Self. It can signify completeness, with

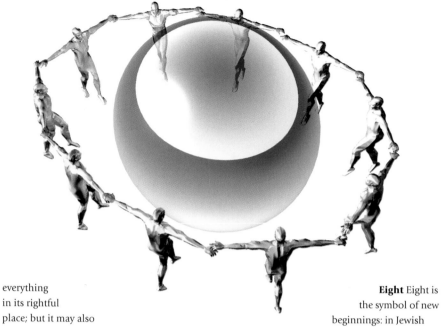

everything
in its rightful
place; but it may also
suggest that one is 'going round
in circles', unable to find a direction. Dancing in
a circle can symbolise good relations in society;
or it may be a surfacing of an image from
prehistory, and represent the desire to have
difficulties solved by some external influence.

In a different context, a circle may symbolise
the female genitalia.

(See also: Ball; Dance; Ring; Sphere)

Crescent The sight, particularly, of the crescent
moon is a symbol of the growing power of the
feminine principle, emotional and mysterious. It
can signify that the individual's life, which has
been starved of emotion, is about to enjoy
spiritual renewal.

(See also: Moon)

Cube A square squared, the cube was one of the
five 'regular solids' described by the Greek
philosopher Plato, and represented earth. Later
it came to symbolise the whole material world,
and so stability.

Eight Eight is
the symbol of new
beginnings: in Jewish
tradition, a baby boy is named on
the eighth day after his birth; and many Christian
baptismal fonts have eight sides.

In numerology, on the other hand, the number
eight represents an ambitious materialist,
dedicated to gaining influence and money.

Five The human body has five appendages – the
head, arms and legs – five fingers on each hand,
and five toes on each foot. The significance of
five in dreams may therefore be a symbol of
physical life.

In numerology, the number five represents an
individual who is adaptable and enjoys change,
who makes friends easily and is good company,
but who is restless and impatient of convention.

Four The simplest solid figure is the tetrahedron,
which has four points, and four triangular faces.
The followers of the Greek mathematician
Pythagoras therefore identified the number four
with solidity and – relating it to the fourth
element, earth – dryness. In numerology, the

number represents a stolid, 'down to earth' individual. It symbolises agricultural labour, or any kind of hard work for little reward.

(See also: Cube; Square)

Green The colour of plants, without which animal life on earth would be impossible, green symbolises vitality, vigour and growth; it is also connected with healing.

At the same time, green can represent immaturity. And it should not be forgotten that it is also traditionally the colour of envy.

Halo To dream that one has a halo is not necessarily a sign of a 'holier than thou' attitude. Many people believe that every human body has an 'aura', a glow of coloured light that can be seen by some, and indicates the state of physical or spiritual health. The colour of the aura, and the patterns of light within it, are essential to the understanding of its significance.

(See also: individual colours)

Helix See Spiral

Hexagon A six-sided figure that is one of only three regular plane figures – the others are the triangle and the square – that can be fitted continuously together without leaving gaps. It is the shape of the honeycomb, and also the structure of graphite.

The hexagon therefore symbolises rigidity and strength – but only in two dimensions: the use of graphite as a lubricant is due to the ease with which one hexagonal level can slide over the next. For this reason, hexagonal symbols in dreams must be viewed with caution: they offer strength at a single level, but instability in depth.

(See also: Six; Square; Triangle)

Line A straight line is the shortest distance between two points, a symbol of the ego, the driving force that carries the individual from one point to another of his or her life.

However, two straight lines – which may be parallel, and seen as a rail track, or diverging – are a sign that there is a conflict between two aspects of the individual's personality or career that cannot be reconciled.

A line can be curved, zigzag, or constantly changing direction, representing indecision. It is also what defines the shape of all plane figures.

Mandala The word 'mandala' means circle, but the term is usually applied to an intricate pattern of circles and squares, which can be used to focus the attention in meditation – as Jung suggested, it is an aid to 'centre ourselves'. Dreaming of a mandala can be a sign that one is entering a stage of important spiritual development. The specific shapes and colours of the pattern will also be of significance.

(See also: individual colours; Circle)

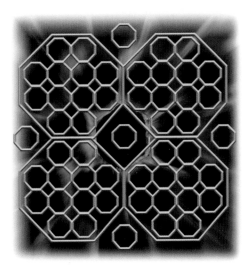

Nine A symbol of things coming to completion: the human child is born after nine months' gestation, and a cat has nine lives. And as three times three, nine has a further magical significance.

(See also: Three)

One For the followers of the Greek mathematician Pythagoras, the number one represented the point, something without dimension. At the same time, because it could not be divided into a smaller whole number, it represented the Infinite God, the first principle of the cosmos.

In numerology – and probably for the dreamer – the number one signifies the self-centred individual, dominant and powerful. As we say of such a person, they are 'all for Number One'.

Orange Traditionally, the colour orange is a portent of good fortune, particularly in its significance as a combination of spiritual and physical health. The colour of the robes of Buddhist monks, however, is said to be a symbol of occult power.

Oval The oval is the idealised shape of the egg, from which it takes its name. Like the circle, it is completely enclosed upon itself, but because of its egg-like form it can also symbolise potential life and creativity.

(See also: Circle; Egg)

Parabola The parabola begins at infinity, passes round a fixed point – its focus – and shoots off into infinity again. Parabolic reflectors are used to focus light, sound or radio waves on a fixed receiver. For the dreamer, the symbol can represent his or her ability to gather information from all sorts of sources, and concentrate attention upon a single project or ambition.

(See also: Comet; Line; Radio)

Pentagon A figure with five equal sides. Like all enclosed figures, it can represent completeness, but the significance of its five points should also be borne in mind. The Pentagon, the headquarters of military power in the USA, is built in this form, and may have a particular meaning for the dreamer.

(See also: Five)

Pentagram The five-pointed star shape of the occultists, which can be drawn as a single line returning to its starting point. The pentagram is regarded as a powerful symbol by practitioners of both good and bad magic. Its appearance in a dream may have a specific significance in this connection for the dreamer.

(See also: Five; Line; Witch)

Point See One

Purple A colour that traditionally represents leadership and power. For the dreamer, it can signify either promotion in waking life, or an important spiritual transformation.

Pyramid Standing firm on its square base, representing the earth, the pyramid has four sides of equilateral triangles, meeting at a single point, and any number of equal pyramids can be packed together without any space between. In this way,

the pyramid represents stability – and the pyramids of Egypt have certainly withstood the ravages of time.

If it was the Egyptian pyramids that appeared in the dream, they may have an entirely separate significance. Some people believe that the dimensions of the Great Pyramid denote not only the whole of past history, but the future to come. Others maintain that the form of the pyramid can concentrate some healing power at its centre. These concepts may have a special meaning for the dreamer.

Red The colour of blood, fire and strong wine, red is a symbol of intense emotion, anger and sexual excitement. In popular tradition, a red dress signifies a woman of 'easy virtue'.

Seven The number seven has a particular significance of mystery and occult power. This is connected with the four phases of the moon, each of which lasts some seven days. In addition, there is a popular belief that the human body renews itself every seven years.

In numerology, the number represents an introverted, thoughtful person, withdrawn from the world to meditate and contemplate mystic matters. The seventh son in a family has long been believed to possess magical powers.

Silver The colour silver in a dream is closely related to white, and symbolises self-knowledge, innocence and purity.

Six Six is a 'perfect' number: it equals the sum of the numbers by which it can be divided – one, two and three. (There are few perfect numbers: the next three are 28, 496 and 8128.) For this reason it represents undying love, marital harmony and peace.

Solomon's seal A six-pointed star-shaped figure made up of two triangles overlying one another in opposite directions. It can be a symbol of the human soul, the inter-relationship of the conscious and the unconscious. It is also the symbol of Judaism.

(See also: Triangle)

Sphere A sphere contains the maximum volume of matter within the minimum surface area – which is why drops of liquid assume a spherical form. It can symbolise the planet earth, or the entire cosmos; in personal terms it signifies perfect completeness, but at the same time a desire to ignore the outside world – as it were, to roll up into a ball.

(See also: Ball)

Spiral Strictly speaking, a helix (the shape of a spring or a circular staircase) should be distinguished from a spiral (a form that winds outwards from a central point), but in popular speech the two are equated. We speak of matters 'spiralling out of control', and this can be the significance of the dream symbol.

Alternatively, the spiral can be seen as a symbol of the evolution of the cosmos, and in this sense it is related to the coiled shape of a snake. A clockwise spiral symbolises creativeness, and an anti-clockwise spiral represents destructiveness. Both are very ancient symbols. A double spiral has its simplest representation in the Chinese yin-yang symbol, representing intercommunication between two opposing principles.

Square The square represents firmness and stability: with the triangle and the hexagon, it is one of the few plane shapes that can be fitted together without gaps. It has four sides – and therefore four corners – and has a similar significance to that of the number four. In Freemasonry it has a particular meaning, and the phrase 'on the square', suggesting truthfulness and reliability, has found its way into popular speech. On the other hand, the implications of solidity and fixed form are found in the slang usage 'square', indicating unimaginative conventionality.

Star Both the pentagram and Solomon's seal are star shaped, but their form is enclosed; the rays of a star are made up of independent, unconnected lines that extend outwards, getting ever further apart. A star shape can symbolise a brilliant

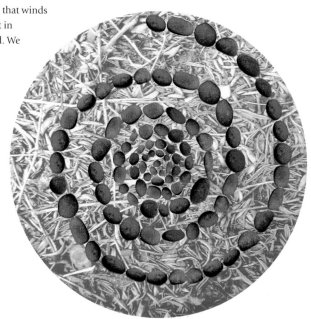

three lines meeting at three points – and has been said to represent the manifestation of God. At the same time, the triangle is often used as a symbol for the male genitals.

Twelve A number with ritual significance, which occurs particularly in our awareness of time: there are 12 hourly divisions on a clock; 12 months in a year; 12 signs of the zodiac; and Christmas traditionally lasts for 12 days, for example. In this way, 12 can represent a completed cycle of events.

Two Historically, two was associated with woman, and so – in a male-dominated society that regarded women as tempting and sinful – with evil. Modern numerologists do not subscribe to this belief, but continue to equate two with the feminine principle. The number represents a quiet, tactful, unassuming person.

White The colour of innocence and purity, the 'white light' of spiritual illumination and wisdom. The very opposite of black. A dream of being dressed in white, or in a white environment, can signify that the individual will be unaffected by the problems that obsess others.

Yellow Bright yellow is a sign of health, either physical or spiritual. However, if the yellow is darkened, it represents betrayal. Remember, also, that cowards are popularly described as 'yellow'.

concept, but one that is unlikely ever to be fulfilled. In the same way, it can represent one of those individuals who is 'full of ideas', none of which is ever developed.

Ten A number that represents the combination of man and woman: sexual intercourse and marriage.

Three A complex symbol. It can represent the Christian Trinity, and has a similar significance in other religions; it may signify the male genitals; and it is also a symbol of rivalry. Three has an important magical connotation, and is regarded as a very lucky number; at the same time, it is a popular superstition that misfortunes also come in threes.

Triangle A symbol with a number of meanings. It is the simplest plane figure that can be drawn –

INDEX

Page numbers in **bold** refer to subjects of dreams; those in *italics* refer to picture captions.

Bibliography

Hans Biedermann, *Knaurs Lexikon der Symbole*; Knaur, Munich 1989

Tom Chetwynd, *Dictionary for Dreamers*; George Allen & Unwin Ltd, London 1972

Jean Chevalier and Alain Gheerbrant, *Dictionaire des Symboles*; Robert Laffont, Paris 1982

J.E. Cirlot, *A Dictionary of Symbols*; Routledge & Kegan Paul Ltd, London 1971

Ivor H. Evans (ed), *Brewer's Dictionary of Phrase and Fable*; Cassell, London 1990

Gustavus Hindman Miller, *10,000 Dreams Interpreted*; Aquarius Books, London 1975

Stuart Holroyd, *Dream Worlds*; Aldus Books, London 1976

Carl G. Jung, *Man and his Symbols*; Aldus Books, London 1964

Julia and Derek Parker, *Dreaming*; Mitchell Beazley Ltd, London 1985

'Zolar', *Encyclopedia & Dictionary of Dreams*; Simon & Schuster, London and New York 1988

The Book of Fate & Fortune; Grant Richards, London 1932

Dreams & Dreaming; Time-Life Books, Amsterdam 1990

Picture Credits